Dogs of Courage

When Britain's Pets Went to War 1939–45

CLARE CAMPBELL AND CHRISTY CAMPBELL

corsair

CORSAIR

First published in Great Britain by Corsair

Copyright © Clare Campbell and Christy Campbell, 2015

A CIP catalogue record for this book
is available from the British Library

ISBN: 978-1-47211-566-9 (hardback)
ISBN: 978-1-47211-568-3 (ebook)

Typeset in Caslon Classico by Saxon Graphics Ltd, Derby
Printed and bound by CPI Group (UK) Ltd, Croydon, CR0 4YY

MIX
Paper from
responsible sources
FSC
www.fsc.org   FSC® C104740

Corsair
An imprint of
Little, Brown Book Group
Carmelite House
50 Victoria Embankment
London EC4Y 0DZ

An Hachette UK Company

www.hachette.co.uk
www.littlebrown.com

Dedicated to 'Gerry' (War-Dog 3055/9458), and all the others

Contents

Preface

It was surely the strangest military unit of the Second World War or any other. We first came across the existence of the 'War Dogs Training School' when researching our book *Bonzo's War* (Constable, 2013), the story of Britain's civilian pets under fire in the conflict.

That book was about domestic pets, cats and dogs in the main, and not those who officially served the armed forces, some becoming medal-winning heroes at the war's end. 'Hero' animals already had memorials and biographies galore. A number of them had been 'mascots,' dogs unofficially adopted by soldiers, sailors and airmen as good-luck charms or cook-house companions at home, at sea and in the field. They had regularly featured in morale-boosting wartime newspaper coverage — depicting dogs smoking pipes or wearing jolly sailors' hats. It was the same with all the combatants on every front — where armies of unofficial canine camp-followers followed the flag and the smell of the mobile field kitchen.

Such accidental combatants were the ones who seemed to have been the most written about at the time and celebrated thereafter. Britain's official war-dogs seemed entirely forgotten. A Freedom of Information request in autumn 2014 to the Ministry of Defence as to the whereabouts of their individual records (logged a decade earlier as being in the care of the Veterinary and Remount Services, Army Medical Directorate, Aldershot) brought the terse response — 'the information is no longer held.' It was as if they had never existed.

Although our last book had been about civilian animals, there had been reason to look into the 'WDTS', which began life in a west London suburb, then moved to a place called Northaw in rural Hertfordshire, because the animals it trained for military purposes turned out to be pets loaned by the public for as long as the war lasted. It was the most extraordinary story, and, as far as we could see, had never been told.

There was a similar school in Gloucestershire run by the Ministry of Aircraft Production (later taken over by the RAF), which also trained pets-on-loan to become brave little soldiers and airmen. It was always intended that these 'volunteers' (on the owners' account, if not the dogs themselves) should return to civilian life when the fighting was over. This would turn out to be more difficult than it sounded.

Both were very unusual operations with mixed civilian— military staff. The Gloucester 'Guard Dog Training School' had a predominance of skilled female trainers, such as the extraordinary Mrs Margaret Griffin and the twin sisters, the Misses Marjorie and Dorothy Homan. By contrast the army school in Hertfordshire was more militarised and employed men to do the training and women in uniform as lowlier 'kennel maids'.

Dog training, along with dog breeding, had already been a 'respectable' outlet for female ambition for several decades. It went along with a cultural shift, among middle-class dogs, at least, that had transformed abused backyard mutts into family pets. To be acceptable in the neat homes of suburbia, dogs needed collars, leashes and walkies. They also needed to be obedient; they needed training.

In the pre-war years, dog training had indeed become an amateur enthusiast 'craze', while no village fête was complete without displays of working-dog obedience and agility. Such things had begun in Britain in 1924 when the 'Associated Sheep, Police and Army Dog Society' held their first event. Three years later, the first obedience trial recognised by the UK's Kennel Club was held by the 'Alsatian League and Club of Great Britain'. In America the first obedience trial was staged in 1933 by Mrs Helene Whitehouse Walker, a woman Poodle breeder.

But British 'Dogdom', as it proudly styled itself, still remained largely a male-dominated affair and with the onset of war, three principal characters would compete for canine glory in this, a more drama-filled arena than even the show ring at Cruft's. They were Lt-Col Edwin Richardson (who favoured Airedales), Lt-Col James Baldwin (an Alsatian fan) and Herbert Summers Lloyd, breeder of champion Cocker Spaniels and multiple winner of Cruft's Best in Show. So, which one would emerge as top dog?

The Hertfordshire operation, for which Herbert Lloyd acted as 'Technical Adviser', was by far the biggest, turning out many hundreds of trained war dogs, or 'disciplined pets', as the Chief Army Vet would call them. To be a vital part of doing just that, a small force of young women had to be recruited.

At first it was difficult to find out much about them, other than that they came from the ATS, the Auxiliary Territorial Service. When it began in 1938, the official duties of an ATS-girl were described as: 'Non-combatant duties with military units. Motor driving, clerical and other services, calling for energy and initiative'. Well, learning how to handle a boisterous Border Collie certainly called for all these attributes, qualities the war-dog girls turned out to possess in abundance.

Although official documents gave only the briefest description of their duties, which at first appeared little more than those of a kennel maid in a Sloaney, peacetime pedigree stud, a wartime account from the splendid *The Dog World* magazine sounded much more intriguing. The breathless writer had been allowed a rare glimpse of this top-secret canine academy somewhere in the embattled Home Counties. He wrote:

> The town of dogs lies hidden in a verdant basin fringed by towering leafy trees. It is in the heart of England, unsuspected by the passer-by. It is still all as hush-hush as it was twelve months ago, except that dogs which have been trained as soldiers are now taking their place in the order of things. The War Dogs School has reaped the rewards of its success. Though a year ago, few women were employed, today we find a body of ATS installed there, bringing a vital and much appreciated feminine touch of warmth and colour to the township of dogs.

Although many of the girls had worked as professional kennel maids before the war, they were by no means all from a doggy background, and varied as much in occupation as in social class. Eve Lowery from Chessington in Surrey had been an insurance clerk, Margaret Beare from Norfolk was a children's nurse. Marjorie Vidgen from Essex had been a civil servant working for HM Customs and Excise, while Ellen Brydon was a hairdresser from Glasgow. Pauline Humphreys from New Malden in Surrey had trained as a ballet dancer, 'but now much prefers life in the ATS'.

In the end it was Herbert Lloyd who would emerge as the most significant human participant in this story and we are very grateful to his daughter, Jennifer Lloyd Carey (still breeding wonderful Cockers), for giving us an insight into the life of this remarkable man.

What is clear is his unshakable faith in his dogs' ability to help win the war. Lloyd's training method, based on kindness and reward, produced amazing results. His 'practical, *doggy*' approach (his own description) was the link between traditional training methods and the new academic science of 'animal behaviour' that had emerged between the wars. He respected dogs as complex and fascinating, not just creatures to be 'broken' to do man's bidding, as the old-time trainers would have it. 'The mere fringe of a dog's mentality has as yet only been touched upon,' he would write soon after the war's end, 'and it is a subject for the deepest interest and benefit to the nation.'

Most of all, he understood and respected the astonishing power locked up on that canine Enigma Machine, *a dog's nose*. By unlocking (some of) its secrets he and his fellow enthusiasts really did help save the lives of many British servicemen menaced by 'undetectable' anti-personnel mines and, by extension, during the revenge weapon attacks on London, the lives of many men, women and children buried under the rubble found by rescue dogs. We dug in files and put together this much, much wider story. Some of it was heartbreaking, much more deeply moving.

This, then, is a story of humans and dogs doing something quite remarkable together. There is sadness, loss and cruelty;

there is tenderness and joy. There is a canine catastrophe when the dogs first go to war in North Africa, a tragic episode long hidden from public view — but the animals' will to survive is unbreakable. Men far from home found the company of dogs irresistible, perhaps too much so. There is intense bravery and there is, indeed, love.

A Note on the Sources

The authors were once again faced with the problem that animals do not leave memoirs. But this narrative comes overwhelmingly from primary sources because, although the detailed records of the War-Dog Training School were in part destroyed, the memoirs of many of the wartime human participants, including many ATS-girls, were gathered by one veteran, bundled up into albums and placed in both the Imperial War Museum and Defence Medical Services Museum, Keogh Barracks, Ash Vale, Aldershot, Surrey.

This fine museum also contains the AV&RS Directorate War Diary in full, plus many more wartime albums, notebooks and diaries on the subject of war dogs, especially the reports by Lieutenant James Davison, CO No. 2 Mine Platoon (Dog) RE, sent from the front line in 1944–5. Also on file are the reports of the US mine-dog experiments, as relayed from the Washington Embassy in 1943, and the secret recruitment of dogs' home strays for the equivalent in Britain in the months before D-Day.

Home Office, Air Ministry and War Office files in the National Archives recount the story of Mr Herbert Lloyd and Colonel James Baldwin's early experiments and the long struggle to get war dogs accepted at all. War Diaries and other reports track their fate in Tunisia and northwest Europe and higher decision making on canines by the General Staff Policy Committee on Weapons and Equipment. The Ministry of Home Security files on the London rescue dogs are extensive and illuminating, as are those on the War Office's tortuous negotiations post-war with the RSPCA and Allied Forces Mascot Club (sponsored by the PDSA) to award (or not) bravery medals to acceptable dogs.

Journals such as *Our Dogs*, *The Dog World*, *The Dogs Bulletin*, *PDSA News*, *Animal World* and *The Tail-Wagger Magazine* were published throughout. We are especially grateful to those wartime veterans and their children who were kind enough to share their remarkable memories of the time when Britain's dogs went to war.

Abbreviations

AES Arms and Explosives Search (British Army, twenty-first century)

AFMC Allied Forces Mascot Club

AMSMVA Army Medical Services Museum Veterinary Archives

A/P anti-personnel

ATS Auxiliary Territorial Service

AV&RS Army Veterinary and Remount Services

BAOR British Army of the Rhine

BEF British Expeditionary Force

BLA British Liberation Army

CD Civil Defence

CMP Corps of Military Police

CO Commanding Officer

CQMS Company Quartermaster Sergeant

DAV&RS Director Army Veterinary and Remount Services

DFD Dogs for Defense

DM Dickin Medal

FV For Valour

GDTS Guard Dog Training School

GHQ General Headquarters

GPO General Post Office

HMG His Majesty's Government

IED Improvised Explosive Device

JIC Joint Intelligence Committee

MAFF Ministry of Agriculture, Fisheries and Food

MAP Ministry of Aircraft Production

MC Military Cross

MDD Mine Detecting Dog (US Army, twenty-first century)

MFH Master of Fox Hounds

M-O Mass-Observation

MWD Military Working Dog (British Army, twenty-first century)

NARPAC National Air Raid Precautions Animals Committee

NCDL National Canine Defence League

NPS National Pigeon Service

NVMA National Veterinary Medical Association

ODFL Our Dumb Friends' League

PDSA People's Dispensary for Sick Animals

PMD Polish Mine Detector

QRWK Queen's Royal West Kents

RAMC Royal Army Medical Corps

RAVC Royal Army Veterinary Corps

RE Royal Engineers

REST Remote Explosive Scent Tracing (demining, twenty-first century)

RIF Royal Irish Fusiliers

RSPCA Royal Society for the Prevention of Cruelty to Animals

SAS Special Air Service

SOE Special Operations Executive

USAAF United States Army Air Force
UXO Unexploded Ordnance
VP Vulnerable Point
WD War Department
WDTS War-Dog Training School
WO War Office

DOG TO JOIN SERVICES OR DIE

A large dog belonging to Mrs Adeline Humphries of 111 Beverley Road, Ruislip Manor, alleged to be ferocious, is to join the armed forces or to die for its misdeeds.

The little girl of Mrs Pym, a neighbour, aged five, was bitten twice on the ankle. Mrs Humphries said she kept the dog because it belonged to her husband, who was serving with the RAF in India.

She [had] heard an appeal on the wireless for dogs and she would like to send the dog to the RAF or the Army rather than have it destroyed.

The Chairman (Mr C. E. King) said the Bench were unanimously of the opinion that the dog was ferocious. They however accepted the defendant's offer to send the dog to the armed forces.

News story, 12 May 1944

SNIFFER DOGS LEAD THE WAY

So great is the demand for dogs that the Royal Army Veterinary Corps must recruit constantly — from homes; animal welfare organisations; breeders — at home and abroad. It still needs more. 'It is getting harder,' one officer said. 'The British have a thing about dogs, and fear that they may be mistreated or put in great danger.'

News story, 20 January 2011

BRAVE ARMY DOG AWARDED POSTHUMOUS MEDAL

The highest military honour awarded to animals has been given to Sasha, a yellow Labrador army dog, who was killed on active service in Afghanistan. Sasha was four years old when she died alongside her handler, Lance Corporal Kenneth Rowe, when both were caught in a Taliban ambush on 24 July 2008.

Sasha the army dog was trained to sniff out weapons and went ahead on sorties to make routes safe for patrols. Kenneth's mother, Lynn Rowe, remarked that 'Kenneth always adored animals and loved working with his dogs.'

News story, 30 April 2014

Prologue

Walcheren Island, the Netherlands, December 1944.

Peggy shivered, even in her little coat made out of an army blanket. She stopped working for a minute, looked round to meet her handler's reassuring gaze, then started 'quartering' the ground again, pacing at an angle, sniffing, pausing, pacing once more, just as she had been taught.

'Ground' was hardly the word. A great sheet of water stretched almost to the horizon, an icy wind whipping its surface into wavelets. A dark hump of raised dyke marked its distant rim with the grey North Sea beyond that. Hoar frost bloomed on the smashed telegraph poles and thin sheet-ice crunched underfoot. Tread carefully … everyone was treading carefully.

Peggy's handler, a British soldier with Royal Engineer shoulder flashes, followed her with wary respect, man and dog inching their way along the railway track on its raised embankment that was the only way through the floods out of the ruinous Netherlands town of Middelburg.

Peggy 'froze', pulling at her leash. Very gently, her handler moved forward to mark the spot on the ground with a little flag. Other platoons had lost lives, limbs and dogs doing this job. No one had been killed in this platoon — yet. There was no doubt. Clever Peggy! Her handler took a little chunk of meat, which he kept in a captured German gas-mask case for this very purpose, and gave it to her. Good dog, clever girl!

Peggy, War-Dog No. 2557/67404, was a bit of everything — Alsatian, Airedale, with some black and tan thrown in. All of No. 2 Platoon's dogs were 'Heinz' dogs, fifty-seven varieties. Only 'Peter' and 'Prince' were what you might call pure bred (they were Black Labs, if anyone cared — the dogs certainly did not). Most of them were once somebody's pet. Peggy belonged to Mrs King of 19 Banchory Road, Blackheath, southeast London, while War-Dog 'Gerry' came from a family in Bromley, south London. For the duration of the Second World War they were on loan to the British Army.

War-Dog 'Smiler' came from the Dogs' Home, Battersea and, as it was said, 'knew no owner but the state'. He would not be going home.

The chums were on the Dutch island of Walcheren. Now it was a vast lagoon. The breaching of the encircling dyke by RAF bombing had put a huge inland tract of 'polder' below sea level.

A month before this had been the scene of ferocious fighting between British and Canadian soldiers and die-hard German defenders as the onrushing North Sea had swept over the land. Enemy snipers were rumoured to be still holding out in barns and attics. Dutch civilians were picking their way back to their flooded homes and farms. Hollow-cheeked children played as they might with sledges and carts made of ammunition boxes. This would be remembered as the 'Hongerwinter'. There was no food, no fuel and no transport. Those in the still-German-occupied part of Holland had it worse.

Middelburg, the beautiful, historic capital of the island, flattened by German bombing in 1940, was marooned in a sea of floodwater. The surrendered German garrison, just taken prisoner, had had to be taken out in rowing boats. 'Here really reigns the terror of war,' wrote one of Queen Wilhelmina's ministers on a despairing visit.

Second Lieutenant James Davison, a twenty-three-year-old medical student from Liverpool, was there on a mission. The task of his curious little command, No. 2 Dog Platoon, RE, was to clear the railway that ran from Middelburg to the port of Flushing, of mines and booby traps, and get it open for civil aid to get in; Flushing had been heavily fortified by the Germans on its landward side.

The railway line was punctured by craters and had been sown with mines along its whole length — including those aimed at men rather than trucks or tanks, like the notorious 'Schrapnell-mine', which jumped out of the ground to spray a wall of shrapnel at waist height, and the even more feared 'Schu-mine', a wooden box of explosives with a primitive pressure trigger — enough to blow off a man's foot. It was loathed by the infantry and by those whose job it was to clear it: Royal Engineer sappers who had to crawl on their hands and knees poking with a bayonet, then lift the horrific thing out of the ground, all the while praying it did not go off six inches from their faces (unless they had a dog to find it first).

And there were big anti-tank 'Teller' mines, made of metal. A mine detector could normally find those but on the steel railway track they simply did not work. That is why the dogs were here. And the dogs were very special — they could smell any mine, even one in a case made of wood. They were extremely good at it too.

Peggy was working harder than ever now, with no break in her rapt attention in spite of the sharp, stony ballast on the track-bed that even a veteran, leathery-pawed mine dog like her, one who had come all the way from the beaches of Normandy, could find distressing.

Smiler was working away happily on the other side of the eight-foot-wide roadway. Gerry was a little behind, with his handler, Sapper Pitkin, sweeping from left to right, looking for mines the first two dogs might have missed.

It was bitterly cold but the sour scent of death, both animal and human, hung in the air. This was a terrible place, a place, so Lieutenant Davison would note that night as he wrote up the unit War Diary, that even the vermin had abandoned.

Peggy stopped. Up ahead was what looked like a farmer's cart blown to bits; a dead horse lay further along the track. There was blood everywhere. The dogs sniffed on, blinking, glancing sideways but staying close to the job, just as they had been trained.

The cold was getting increasingly intense; the winter sun was dying. Very soon it would be too dark for the men to see. The dogs, in their sensory realm of smell, did not care. Lieutenant Davison ordered stand down.

Five thousand square yards had been cleared; they would go for more tomorrow.

Part One

'SIT!'

'In their great struggle, it was to some purpose that the British were a nation of dog lovers.'

Herbert Summers Lloyd, 1946

I

Dogs in the Service
of the State

The new recruit was not quite what they were looking for. On his first day at work he had taken fright at the sight of a wardrobe being manoeuvred down a street by removal men, then 'cowered down, run off, knocked over a small girl and hidden behind a woman's skirts'.

'Smut' was clearly not going to make much of a mark on history. An agreeable black Labrador, his place in this story is assured, however, by a report held in the files of the Metropolitan Police on his, and some other remarkable dogs' adventures on the streets of London, not long before the outbreak of the Second World War.

It was early summer, 1938. Smut had set off with his minder from the village of Washwater in Berkshire, heading for the capital by the Great Western Railway. With him was his kennelmate, 'Nigger', another black Lab, both dogs judged by their trainers to be ready at last after months of training for their grand debut.

It had been a long time coming. For decades, it seemed, British officialdom had been considering the use of canines in the maintenance of law and order. Enthusiasts had been campaigning for 'police dogs' since the days of Queen Victoria — without much success. Continental coppers, especially in Germany, had long found certain breeds of dog ideal for nabbing miscreants. A German, Konrad Most, a police officer in Saarbrücken, published his hugely influential book, *Training Dogs*, in 1910. Establishing dominance of human over the wolf-descended canine was the key thing, according to Most — hence the need for lots of conditioning to create an obedient working animal in the service of the state. Although it was not all pain, there should be primary inducements too — especially 'food and fondling' — to result in a dog who flawlessly obeyed spoken commands or hand signals for action.

Why not in Britain too? The Airedale enthusiast, Colonel Edwin Richardson, had been one of those long advocating, without much success, using dogs for police and government work — but his time had come at last in 1917 when the British Army, following the German example, formally agreed to the idea of using dogs to carry messages around the static trench lines of the Western Front. Lt-Col Richardson and his wife Blanche had trained them (they came from stray dog-pounds or were presented as gifts from patriotic pet owners) at the 'War Dog School' at Shoeburyness, Kent (see pp. 15–19) before they were sent to France.

At the war's end the school had been disbanded and the Army forgot all about dogs. An attempt in 1919 by the Colonel to interest the War Office in deploying his canine force against the rebellious Irish came to nothing. 'All the dogs were returned to their owners or found good homes,' Colonel Richardson would write. Hundreds of applications to keep them came from their former masters in uniform, officers and other ranks. A mix of charity and official money paid for quarantine while the RSPCA insisted on the humane destruction of 'those who could not come home'. Official attention was rather on all those mascots and stray adoptees brought back by soldiers from France and the Middle East which, in spite of precautions, caused serious outbreaks of rabies in Britain.

Peacetime civilian authorities continued to show no interest in 'police' dogs. However, in 1935 a small Home Office committee chaired by the dog-loving Lt-Col David Allan, HM Inspector of Constabulary for England and Wales, had begun to reconsider the idea. But they had turned in the end to Mr Herbert Summers Lloyd, the most famous breeder and trainer in British Dogdom, author of *The Popular Cocker Spaniel* and proprietor of the 'of Ware'[1] stud. An experimental police dog academy was established at Washwater, near Newbury, on 200 acres of chalky upland on the Highclere Estate that Mr Lloyd was renting from the Earl of Carnarvon, for the training of gun-dogs. Mr Lloyd's thriving commercial kennels at Ickenham, west of London, would also be progressively turned over to the government work.

Lloyd's brief was to determine the best breed for the job and the optimum method of training. The fee was £500 per annum — with a five-year contract stretching to March 1940. His chief handler was the noted gun-dog trainer Mr Reginald Hill, 'a man

---

[1] The Lloyd kennels were at Swakeleys Farm, Ickenham in Middlesex. The 'of Ware' suffix was retained in tribute to his father, Richard Lloyd, who had founded the famous kennels in the Hertfordshire town over three decades before. According to his daughter, Jennifer, speaking over seventy years later: 'My father was born in Ware. His father had been born a Cockney, in the sound of Bow Bells. Dad had been through the First World War, where he worked with horses as well as in the training of messenger dogs.'

who has spent a good deal of his time in big-game hunting in Africa'.

A police dog, it was considered, must be good at two things. Tracking, for running down criminals or tracing the whereabouts of lost persons, and more generally, aiding and defending his blue-uniformed master, especially on night patrol. Could one breed or crossbreed do both?

It was reported: 'Breeds such as Bloodhounds, Otterhounds crossed with Bloodhounds, pure Doberman Pinschers (a German breed) and crossed Doberman Pinschers, all gifted with superfine scenting abilities, have been enrolled for tracking down criminals and gaol fugitives, while collies, French poodles, and retrievers crossed with Border terriers, are being taught how to disarm and hold down assailants for arrest. A special breed is also being selected to identify wanted men ...'

'"Mouse", a cross-bred retriever, can vault a 6ft fence, and in a trice, bundle over a 14 stone man. He is the only stray so far to be given a police collar,' said a newspaper report.

A bedraggled Mouse had presented himself three times at Banbury police station (they had simply cast him adrift each time he showed up) and only dodged the lethal chamber[2] when kindly Lt-Col Allan himself heard of his plight. 'Although

---

[2] Under the Dogs Act (1906) police had the authority to detain dogs believed to be strays but they had to retain them for seven days (which under wartime emergency legislation would be reduced to three), within which the dog might be claimed or found a new home before it was humanely destroyed. The Act forbade sale for the purposes of vivisection. Detention and destruction was normally a task for pet welfare charities. In London, Battersea Dogs' Home and Our Dumb Friends' League, which ran the North London Dogs' Home in Willesden, were contractors to the Metropolitan Police, destroying unclaimed and diseased dogs on an industrial scale. For half a century Battersea had used chloroform in its famous 'lethal chamber' – until installing a battery of 'eletrothanaters' in 1932.

unruly at first, he showed such aptitude that he is now a "key" dog and is used to set an example to other dogs,' it was reported.

'Kindness is the secret of the training at Washwater,' it was reported, and the 'handlers who put the animals through their paces talk to them almost as if they were human. There are no harsh words of command, no special code words or elaborate technique, and willing compliance with instructions is rewarded generously with tit-bits of raw or cooked meat'. That was Herbert Lloyd's style.

But just one super-breed, all-purpose police dog could not be found. After a further year of trials, it was reported: 'Before long the conclusion became inevitable that tracking and other work would have to be divided. Hounds are so highly specialized that they are not suitable for anything but hunting. It was altogether different in deciding upon the kind of dogs most fitted, for liaison and what for convenience may be called detective work. Many different breeds were submitted to the test. Eventually it was decided that [for utility work] nothing was equal to Labradors'.[3]

Smut and Nigger's big day was drawing near. Two volunteers from the Met, PCs Smith and Allen, had trained with them for the past four weeks. The press were invited to wintry Washwater to see dogs scaling ladders, guarding police bicycles and fighting off (but 'not savaging') a constable's well-padded assailant. Their training was now complete.

[3] In his 1938–9 experiments for the Home Office, Herbert Lloyd had defined the difference between a 'dog', which 'worked for the sheer love of pleasing his handler', and a 'hound', which worked 'only to please himself'. A hound 'would give up if distracted', he concluded, whereas there was 'no limit to a dog's intelligence and desire to please'. According to him, the most 'pliable and humanised dogs' were Labradors although according to Jennifer Lloyd: 'I remember Dad telling us that German Shepherds [Alsatians] were "one-man" dogs and that Labradors could become over-friendly.'

On 11 May 1938, the chums were taken by train to London, where they were to live for a little while at least with their minders at their homes in Balham and Lewisham in backyard kennels provided at public expense. Leads, brushes, dog food, etc. were obtained by the PCs from local stores, but the weekly cost of 9s 10d per dog should be reimbursed, it was recommended.

A few days later, a photographer snapped the two black Labradors ('Britain's first official police dogs') with their portly looking handlers in their Victorian uniforms on arrival at their new operational quarter, No. 4 District of the Met, at 47 Cavendish Road, Balham, in south London.

It was then that PC Smith took the Labrador for his first day out in the Big Smoke. But it was all a bit big and scary for Smut.

'He seemed very nervous in his new surroundings,' it was reported, while his handler kept him on a lead and encouraged him every way possible. But 'a man ran out from a doorway' and Smut ran into the road in fright. Next came the toddler-toppling incident – after which the unfortunate Labrador ran out into the road once again and was struck by a car.

Nigger meanwhile was proving a very different kind of dog. He was 'satisfactory in every way and working very well'.

Nervous Smut was patched up and despatched back to Washwater. His replacement was another Labrador, 'Tint', who, said PC Smith, turned out to be a more reliable and steady animal. Tint gave Nigger a nasty nip in the neck but that did not seem to count against him too much.

The crime-fighting duo of Tint and Nigger proved a success on the streets of London as far south as Croydon, but no more

Berkshire-trained dogs would be coming to join them anytime soon. The 'Munich crisis' of September—October 1938 had given the Home Office more pressing concerns in organising air raid precautions and mass evacuation of Britain's cities than experimentation with police dogs. Whatever Herr Hitler might have promised, whatever fatuous assurances about 'peace in our time' might be in the air, it was clear to political realists that a new European war was coming. Better plan for the worst.

But where were the Washwater dogs in all of this? Mr Lloyd told the Home Office by letter on 15 April 1939 that he had 'quite a number of Labradors ready to go out to the County Police'. But, 'in view of the present crisis [Britain and Poland had just signed a military defence pact] is it possible that my dogs and staff might be used for Army training purposes,' he asked, 'for which they are fit to go at any moment, their police training being easily converted into army training?'

An official noted it was lack of finance that was holding back chief constables in taking more Labradors, rather than any doubt as to their usefulness. But he had heard, meanwhile, of an Air Ministry interest in guard dogs for so-called 'Vulnerable Points' — transmitters, airfields, etc. — which could be targets for sabotage, should war come. The War Office might also be interested. Otherwise spurned by the police, the Washwater dogs spent an uncertain summer of 1939, along with the British public. The number of people who thought that war could be avoided was dwindling by the day.

No more newspaper reporters came to see the dogs going through their paces. The Otterhound-Bloodhound crosses had not turned out as useful at tracking as had been hoped. The police generally had other concerns.

Tint and Nigger meanwhile would shortly depart the capital to take up duties with the Cheshire Constabulary. 'Nigger is a great dog,' it would be reported in September 1939.

Mr Lloyd's government contract would soon expire and there would arise the question of paying for dog food and staff. Nevertheless, for a British dog, the Grandmaster's kennels were a much safer place to be than anywhere else, for now at least.

Police dogs had no place in the intense planning going on that summer in Whitehall to meet what now seemed an increasingly inevitable war with Nazi Germany. But domestic dogs, horses – and indeed cats – most certainly did. In spring 1939 the Home Office had begun to prepare for the time when Britain's cities were attacked from the air with an opening thunderclap of high explosive and poison gas. What would the nation's pets do then? Surely they would go barking mad at the first wail of a siren. It was noted:

> During an emergency there might be large numbers of animals wounded, gassed or driven frantic with fear, and destruction would then have to be enforced by the responsible authority for the protection of the public.

There were consultations with the mutually suspicious animal welfare charities and with the National Veterinary Medical Association. A semi-official umbrella body, the 'National Air Raid Precautions Animals Committee (NARPAC)', was formed in early summer 1939, which produced a series of soothingly worded pamphlets and press announcements, including one given out in daily newspapers and on the BBC on 26 August that pet owners could not take dogs and cats into public air raid shelters.

If you could not 'send your pets to the country in advance of an emergency', 'it really is kindest to have them destroyed,' so it was advised. The pet welfare charities had already declared themselves ready to carry out mass euthanasia. Meanwhile the story of the great disaster which overtook Britain's companion animals in the first week of war has been told at greater length elsewhere.[4]

It was not surprising, therefore, that in the transition to war of late August, many people took the horribly flawed advice seriously, rushing off with their pets to their local vet or animal welfare charity, or even abandoning them altogether. On 3 September came the grave announcement: Britain was at war with Germany. It was a Sunday morning.

That same day Herbert Lloyd wrote to the Home Office: 'I'm a bit in the dark as to where I stand with police dogs. The question of both food and [now rationed] petrol arises.' He and his staff were 'ready to quickly train messenger dogs should the War Office wish to make use of our services.'

Still the pet killing continued. By the end of the first week of war, 750,000 animals, mostly in the capital, had lost their lives, their bodies piling up in the yard of a commercial renderer beside the River Lea in east London. The bodies were taken by night to a field behind the PDSA (People's Dispensary for Sick Animals of the Poor) cemetery in Ilford and buried in pits.

But it was not all heartbreak. Even before the first siren had sounded, there were some who declared themselves ready to shelter pet refugees from the imperilled cities, in their thousands, if necessary. One such was veteran 'animal defender', Nina,

---

4   See our book, *Bonzo's War*, 2013.

Duchess of Hamilton, who sent her staff in the ducal Daimler onto the streets of London to rescue abandoned animals — and declared the family country estate, 'Ferne' in Wiltshire, and her St John's Wood mansion to be sanctuaries for the pets of the poor. She took to the wireless to make a plea for others to take in refugee companion animals from the cities — and it would be acted upon.

2
A Splendid
Collection of Dogs

The pet-killing frenzy of September 1939 was burning out. At a stormy meeting of the NARPAC executive on the 12th, everyone had threatened to resign. The despairing Home Office representative thought it a miracle the strange organisation had survived the outbreak of war at all. The Battersea Dogs' Home defected from the organisation as soon as it could. Similarly unenthusiastic, the RSPCA would pull out altogether after a year. The PDSA and Our Dumb Friends' League, in contrast, were determined to continue.

While the internal rows continued, NARPAC desperately tried to turn back the damage that its own ill-considered advice had triggered. Vets, animal welfare charities and pet owners recoiled at what had happened. 'The day of hysterical slaughter has gone,' declared *The Dog World* magazine, 'it was but a transient, mistaken phase.' Meanwhile stoical dog breeders declared their intention of carrying on as best they might.

In fact it was not food (not yet) that would concern dog owners most. In cities it was the universal blackout — as the autumnal days shortened. The officially enforced gloom, meanwhile, was natural cover for burglars and prowlers. What better than a dog to provide reassurance to a woman whose husband was away at the war? Who would not feel safer with a trusty dog at heel when opening the door to strangers? Mr Lloyd's experiments for the Home Office had shown the way, according to the canine press. What the nation needed were lots of intelligent trained dogs as a safeguard in this new time of trial.

Far-sighted dog owners could also see that feeding their pets might one day be a major problem.

Poison gas attack from the air was the other great unknown. Millions of gas masks had been distributed for men, women and children. Could not the same be done for pets? According to *The Veterinary Record*:

> In the case of dog masks, there are many difficulties to be overcome. In the first place, to get the animal to tolerate the mask. Secondly, there are the various shapes and sizes of dogs' heads which would necessitate a large number of different sized masks. The sense of smell is the guiding sense of the dog, which is completely excluded by the application of a respirator.

When, a little later, it would be decided to experimentally recruit dogs for some kind of military service, much effort would be expended on the quest for a workable gas mask.

But instead of being simply rescued or evacuated, could not blacked-out British dogs who had survived the mass culling be somehow enrolled in the defence of the realm as they had been in an earlier war? In 1917—18 food shortages and rationing (for humans) had occasioned a very nasty hate campaign against dogs. One MP had declared he would not be happy until the last Pekingese had been turned into a meat pie!

In the first months of this new conflict there were scattered reports of dogs doing their bit — by more than being just 'mascots' or 'regimental pets' (see p. 139). Could they not guard things? From the Duchess of Hamilton and her pet rescue operation came news that: 'The officers and men at a wireless station somewhere in England have, owing to the efforts of one of their police staff, come forward with an extraordinary offer to help and several evacuee [dogs] have been placed with them.'

While Herbert Lloyd waited for a decision on what to do with his unwanted 'police dogs', in a different corner of the country another stalwart of British Dogdom was stirring for action. When the Home Office had first embarked on its canine law enforcement experiments, it had overlooked the nation's greatest expert on the matter. Lt-Col (retired) Edwin Hautonville Richardson had been in the working-dog business for almost half a century but, aged seventy-five when the government contract had been issued, he might have seemed a little past it.

Emphatically not so, as far as the inspirer of the British 'War Dog School' in 1917 was concerned. Once famous, now it was forgotten.

Richardson had written a spirited history of the strange enterprise in 1920 under the title *British War Dogs*. He explained where the dogs had come from:

> At first the only supply was from the Home for Lost Dogs at Battersea. Then the Birmingham, Liverpool, Bristol and

Manchester Dogs' Homes were invited to help by sending
any suitable dogs to the school. Many a homeless, deserted
'stray' was saved from the lethal chamber, and transformed
into a useful member of His Majesty's Forces. Later, the
Home Office ordered the police all over the country to send
all stray dogs of certain breeds to the school. Finally, when
even these sources were not sufficient, the War Office decided
to appeal to the public for gifts. The response was exceedingly
generous. The country was, at this time, passing through
especially serious times, and many people were only too glad
to help by sending their dogs.

The Colonel's kennels at Horsell Common near Woking, Surrey,
were still famous among those who cared about these things. But
Colonel Richardson was not done with yet – and nor were his
dogs.

Indeed in a lifetime of breeding dogs, training dogs and writing
about dogs, he was still campaigner-in-chief for their useful
employment by the authorities. His approach was scientific and
practical – the Colonel, for example, was a Fellow of the
Zoological Society, but he was not a member of Dogdom's social
Athenaeum, the Kennel Club.

His engaging book had dwelt at length on the right match of
handler and dog. Other factors, such as social background of
handler or breed (although he himself favoured Airedales), were
not so important. It was human–canine understanding that
mattered.

Richardson insisted any dog with 'proper character' could
undertake the work. And, as his furry army of mongrels and
dogs' home strays had come together for war service a quarter of

a century before, he had imbued them with all the Edwardian sensibility of a schooldays' story that readers of the boys' comic *The Gem* might recognise. He wrote:

> A splendid collection of dogs was daily assembled. Many of them were fine show specimens, while others of humble ancestry nevertheless came with wise faces and willing hearts. They were one and all welcome, and were made to feel so. The attitude of mind was in most cases that of a schoolboy plunged into a large public school, bewilderment and sometimes homesickness, but as [they found that] kindly human voices were all around, and that excellent dinners were going, they soon became quite at home.

Richardson's dogs had feelings of 'justice, and honourable dealing'. For example, if a message dog was rewarded with a piece of meat, the response of his kennelmates would show 'no attempt to snatch and a distinct understanding that it was a definite reward for good work done, and, therefore, to interfere, would be a most unsportsmanlike act'.

And as for the handlers (he called them 'keepers'), working with animals required 'a decidedly special gift in the instructor', most often described as 'a natural love of animals' — 'Affection must exist between dogs and keeper, and the man whose only idea of control is by coercion and fear is quite useless,' he wrote.

Meanwhile his commercial kennels prospered up to the eve of war — when on any day one could read his press announcements in *The Times* personal columns: 'Dogs Airedales Lt.-Col. Richardson. For house protection, ladies' guards, companions, exhibition, pups, adults. Export all parts'.

With a new war coming, all the press attention meanwhile had
been on Herbert Lloyd and his insufferable Labradors. Bizarrely
perhaps (it was certainly a way of getting attention), in 1939
Colonel Richardson and his wife Blanche began a freelance,
war-dog experimental establishment in leafy Surrey featuring
Airedales in gas masks, Airedales bearing first aid pouches and
Airedales bearing carrier pigeons in wicker baskets. The press
could not get enough.

The RSPCA's *The Animal World* magazine reminded readers
of his method of training 'based on a dog's love for its master' —
and could report: 'At Woking Major Richardson is training
Airedales and Collies to wear gas masks although the difficulties
are great as dogs perspire through their panting mouths and the
soles of their feet, not through their skin like most animals. The
main difficulty as with most pets is to keep the device on their
heads'. Such difficulties would continue.

Following the Declaration of War when the first contingent of
Canadian soldiers arrived in Britain (the Toronto Scottish — who
would a little later mount guard at Buckingham Palace),
Richardson invited them to Woking via an old wartime chum,
their commanding officer Colonel Thompson. Pictures of these
camera-friendly outings in Surrey woodland, featuring troops in
Glengarry bonnets and British battledress, have appeared in
publications ever since as 'British war dogs'. The BEF (British
Expeditionary Force) in France meanwhile had not one official
war dog.

Richardson himself would write: 'Some excellent work was
done [in winter 1939—40] on Horsell Common outside our house
and a contingent of army nurses was kind in helping with the
Red Cross dogs. We were not working officially and I could see

that someone younger or more capable of the strenuous work involved in the command of a war-dog training school, than me, was necessary.' It was a noble thought but in fact he had no choice. His pleas to be allowed back into this new fight had gone unanswered.

As he would later confide in a letter to the War Office: 'When the war broke out, I urgently asked that I might be allowed to collect and organise the dog power of this country but could not get in touch with anyone who sufficiently understood the value of these animals.'

The Colonel had had much experience of being ignored.

3
The 101 Alsatians

There was another frustrated enthusiast who would not take no for an answer. Lt-Col James Y. Baldwin had been a moving spirit behind the 'Alsatian' boom in pre-war Britain. The 'Alsatian wolf-dog', as the Kennel Club first recognised it, had come from nowhere to be a hugely popular breed. Baldwin would tell the story of how, as an officer on the Western Front, he had come face to face with a German Army dog in an abandoned trench and 'thought it was a wolf' – he was smitten. He and his friend, the pioneer aviator and Conservative MP, Lt-Col John Moore-Brabazon, had jointly promoted the Alsatian (a suitably un-Teutonic name for a dog which actually found its origin in southwest Germany) through pre-war controversies and bids by rival 'Alsatian Leagues' to seize the canine crown.

As the most famous exponent of this evidently militarily useful dog, Baldwin had proposed on the outbreak of war a register of disciplined canines as the 'Volunteer Trained Dog Reserve' and been ignored by the authorities. Alsatian owners who had offered their dogs for military service had been dismissively 'told to enlist as Police Special Constables,' he would later complain. That was not to be the end of the matter — Baldwin would later tell a wartime audience:

> It is a peculiarity of the English, that we will give up our sons to military service, our wives and daughters to industry, our money to taxation, and our homes to billeted strangers, but when I pointed out to the authorities that they had 3,500,000 dog licences, and suggested that some of the dogs should be conscripted, I was warned that the public would not stand it!

Doggy stories from the wintry front in northeast France, where the British Expeditionary Force had begun to take up position in mid-September 1939, bloomed in the press desperate for something to report about what, for its lack of purposeful activity, was being called the 'Phoney War'.

First, there were tales of how the beastly Germans had seemingly limitless dogs, just as they had had in 1914. Their own Nazi-controlled canine press could not help but boast about how Germany's dogs were loyally serving the Fatherland as they had done since the days of Bismarck.[5]

---

[5] In March 1889 E. E. Bennet of the Army Veterinary Department had delivered a much commented upon lecture, the 'Employment of Dogs for Military Purposes'. The first public demonstration of a 'war dog' in Britain came a year later at the 1890 Military Tournament at the Agricultural Hall, Islington. The dog, a smooth-haired Collie, 'was borrowed for the purpose of testing the value of the German system of sending messages by these useful creatures in time of war,' it was reported. 'The dog was attached to a cyclist who rode the whole length of the hall — over bridges, ruts, and other difficulties in the way — the animal following him. Then the cyclist wrote a message, and tied it round the Collie's neck. The way was pointed out to him, he took a silent view of the road before him, and then, with a sudden bark, away the Collie went, and delivered the despatch safely as required.' The Collie (name unknown) had been borrowed from the Home for Lost Dogs, Battersea. After the performance it was acquired by a kindly officer, a certain Major Crabb.

Neutral sources relayed a story from the Berlin dog paper, *Die Hundewelt*, reporting on a grand recruiting rally in Berlin that had added 15,993 Airedales, Boxers, German Shepherds and Doberman Pinschers to the Wehrmacht's ranks. A fabricated story of a supposed German rations-only-for-war-dogs decree appeared in an outraged British press.

The British military attaché in Tokyo had also long been filing reports to the War Office of the keenness of the Japanese Army (as yet still only a potential enemy) for using dogs in their Chinese incursion, as scouts, for finding casualties, and for pursuing 'guerrilla bandits'. Dogs were donated by patriotic owners who were encouraged by the Imperial Military Dog Association to write to their army handlers for news of their former pets. Comics and films about war dogs aimed principally at young girls were very popular.[6]

But look how resolute the Germans were being in employing canine soldiers. The British Army was plainly missing a trick. There was the story from the front of how infantrymen of a Yorkshire regiment manning a front-line outpost had been alerted by a 'snuffling sound', when a dog (not on a leash) 'crawled under the barbed wire'. Sensing danger, 'it then retreated the way it came'. It was an enemy dog! Not far behind came its handler, leading a German patrol that was 'beaten off by machine gun-fire'.

From the detachment of the BEF in the Saarland around the Maginot Line came more news of Hun dogs. 'Dogs — usually

[6] The 1938 film, *Sensen ni Hoeyu* ('Barks at the Battlefront'), featured 'Esu' (Ace), a German Shepherd donated to the Army by a teenage girl from a wealthy family, who teams up with 'Doru' (Doll) in Manchuria to apprehend a spy — before expiring amidst a hail of Chinese nationalist bullets.

Alsatians — are used a great deal,' ran one story. 'Quite often the dog advances alone to discover a way through our wire and between our posts. It progresses forward, makes a detour, returns to its masters, and then leads them forward by the route it discovered. That is why all strange dogs seen by our advance infantry are shot'.

Britain's French allies had war dogs, which 'many times [have] saved whole regiments from walking into an ambush,' so it was reported. These were not brutalised attack dogs, but 'sensitive animals, which could scent a nearby enemy or the presence of gas or find the wounded.'

Herbert Lloyd envied the 'ever-practical Germans' and the time and effort they dedicated. He would write:

> Their method was for the trainer to start on the ground floor with the dog, taking him right through his training courses [and] continuing to handle him whilst on his active service career. The German dog was always worked loose, having been trained for probably a year, as against the British Army's hurried three months. The Hun dog relied on his nose to get direction and, creeping silently forward to confirm his suspicions, returned to his handler, who put him on a lead and followed on with the patrol.

There was meanwhile not a single official dog with the British Army in France. But there were some unofficial ones. As the BEF dug in deeper for the winter, there were some dashing officers who sought to relieve the tedium — such as Lieutenant A. C. Fane of a county infantry regiment, who announced in a sporting journal: 'The officers of this regiment hope to start in the near future a pack of beagles "somewhere in France", where hares are plentiful.'

Did anyone have any to spare? Aroused *Horse & Hound* correspondents piled in from elsewhere in France with stories of how the beastly local authorities had banned such a move on their behalf, along with 'shooting' (birds, presumably) — because 'they would rather the English treat the war in a more serious way'.

'Foxhunter Abroad', an English expatriate living in the Hautes-Pyrénées, revealed that, inspired by the donation of some two thousand footballs to the troops by Lord Rothermere, proprietor of the *Daily Mail*, he had been trying to organise a pack of 'foxhounds for British officers and beagles for all and sundry,' which could tour the rear areas of the front 'like a travelling circus'. The French authorities had been outraged.[7]

Captain Leonard Frank Plugge, extrovert commercial radio entrepreneur and Conservative MP for Rochester, struck a more sombre note in the Commons on 9 October 1939, when he asked the 'Secretary of State for War whether his attention has been called to the French system of training dogs for war service; and whether his Department is also adopting this policy?'

'The question of employing dogs for appropriate purposes is being examined,' Mr Leslie Hore-Belisha replied.

He was not being entirely untruthful. The War Office was indeed considering a response to Mr Lloyd's pleas that his trainee

[7] Some English dogs clearly did reach the army in France. A hunting historian recorded: 'Major Montacute Selby-Lowndes R F A took a pack of beagles to France with the British Expeditionary Force,' while Freddie Edmeades, whipper-in for the Royal Artillery Harriers, and his friend, Algy Hewitt, 'managed to smuggle a couple of harriers with them to France and enjoyed several weeks' hunting until apprehended by the Gendarmerie and hauled before the Army Commander'.

police dogs might have a place in this new war. On the 10th the Grandmaster was at the War Office to explain how his operation worked. The best dogs were Labrador crosses but any dog of the right temperament was suitable, so he told the gathered generals. Getting hold of them was no problem either — 'Dogs' homes could provide all required.'

Under the Home Office contract he had sixty dogs at Washwater and 250 dogs at his own kennels at Swakeleys Farm tended by a staff of eighteen — plus a transient population of twenty to thirty policemen, who stayed for two- to three-week courses. That is how it had been before the police work was stopped on the outbreak of war. After the ten-day selection period, 60 per cent of the canine candidates might prove suitable — and would go on to a further two months' specialist training. Rejects might make it as messenger dogs.

Suitable dogs could help to guard so-called 'Vulnerable Points' (VPs) at home, explained Mr Lloyd, or even act as 'patrol' dogs accompanying soldiers into action on the front line, just as the Germans and French were already employing them, as had been widely reported. But all agreed it was better to start experiments at home, seeing if dogs could help guard the arms dumps, airfields, headquarters and other VPs now sprouting around London and across the country, the security of which was monitored by the highest level of government. A special concern was securing isolated Range and Direction Finding sites — 'RDF' — later known as 'radar'. Saving manpower was the immediate goal. It was noted in the Cabinet Office that 32,000 troops were on guard duty at home, 2,000 of them watching over railway tunnels.

There was not a single dog employed by them. The 'saboteur tendency', as it was described, was reckoned at '100 or so IRA men' and 'an extremist section of the public with communistic tendencies' (but seemingly no British Fascists). There was no immediate fear of German saboteurs landing by parachute or submarine. And there was no intention, yet, of supplying dogs to the British Expeditionary Force in France.

As Herbert Lloyd told Colonel Cox of Eastern Command on 27 October: 'I believe you will find the patrol dog of the greatest value where you have <u>permanent</u> night staff. But of course, it is useless handing the dog over from one owner to another.' The one-man, one-dog principle, was paramount — and would stay that way throughout the war. It was also going to be a very big drawback in the employment of war dogs at all.

But, so Mr Lloyd added, a 'pinioned' dog on a long-running chain would be ideal for guarding petrol dumps and key positions. 'Such a dog can be very fierce and dangerous,' he said. A system with four men with four 'liaison' dogs running from 'corner to corner' of a defended area had proved promising in experiments.

'The Home Office are prepared to transfer me to the War Office,' explained Mr Lloyd, although the kennels at Washwater remained his property. As to cost, guard dogs cost £12—15 to buy on the open market, he said, but 'if I was taken over, I could possibly get a lot of material from "the lost dogs" homes and train these with the staff currently at my disposal.' He offered 'a man and a dog' for a week-long trial, 'at no expense to yourselves'.

And so it came to be. Britain's first war dog of this new conflict (name, breed, sex and origin unknown — but presumably from a lost dogs' home) was set to stand guard, along with the men of HQ Company, 1 Battalion, the London Rifle Brigade, over the very secret 'range and direction finding' apparatus attached to the RAF aerodrome at Northolt, west of London.

It all sounded rather jolly. From his suburban command post at Aspidistra Villa, 53 Woodland Avenue, Ruislip, the battalion's Commanding Officer, Major John K. Shanson, reported after two weeks: 'The dog supplied proved to be friendly with all the men of the Guard Post and although occasionally barking during the night, it did not appear certain that he would do so at the approach of any human being. It is of course possible another dog might do this.' Mr Lloyd had written, meanwhile, that 'he believes the dog has carried out his duties exceptionally well.'

There was evidently a second dog. While dog number one was 'so friendly it could not be relied on to bark at the approach of an unauthorised person', another was 'so fierce it was a danger to the general public, whether innocent or guilty'.

The War Office concluded: 'It is doubtful whether it is worthwhile pursuing any further.' As guard dogs, Britain's canines looked pretty useless. And the war was only six weeks old. And that, for now, was it. There would be a flicker of interest from the RAF, in February 1940, for dogs to guard airfields, where 'intended saboteurs' could lurk in 'copses and hedgerows before affixing time bombs to aircraft,' but the War Office was unmoved.

No dogs, please.

4

'Army Dog No. 1'

The British Expeditionary Force in France was proving a magnet for dogs. As with armies through history, the smell of field kitchens and the attentions of playful young men looking for companionship proved irresistible. In late 1939 there was an official rabies fear, that somehow soldiers coming home on leave would bring such foreign adoptees with them. The issue of smuggling of 'regimental pets by dominion or colonial troops, the source of so much trouble in 1914', as a stern memorandum reminded everybody, was not to be repeated. And this time pets might be breaching the nation's defences not just by troopship, tucked inside a greatcoat or soldier's kitbag, they could be flying in. In early 1940 the Air Ministry amended King's Regulations with orders to 'prevent the movement or importing into this country by air of dogs and cats'. That rule would be much flouted in the years to come. Flying pets would be a big feature of this new war and greatly vex ministerial inspectors.

Unwanted by the military back home, the nation's dogs adjusted to the deepening uncertainties of war. With no bombing and no actual fighting (except at sea), dog-lovers' anxieties at home now centred on the issue of food. On 8 January 1940, bacon, butter and sugar were rationed; meat would surely be next. In addition, on the first day of the New Year, the National Poultry Council expressed 'grave concern at the large quantities of feeding stuffs which are being consumed by hunters, packs of hounds, dogs, etc., not engaged in war-work.' It was reported in February that the breeding of pedigree puppies 'is to be discouraged because of too many dogs when protection of pets from air raids is already a problem.' Anti-dog sentiment was growing by the day.

Meat was declared rationed on 11 March 1940. It was done by price rather than weight, to the value of 1/10 per person per week. There was to be none for pets. Sausages, of dwindling meat content, were not rationed, and nor was offal (but that did not mean you could get it). Tinned dog foods, such as Chappie and Red Heart, were not restricted (yet). The Cabinet Food Policy Committee decided that impending shortage was to mean reductions all round for 'non-essential' animals. Horse and greyhound racing and hunts would be rationed to one-sixth of the pre-war level of feed for hounds (including beagles) and one-tenth for hunters.

The harmless-sounding 'Milled Wheaten Substance (Restriction) Order', made on 2 May, forbade the use of such products for anything but human food without special licence. It was a disaster for dogs. Where were their biscuits to come from now?

How to reduce dog numbers was becoming a direct concern of the government. Raising the cost of the dog licence was considered in May but it was noted for the minister that this 'would fall on the lower classes', who fed scraps to their pets. How very true!

The anti-dog whispering campaign was becoming a hate-filled rage against the furry fifth column. Grumpy farmers were already advocating the destruction of all domestic pets — while their own working dogs were exempt from licence. And in Britain's towns and cities, so *The Tail-Wagger Magazine* advised, there were 'dreadful people' abroad leaving lumps of poisoned bread in the streets. The 'anti-doggites' were winning everywhere, it seemed. But where and how might British Dogdom do its bit? By joining up. There were already several freelance examples.

A report from Nottingham in March revealed that the intrepid Flying Officer G. Ricks had acquired seven Alsatians and seven Airedales to guard his airfield. The dogs had been granted an allowance of 2d a day for food, plus scraps from the mess. They were guarding the main gate by day and the hangars and control tower by night.

Why could such initiatives not be made official? Wake up Dogdom, your country needs you! Mr Lloyd (still working under government contract) had to keep quiet. The noisy public entreaties of the war-dog enthusiasts, Messrs Baldwin and Richardson, were still being met by official silence but they had friends in the press and Parliament to help raise the canine rumpus.

Newspapers were as full as ever of sentimental stories about war dogs. The story of 'Bobby', for example, described as 'the first messenger dog of the French Army on the Western Front to be killed in action', was reported in April. Brave Bobby's body had been retrieved from no man's land under fire.

Bobby's demise 'on the field of honour' reminded one correspondent of the once-famous British 1918 war dog, 'Bing', who on his death, twelve years later, had been buried with 'full

military honours having time and again warned his battalion of
the coming of gas, and thus saved countless lives'.

From the frozen north came a stirring example of canine
sacrifice. *The Animals Defender* newsletter reported in May:
'Madame de Gripenberg, wife of the Finnish minister in London,
writes of [a dog] facing the shells, bombs and bullets of the cruel
Soviet masses standing still by his master in that cold climate of
Finland, where it has been 50 degrees below zero. [She describes]
with touching sympathy the faithful little Finnish Spitz dogs, as
clever as messenger carriers in their ability to find their masters in
the snow. At the time of writing these lines there is anything but
certitude that the hard-pressed Finns will be able to hold out
much longer'.[8]

The Phoney War altogether was ending with a bang. On 7–9
April 1940 the Germans overran Denmark. German naval and
air landings rapidly seized southern Norway. British and French
troops hung on perilously where they could.

The War Office was still deeply sceptical about war dogs as
'VP' guards or any other kind of military duty, but senior figures
at General Headquarters of the BEF in France were evidently
less so. They wanted German-style dogs for night reconnaissance
operations to 'prevent the patrol falling into ambushes', plus
'stationary dogs to give warning of an enemy approach'.

Thus it was that the Director of Military Training directed on 29
April (just as central Norway was being evacuated by British
troops) that an 'Experimental War Dog Section' should be formed

---

[8]   There was outrage among British dog-lovers in 1940 at reports that the Russians were
      using dogs to run under Finnish tanks with satchels of explosives attached to them
      before being blown up. Authoritative sources state that Soviet 'AT dogs' were used
      with limited success until at least 1943. The Soviets would claim it was all German
      propaganda, a position reinforced by the RSPCA.

'for service with British Expeditionary Force' consisting of an officer, an NCO and four men who 'should be trained for several weeks', at Mr Lloyd's kennels at Washwater, near Newbury.

On 7 May, 'the Norway debate' in the House of Commons made clear that after the Scandinavian fiasco, Prime Minister Neville Chamberlain must go. On 10 May the Germans invaded the Low Countries, parachutists seizing airfields and water crossings. The BEF was ordered into neutral Belgium.

Winston Churchill formed a coalition government in London. By the 13th, the Germans were across the River Meuse. The next day a new home defence force was announced for men between the ages of fifteen and sixty-five, to be called Local Defence Volunteers (soon to be renamed as the more evocative 'Home Guard').

Now the war-dog enthusiasts were barking louder than ever. The day Chamberlain quit, the House of Commons heard Mr Daniel Lipson, independent Conservative MP for Cheltenham (James Baldwin was his constituent), ask the Secretary of State for War somewhat bizarrely: 'Why the offer at the beginning of the war of the British Alsatian Training Club to supply working dogs for patrols was refused; and what societies that specialise in training dogs for war purposes have been consulted?'

The minister seemed baffled – there were more pressing concerns. 'The employment of patrol dogs is still in the experimental stage,' he replied and 'the police authorities and the Guide Dogs for the Blind Association have been consulted.' There was no mention of the prospects for Herbert Lloyd's Lilliputian canine unit in Wiltshire.

But Major Baldwin was not to be appeased. He expressed his anguish in *The Dog World* magazine – in an article on 3 May condemning the 'British government for saying no to dogs which can help to win the war.' An old War Office chum had dismissed him as a nostalgist: 'You see, my dear chap, how different things are from what they were last time,' he told him at the club as the German Panzers romped towards the Channel ports. What use were 'message dogs' in any of this? Alsatian owners who had offered their dogs for war service had been told to enlist as police Special Constables. A proper start on mobilising the nation's dogs must be made now, insisted the Colonel.

In fact it had been. On 17 May 1940 Britain's war-dog operation was formally activated. The first animal registered as 'Army Dog No. 1' was called 'Prince'.

On 21 May, Mr Lipson MP renewed his parliamentary assault with a Baldwin-prompted question asking the new Secretary of State for War, Anthony Eden, whether he 'has now informed himself of the use made by the French and German armies of patrol dogs; and whether he will take steps to see that patrol dogs are provided for British troops on a commensurate scale?'

'I am aware of the use of patrol dogs,' Mr Eden replied. 'The extent of their use with British troops is dependent on the result of training experiments now in progress.'

'Is he aware that the Germans have something like 100,000 dogs available for this purpose?' he was asked. The minister was indeed aware. He, however, did not admit to the fact that Britain's war-dog section was just four-strong. Nor did he mention 'Prince' — he was surely a military secret.

The same day Lt-Gen Alastair MacDougall, Deputy Chief of the Imperial General Staff, gruffly minuted that there was nothing to be gained from employing dogs on Vulnerable Points. He clearly had other things on his mind. The Belgian Army surrendered on 28 May. The British Expeditionary Force hastened its retreat to an embattled pocket on the northeast French coast, picking up a four-footed army of refugee dogs as it did so.

The German animal welfare magazine, *Reichtierschutzblatt*, meanwhile showed the triumph of the Blitzkrieg with photos of Hitler, the 'animals' true friend', patting a French Army horse on the forehead and reaching out to stroke 'a French battlefield stray' dog on his journey to conquered Paris.

In London a secret propaganda committee agreed on 10 June to fire up an 'anger campaign' to rouse the people against the 'fundamental rottenness of the Germans'. The result was a bizarre story planted in neutral newspapers that 'three million dogs were to be compulsorily destroyed' in the Fatherland, because they 'eat food that might otherwise be used for human consumption'. British dog owners were appalled.

The rout in France meant that no war dogs would be joining the BEF. But the tiny unit at Washwater had indeed been declared formed, on 3 June, under the command of a Lieutenant H. A. Buxton of the Rifle Brigade. Its HQ was now at stately Woolton House, Newbury, otherwise the home of Lady Buckland, sister-in-law of the proprietor of the *Daily Telegraph*. Britain's youthful war-dog commander sent out an urgent request for stores, blank ammo, flare pistols and twenty-five 'noisy but harmless bombs as used at the Aldershot Tattoo to accustom the dogs to the noise of battle'.

It was clear that this new canine force would not be doing much patrolling. They would instead be guarding things, something they had failed so miserably to do when officially tried out a year before. Now everywhere in the land, it seemed, was a

Vulnerable Point. While invasion panic gripped coastal towns, triggering a renewed wave of pet killing, a new scare stalked the wider nation — parachutists. The Home Guard had been formed in summer 1940 to confound them. The company of dogs seemed ideal; the war-dog enthusiasts had opened a new front.

The Dog World magazine picked up the war-dog rumours referring to the 'experimental work being done by Mr. H S Lloyd'. 'One can easily imagine an Alsatian dashing forwards and attacking a parachutist,' said the journal. Just look at how clever dogs had been in pre-war dog shows and intelligence tests. Displays of Alsatian agility had become star attractions at fêtes and carnivals — although they were still very much a novelty.

Our Dogs would comment: '[T]he people best suited to guard us against the possibility of surprise landings are those men and women who know the country well [and] can ride across it. Shoot straight and command a following of powerful well trained and loyal dogs.' Fox hunting enthusiasts might yet find a patriotic role.

From Woking, Colonel Richardson sent the War Office a stream of telegrams. On 20 May: 'I offer my services immediately for mobilisation of dogs for guarding vulnerable points and other war services at home and overseas'.

'Dogs are invaluable for defensive guarding all vulnerable, secret and dangerous places,' he messaged on 11 June. 'Apologies for wiring but can get no attention paid.' Sceptics and dog enthusiasts alike bounced memos around the War Office. On the 25th, Brigadier Harold Eady, Deputy Director of Military Training, told GHQ Home Forces, 'There is something in the smell dog idea and we should hear the views of the experts.'

But two days later the War Minister was yet again asked in Parliament about dogs — which were apparently 'the only means of finding strange troops in wooded places,' according to the questioner. The minister replied wearily: 'The question of the use of dogs in home defence has been carefully considered and it has been decided that their value is not sufficient to offset the difficulties which their employment entails.' He was none too sure about strange men in woods, anyway.

But it looked like he was reading from an already outdated script. The 'smell dogs experts' would indeed be consulted and they seem to have been convincing. What was there to lose by continuing experiments? There were, after all, only four war dogs in the entire British Army.

5

The Dismal Jimmies

Lieutenant Buxton's Dog Section pottered away in Wiltshire through the autumn of 1940. In spite of earlier ministerial pronouncements, it all looked rather hopeful. If they were judged to be no use as static guards, in November it was decided to 'experiment further with dogs for active patrol work at night', while consideration was 'being given to the establishment at an early date of a War-Dog Training School,' according to War Office memoranda.

But what were dogs without men to handle them? Southern Command was told by the Director of Military Training to 'secure particulars of Other Ranks who have expert experience of handling dogs'. Lists of candidates from all regiments and service branches were ready by the end of November, to be weeded down to those with 'bona fide dog experience'. There were scores of suitable applicants.

Sapper S. J. Shepperd, aged twenty-six, of Brighton, East Sussex, for example, had ten years' experience 'working lurchers and whippets over the South Downs at night'. It sounded exotic.

Driver L. Leedham had 'night estate work with retrievers and gun dogs in the employ of Colonel Hardcastle of Bradshire Hall, Bolton, Lancs'. As well as experience with 'lurchers, breaking terriers and of rat and rabbit catching', he had 'basic veterinary skills'. Meanwhile Private Dennis Houle of Wainstalls, a village near Halifax, Yorkshire, was 'used to cross-bred dogs and curs'.

It was not all shepherds and gamekeepers (and indeed, poachers). Private C. Vyfius of Georgetown, British Guiana, had 'trained dogs for big game hunting'. And Pte H. J. Thacker of New Cross, southeast London, had 'four years experience with Alsatians as a breeder and seller'. Pte A. Hale had worked at East Ham greyhound track, while Sapper W. Pinching had trained performing dogs. Sapper W. J. Phillips owned a pack of Australian bush dogs, 'for hobby and profit'. The British Army was clearly full of untapped canine-savvy talent.

Eager candidates kept coming. There were plenty of good dog men, evidently, but from where would the Amy get the dogs? And what were they supposed to do?

The whole war-dog venture had begun on the premise that because the beastly Huns (and the less beastly French) had patrol and message dogs, then so too should the British Army. But the expulsion of the BEF from Dunkirk ended that idea. Dog-borne messages might be sent by Air Raid Precautions (ARP) posts or Home Guard platoons at home, but this was amateur stuff. Embattled Britain was now a war front of its own — a collection of 'Vulnerable Points' from the Boat of Garten in the Highlands of Scotland to Bletchley Park in Bedfordshire, all of which needed round-the-clock guard. And not a single dog was officially sent to help in the task.

As the Cabinet Office internal history put it: 'No longer was the danger that of an internal saboteur, [instead] attack by enemy agents or armed parties landed from the sea or by air seemed imminent'. It meant that in spring 1941, 60,000 troops were standing around guarding things — which meant that the 'Field Force', the active, mobile component of the Army, could not train for offensive action that it might one day take the fight back to the enemy.

The enthusiasts still banged on that the nation's dog power should somehow be harnessed to meet this obvious need, but the anti-doggites at the War Office were still ascendant. Herbert Lloyd would describe them as the 'dismal jimmies', who used 'the usual shuttlecock methods to dispose of such offers'.

At the end of an inauspicious year, Lt-Gen Sir Guy Williams, Commander-in-Chief of Eastern Command, told GHQ Home Forces that there was a general demand in the Corps under his command for about 'a hundred police dogs' able to detect movement at 300 yards, so as 'to lighten the duties of winter night patrols'. The War Office Vulnerable Points director wearily replied:

> It seems that dogs need careful handling by one person and will bark at all others be they friend or foe. It would be impossible to train a dog to differentiate between a British soldier and a German parachutist or saboteur.

But General Williams refused to give up. In spite of all doubts he was still anxious to try them out. His request was again turned down. 'The standard of dogs is not reliable,' so trials had proved,

according to GHQ Home Forces. 'It had all been thrashed out
and was not worth raising again.'

The immediate threat of invasion receded. The central drama
of the second winter of war was the bombing of Britain's cities,
the 'Blitz'. It had begun in earnest in September 1940. The
long-held assumption that dogs would go berserk in air raids
proved false. Instead dogs (and indeed cats) seemed positively
serene under fire – it was their owners who panicked first.

Nevertheless, as cities burned, the resources of NARPAC and
the animal welfare charities were tested to the limit, with a new
wave of mass abandonment and destruction of pets. The Dogs'
Home, Battersea, had to bury hundreds of animals in 'a large
hole' in its own garden.[9]

The nation's dogs were having a tough time of it generally.
Newspaper headlines had broken the truly appalling news on 6
August 1940: 'Penal Offence to Waste Food: Warning as to Meat
for Dogs'. It could not have been more ominous: 'The Ministry
of Food to-day made an order coming into force next Monday for
preventing [the] waste of food and carrying with it penalties
against offenders. It will be an offence to waste food, which is
described as everything used by man for food or drink other than
water'. In great secrecy the War Cabinet Committee on Civil
Defence considered measures to 'reduce the dog and cat
population generally'.

On 1 January 1941 there was a new humiliation for pet owners,
an order that 'all meat which is unsuitable for human consumption
must be dyed green'. 'The special dye is stated to have no harmful

9   Destruction at Battersea peaked in 1940, with 17,347 dogs destroyed under police
    contract. The 1941 figure would be 11,446. Surely a better use might have been made of
    such animals than rendering their bodies down for glycerine?

effect upon the animals to which it is fed and the colour cannot be boiled out of the meat,' it was reported. After much protest, all the Ministry of Food had come up with was a statement: 'Dogs and cats must subsist on the limited supplies available eked out by inedible offal, horsemeat and the like'. It all sounded horrible, but at least pets were getting something.

Dogs were now openly portrayed as the enemy within. The canine population was estimated at three million licensed and half a million more outlaws. They consumed 5 oz per day of biscuits and 3 oz of protein. How to have fewer? Raising the dog licence perhaps, as had been suggested before, or reducing the grace period for strays on police hands before they were destroyed by dogs' home contractors. That was not nearly strong enough.

A meeting to review the 'Food Consumption by Dogs' at the Ministry of Food took place on 1 April 1941. All the ways and means proposed over the past year to reduce the canine population were looked at again. But the effect on national morale of 'doing away with all pet dogs would have a worse effect than the loss of a military campaign,' was the personal view of the legal adviser to the ministry.

Ruled out for guarding things, and with no chance to show if they could go on patrol or carry messages on the battlefield, or even hunt down parachutists and saboteurs, dogs seemed pretty useless all round. Pro-doggites pointed out the companionship they afforded lonely women whose husbands were away at the war. There were lots of stories from the Blitz of hero dogs scrabbling at the rubble. But the anti-dog lobby generally were winning. A government committee was measuring them up for the chop — if they did not get into this war soon, the outlook was very grim for dogs.

That summer of 1941, the public opinion sampling organisation, Mass-Observation, came out firmly on the side of dogs. 'There should be more done to show the ways in which dogs are helping the war effort,' M-O researchers commented. 'There have been singularly few dog heroes in this war.'

On both counts, that was about to change.

Part Two

'SEEK!'

'To Arms, To Arms, You Dogs Of Britain!'

The Dog World magazine, 22 May 1942

'Nothing will teach the normal British [infantry] unit not to make a pet out of a dog.'

General Staff Policy Committee on
Weapons and Equipment:
Employment of Dogs for War Purposes, July 1943

6

'The War Office invites
dog owners ...'

'There have been singularly few dog heroes in this war,' Mass-Observation had reported. That could change, and it would. Thus far pets had got on with enduring the Blitz at home along with everyone else.

There was, however, a dusty cockpit of war where British forces were actually on the offensive. And there were dogs there in abundance. They were not exactly 'war dogs', but in the circumstances they would have to do.

Since September 1940, the British had been busy fighting off the Italian Army's attempt to invade Egypt from their Libyan colony. The PDSA hospital in Cairo was, so it was reported, 'full of dogs which had belonged to the Italians and had been stranded during the ebb and flow of the fighting' — 'Some of them were very well bred, Belgian sheep-dogs, Italian Pointers and Setters, the majority however were pariahs'.

In February 1941 the Commander-in-Chief Middle East, General Archibald Wavell, was ordered to halt his all-conquering counter-attack into Libya and send troops across the Mediterranean to Greece — also the victim of an Italian invasion. It would end in disaster. On 12 February an obscure German commander called Erwin Rommel arrived in Libya with a small battle group to stiffen Italian resistance and very soon went on the attack. The 'Afrika Korps', as it would soon become known, brought a number of trained military dogs with them.

The German intervention changed everything. Commonwealth forces were trapped in the besieged port of Tobruk. Expelled from Greece, meanwhile, by the German drive into the Balkans (unable to escape by sea, a complete RAVC field hospital unit surrendered on a beach), those British forces that could get away had taken refuge on the island of Crete, only to be evicted again by German air landings and once more rescued by sea.

A collection of animals picked up en route were with them all the way, according to the PDSA's wartime history, 'smuggled out in boxes and kitbags'. British troops in Libya, meanwhile, fell back into Egypt and moved into Iraq and Vichy-French-controlled Syria, lest the whole position in the Middle East be lost.

The ever-expanding desert war became a vast canine arena, with swarms of both ex-colonial posh dogs and outcast 'pi-dogs' (pariahs) following the warring armies in barking rabbles. In Cairo, as the PDSA's own history put it, 'batches of dogs appeared and with them foxes found in the desert. It was a common sight in these dark days to see lorry loads of our soldiers coming in bearded and dusty with their new pets riding with them'.

The story was told of 'one little dog which had been captured from the Italians, sent across to Greece, evacuated to Crete, from Crete to Cairo, then to Syria and Palestine and back to Cairo —

where it arrived on a 15 cwt lorry with eight big infantrymen and a corporal'.

The 'rough-coated brown and white dog of unknown breed' had had five puppies. 'Instructions were left at the PDSA Hospital that should no one come and collect the dog and her family after one month, the puppies would be put to sleep and find the mother a new home. The platoon did not return,' it was reported starkly. Another, homelier account has the 'little dog finding a home with another soldier' while her 'babies were painlessly put to sleep'.

There were two dogs 'belonging to Tommies,' so Hans Bloom, director of the PDSA Clinic in Cairo wrote, which had been brought back from Dunkirk and had seen both Wavell's and the Syrian campaign. 'They had changed hands many times.'

Superintendent Bloom painted a lyrical picture of kindly soldiers – British, Australians, Rhodesians – all selflessly rescuing pets and easing the burdens of abused pack animals, while 'puppies for sale in the streets of Cairo by boys are bought out of sympathy for ten piastres each.' A Polish soldier had adopted a young desert fox, while a wounded Greek soldier was adopted on the battlefield by a 'German police dog', which had crossed the front line. He had woken from unconsciousness in a shell hole to find the dog licking his face. After that they were inseparable.

These dogs of war in North Africa were entirely unofficial. No graduate of the War Office's modest 'War Dog Section' under Mr Lloyd's direction at Washwater had yet joined the ranks. It carried on, all but forgotten until early in the New Year when it moved to improvised quarters in the old Cavalry Barracks at Aldershot and eight army personnel rather than civilian trainers were taken on from the big dog-loving personnel trawl of the winter before. The bespectacled Lieutenant J. H. Clarke was appointed commandant and Herbert Lloyd engaged as 'Chief Instructor and Technical Consultant'. He remained a civilian.

The War Office correspondence file on the matter goes blank after 19 January 1941. Then suddenly, on 5 May 1941, a stirring appeal appeared in British newspapers:

> The War Office invites dog owners to lend their dogs to the Army. The breeds most suitable are Airedales, Collies (rough or smooth), Hill Collies, Crossbreds, Lurchers, and Retrievers (Labrador or Golden), although intelligence and natural ability will be the deciding factors in selection.

Dog-lovers offering their family pets were further assured that:

> Dogs offered will be given an intensive course of training. Those not passing the test will be immediately returned to the owners; selected dogs will be retained for the duration of the war. Owners can have every confidence that their dogs will receive skilled care and attention. The War-Dog Training School is at Willems Barracks, Aldershot, to which offers of dogs should be made by letter.

What prompted the announcement is mysterious. Herbert Lloyd just seems to have written to newspapers of his own volition. *The Tail-Wagger Magazine* for May ran a longer version of the appeal it had received as a letter, reported to be 'signed by Mr H S Lloyd, Chief Instructor'. He had added this: 'It is confidentially anticipated that by the co-operation of the doggy fraternity this scheme will produce the number of dogs required and prove of the greatest value to the fighting services.' The appeal did not mention Alsatians, the modernist über-dog that still remained controversial among more traditionalist members of the Kennel Club.

There is nothing about it in War Office files, no register of dogs offered or taken in. Just a series of press cuttings climaxing four days later in a report that there had been 'thousands of offers from all parts of the country, dogs ranging from Cocker spaniels to Pekingese'.

The story went round the world. The *New York Times* reported the heart-warmingly eccentric doggy tale from embattled Britain for neutral America. Australian papers picked it up. In fact, so great was the response that the War Office had to make urgent press announcements for people to stop sending offers of dogs.

But some suitable dogs evidently did get to Aldershot, or rather letters about them did – thousands of them. Herbert Lloyd, in a post-war memoir, recalled: 'It was the opinion of those [in Whitehall] who had little faith in the project that no good purpose would be served by asking for volunteers. The dismal jimmies however were indeed surprised at the response from the public as, within two weeks, the skeleton staff were snowed under with 7,000 offers of dogs, owners only asking that their dogs should be given the chance of proving their worth.'

'There were many heart-rending letters,' he recalled, 'one writer saying "my husband has gone, my sons have gone, take my dog to help bring this cruel war to an early end".'[10]

In fact, food, or lack of it, was the overwhelming issue. 'Few of these dogs would have been transferred from being pets to the military but for the difficulty of getting dog food these days,' the *PDSA Journal* observed in a report from the sharp end. Feeding big dogs was especially hard, and big dogs were what the Army seemed to want. In fact the Dewsbury Road, Leeds, branch of the veterinary charity had physically mustered all sorts of dogs in response to the strange appeal. 'Some have been given, some have been lent and some have been sold,' it was said. Of the dogs in question, 'Mick', an Alsatian, did not know any special words of command, according to his auxiliary fireman owner, but 'he'll answer to "Oi!"' The owner of 'Toby', a Spaniel, was on 'long hours and war work, and that's the main reason little Toby goes into the Army.' Other hopefuls were 'Peter', a Spaniel cross and two more Alsatians, 'Dan' and 'Rover'.

The doggy queue was getting longer. Alerted to some unusual goings on, a few days later a *Yorkshire Post* reporter found more dogs mustered in Dewsbury Road, including 'Dante', who 'cocked his wolf-like ears, glanced with bright, intelligent eyes about him, and growled querulously'. Mr J. Burdekin of Ossett had 'brought his majestic English mastiff bitch, "Bess", with a pedigree as long as your arm'. And Mrs A. Cunningham had turned up with her black Alsatian, 'Tony', whose 'grandfather

---

[10] Colonel Richardson's 1920 book, *British War Dogs*, recounted the very similar response to his appeal made in an earlier war: 'Some of the letters received at this time [1918] testify to the unselfish spirit in the country. A lady wrote: "I have given my husband and my sons, and now that he too is required, I give my dog." From a little girl: "Let Daddy go to fight the Kaiser, and now we are sending Jack to do his bit".'

had served as a message-carrier in the last war'. 'Tony has had some training already, and, although I shall hate to part with him, I'd like to think he was doing his bit,' said Mrs Cunningham.

What was going on?

'White-coated, Mr. W P Hirst, of the People's Dispensary for Sick Animals, introduced each dog in turn to the examiner – Mr. H S Lloyd, Chief Instructor of the War Dogs' School,' said the report, 'who on behalf of the War Office was attending the Leeds branch of the PDSA to inspect dogs offered for loan or for the army.'

Leeds was as good a place as any for testing the mettle of British dog power. But if, as it seems, the appeal was some sort of freelance stunt by Herbert Lloyd as a dry-run test of public reaction, then it worked. And at the time, with ministers considering drastic anti-pet moves under the Waste of Food Order, that the state offered some kind of refuge for dogs could be politically useful.

Whoever was behind it, Herbert Lloyd's army was on its way. One account says that forty dogs were in training at Aldershot after that first appeal until, in July 1941, the school moved to Mr Lloyd's commercial kennels at Swakeleys Farm, Ickenham, in the west London suburbs. Brackenbury Kennels at Harefield, a few miles to the north, was taken over as a sanatorium for 'sick dogs'.

Swakeleys was a redbrick Queen Anne house, smartly modernised with rambling barns adapted as kennels. Still a much-reduced commercial breeding operation of the famous 'Of Ware' Cocker spaniels, it was also the Lloyd family home.

Herbert Lloyd's daughter, Jennifer, remembered after over seventy years:

I remember my father telling us, just after my fourth birthday in July 1941, that we all had to move out of Swakeley's Farm to another house called White Lodge. Dad said it was because the war dogs were going to be moved into the farm. Although at the time I didn't really understand much about what was going on, I did realise these were dogs that my father was going to train to help in the war effort in some way.

War Office correspondence, in fact, shows a total lack of interest in Mr Lloyd and his war dogs throughout that nervous summer. But the tidal wave of public offers could not be ignored altogether. When, at the end of July, the evidently pro-canine Maj-Gen Sir John 'Ginger' Hawkesworth, Director of Military Training, raised the point, 'that the Italians had used watch dogs in Libya with considerable effect,' he was told gruffly by GHQ Home Forces: 'Patrol and VP dogs had already been thoroughly thrashed out last year [and turned down], it is not worth raising the issue again.'

Attitudes mysteriously changed in August when a handful of dogs were issued to XII Corps on anti-invasion exercises in southern England for one last try as tactical animals. Pro-doggites at the War Office ensured an army photographer was on hand to record Alsatian 'Mark' doing his bit as an ammunition carrier in Eastern Command, boldly bringing up the magazines for Bren and Lewis light machine-guns.

'Mark', went the story, was 'presented to the British Expeditionary Force by the First French Army and was in active service from November 1939 to June 1940.' The picture and caption featured in news stories around the world and the sequence still turns up, along with Colonel Richardson's Airedales, as somehow showing British war dogs in action.

While Mark was bringing up the ammo, the war had
dramatically moved on. In June Hitler's forces had invaded the
Soviet Union – and the threat of more bombing and invasion of
Britain itself receded. British forces on land only engaged the
enemy at the desert margins. No one outside a small group of
doggy cranks was really that interested in 'patrol dogs'. There
was, however, still a great deal of mind-numbing 'guarding' to do
across the embattled nation. For lonely units[11] patrolling some
God-forsaken Welsh reservoir, the presence of a dog might add a
bit of cheer.

A big doggy boost, meanwhile, was coming from a completely
different direction to Mr Lloyd and his army dogs. It was down
to that veteran canine campaigner, Lt-Col James Y. Baldwin,
now a reserve army officer, recalled to active duty as local
defence commander at Staverton aerodrome, Gloucestershire.
He was busy opening up a second war-dog front with some very
astute string pulling. The imminent threat of airborne invasion
might have receded, but southern England was now dotted
with factories and aircraft supply units (ASUs) packed with
new-made fighters and bombers, glaringly open to sabotage.

The factories and satellite storage sites were the concern of the
Ministry of Aircraft Production (MAP). The newly appointed
minister was Baldwin's old chum and fellow Alsatian enthusiast,
John Moore-Brabazon. Guarding the sites was the Army's
responsibility.

---

[11]   In early 1941, the 'Vulnerable Points Wing' (the so-called 'Blue Hats') of the Corps of
Military Police was formed with 'men of lower medical categories to patrol and guard
key installations'. Their role was to defend bridges and railway tunnels, etc. against
'sabotage by stealth'. They were armed but not expected to counter commando-style
raiders.

The area commander for the South Midlands (lots of aircraft factories) admitted the handful of men available and the scale of the task made it a 'farce'. Staverton itself, where Baldwin was in charge, was rather special. It was where Rotol[12] airscrews were made — the RAF would not be going very far without them.

Baldwin had been a whirl of activity. At the beginning of August, he had proposed setting up his very own guard dog school, and 'had earmarked 8 to 10 women and men, experienced instructors in dog management who would form the instructional staff.' The Army, he proposed, would send guards to the school, be matched up with a dog, trained and sent back on duty. There would be no difficulty in getting dogs — 'we have already had offers from many owners,' he told his friend, the minister. 'I understand some such school has started at Aldershot,' wrote his superior officer (and evident enthusiast for the plan), Brig McMullen, 'but it will be years before this Area will gain any benefit.'

Thus it was that on 11 September a parade of staff cars in Army khaki drab and RAF grey rolled into Staverton airfield at 1100 hours to see a splendid demonstration of guard dogs in action. The demonstration was attended by Lt-Gen Edmond 'Teddy' Schreiber, the Commander-in-Chief Southern Command and a glittering roster of Army and RAF brass.

Concealed saboteurs in padded clothing were routed out of the hedgerows in a display of Alsatian determination that would become a regular fixture of Colonel Baldwin's highly press-

---

[12] The Rotol Company was formed on 13 May 1937 by Rolls-Royce and Bristol Aeroplane Company. Rotol produced over 30,000 airscrews for Hurricanes and Spitfires. By the end of the war, a total of 100,000 airscrews had been produced.

friendly operation. Attendees were advised to book a table at the
Plough Inn in the village for an agreeable luncheon afterwards.

It was a triumph. Lt-Gen Schreiber wrote that afternoon to
General Sir Alan Brooke, Commander-in-Chief Home Forces
(later to be Chief of the Imperial General Staff), that he 'had just
seen a most convincing demonstration of the value of dogs of the
protection of dispersed aircraft.' The 'prime mover' in the scheme
was an 'Aerodrome Defence officer' in the South Midland
Command Area, he added. 'He can get the necessary dogs given
to him and trained by voluntary effort.'

Recruiting pets from the public would mean minimal cost.
The Treasury was still being sticky but Baldwin's back channel
to the Minister of Aircraft Production would overcome all
resistance. 'We requisitioned the big kennels at Redditch,' he
wrote, 'also a big house near here which would accommodate all
the trainers etc.'

'I have been paying some of the trainers myself,' he confided,
'and have about twenty dogs to be sure of a really good start.'

The highest levels of the British Army were, it seemed, now
dog-lovers to a man. Lt-Gen Harold Alexander, newly appointed
GOC-in-C [General Officer Commanding-in-Chief], Southern
Command, informed GHQ of a factory being guarded by 'a
single woman and a dog', which 'exhaustive trials had
demonstrated was far more effective' than the local Home Guard
platoon.

The Army must get back in the canine game. On 28 October
Southeast Command was ordered to restart 'intensive troop
trials' with the XII Corps dogs already trained by Mr Lloyd and
'report on their usefulness as patrol and messengers' within a
week. 'The dogs have proved in night patrol trials to be of the

utmost value in detecting the presence and direction of enemy personnel,' the War Office was told on 3 November, 'except where [exercise] umpires or civilians had lain a false scent. Message dogs seldom fail to find their way back.' It was all down to that mysterious thing, a dog's nose.

After the debacle of the May 'lend-your-dogs-to-the-Army' appeal, it was time for some positive PR. Pathé news cameramen arrived at Swakeleys Farm that November to film Alsatians jumping over gates, carrying messages, 'smelling out the enemy' and generally being warlike as they were led by handlers in battledress through suburban woodland in a newsreel sequence dubbed 'Canine Warriors'. *Illustrated* magazine ran a three-page photo spread under the startling headline, 'Pets Train for War'. 'Men and dogs are firm friends,' ran the report, 'and although the dogs are not petted at all, you have only to see a great Alsatian putting his long muzzle into a khaki pocket to know that endearments are unnecessary.' Among the dogs encountered were 'Max', 'Zena', 'Judy', 'Bob', 'Sandy' and 'Piper', all 'once ordinary household pets'. Should they so wish, their owners might come and see them, 'although were not encouraged to do so'.

'Here, at the Army School of Dog Training, the officers and men of the establishment are all "doggy" people,' reported *The Times*, 'expert in the management and training of dogs. It is to the credit of the Army authorities that, having decided to start this school, they took these men from other units so that their special knowledge might be usefully employed.' As for the dogs, 'they are on loan (like binoculars) from a generous public ...

'Already this school has supplied many trained dogs for home defence work,' the report continued somewhat misleadingly, 'and its programme for the future aims at still more advanced work. The dogs are mostly Alsatians, the Airedale is unfortunately rare these days, and Collies of different varieties'.

And then there was this: 'There is one dog kept at the school for another phase of work that is as yet only experimental. He used to belong to a gas company and was used for tracing leaks in their mains'.

As it would turn out, the gas company dog would prove a very important dog indeed.

In deepest Gloucestershire, meanwhile, Colonel Baldwin's air dogs were by now outpacing everybody. His stream of upbeat reports to the Minister of Aircraft Production continued. 'The thing we want the dog to do is scent any stranger within 200 yards,' he wrote and by November 1941 he could report, 'everyone is dying to get at it, although a very large number of dogs will be required.' Flight Lieutenant Hugh Bathurst-Brown, the Adjutant at Woolton-Staverton, otherwise a country solicitor, was appointed commandant. Baldwin himself would be 'Dog Advisor' and 'Chief Training Officer'.

His political patron, John Moore-Brabazon, was in trouble, meanwhile, for allegedly saying what a fine thing it would be if Nazi Germany and the Soviet Union fought each other to death, leaving Britain as the master of Europe. He denied this allegation, but it would later claim his career.

The Treasury approved Colonel Baldwin's 'experimental' dog scheme on 17 November 1941. Kennels were quickly erected by the Royal Engineers on an Army-run AA gun site at the existing Staverton aerodrome. Challenged by this new rival, any lingering doubts at the War Office were swept away. It had been agreed that the Army would have 'tactical' dogs to actually go into battle. But if the Ministry of Aircraft Production could have its own canine sentries to bark at intruders, the Army would have them too — it was a lot more straightforward than training them for combat.

7

'... To lend your dog to the Army'

On 7 December 1941 Japanese aircraft attacked the US naval base at Pearl Harbor in Hawaii. Germany declared war on the United States. A sleeping canine giant had been roused.

The next day Japanese infantry attacked the British Crown Colony of Hong Kong. Among the defenders were troops from the Royal Rifles of Canada, who had arrived by ship a few weeks before. With them was an enormous Newfoundland dog, 'Gander', once a family pet called 'Pal', who had been adopted as a mascot. The outsize dog had crossed the Rockies and the Pacific Ocean completely unofficially. At the fighting for Lye Tun, the inlet separating Kowloon from Hong Kong Island, it was said that he met his end by running off with a Japanese grenade in his mouth. Gander was a mascot, not a war dog, but he had died in action alongside Commonwealth forces and merits a place in this story. His exceptional bravery would be remembered in exceptional circumstances much later with the award after sixty years of the revived 'Dickin Medal' (see p. 139).

On Christmas Eve, 1941, the Hong Kong garrison surrendered. The same day, Lt-Gen Sir Bernard Paget, Commander-in-Chief Home Forces, gave the War Office his reaction to Southeast Command's canine experiments featuring 'Mark' and his pals. It was positive: 'This XII Corps report fully justifies the adoption of dogs for patrol and message carrying,' he wrote. He suggested that this would require 'initially two each for the infantry battalions. This will involve a commitment of 460 dogs of each type for Home Forces. The first should go to divisions on the coast.'

As for guard dogs, an exhaustive audit of Vulnerable Points and the numbers of dogs required to protect them was drawn up – hundreds of sites stretching from the Boat of Garten in the remote Cairngorms (two dogs) to Overton, Hampshire, where the Bank of England had been evacuated.

Fuel dumps, truck parks, RDF stations, BBC transmitters, locks, docks, bridges were laid out in a very secret document with three hundred four-footed defenders allotted. The overall calculations were done. No fewer than 1,220 dogs were wanted for the British Army as soon as practicable.

Tails were wagging everywhere. The RSPCA's *Animal World* magazine that month reported on how Britain's gallant Soviet ally was using 'Airedales as ambulance dogs' during the dramatic winter defence of Moscow — 'dragging wounded back through the snow on little sledges'. Would the British Army do the same if the need arose?

Dogs doing brave things in the snow always excited dog-lovers. After being expelled from Norway in spring 1940, there was no wintry front on which Britain might take the enemy to war, but there might be in the future, and there was always Iceland, occupied since 1940 by British forces to forestall a German invasion. In May 1942 the DAV&RS War Diary recorded a request from the force commander in Reykjavik, that 'sled dogs be trained in Britain during the summer months'. The US would soon thereafter take over the defence of Iceland but a big idea had taken root. A month later the requirement would be increased for no fewer than six hundred sled dogs, for unspecified purposes, but nothing to do with Iceland. How to obtain as many as that was clearly a problem; the most obvious source was North America.

By July these still-to-be delivered animals were earmarked for some form of 'winter and arctic' warfare training in Britain, to be handled by 'experienced Norwegian personnel'. Major R. F. Wall of the British Purchasing Commission in the USA was ordered to ascertain the speediest method of obtaining them — while the Scot Polar Institute in Cambridge was approached as to whether they could be found from 'Iceland or North Russia', along with sledges and harnesses. Major Wall cabled back, he could 'only get 120 dogs due to intensive buying by the US Army'. Nevertheless the strange plan to get hold of suitable winter war dogs would proceed.

In the Cotswolds, meanwhile, Colonel Baldwin had already outpaced everyone in getting his Alsatians ready for action. On 20 January 1942, he had been formally seconded to the MAP as 'dog adviser' and installed in an agreeable HQ in the requisitioned stables and outbuildings of 'Woodfold', a rambling country house six miles from Cheltenham. The nearby Staverton aerodrome kennels were formally transferred from the Army to the RAF — it would be called the 'Guard Dog Training School'.

It was clear to the Treasury that to have two war-dog operations running at once might be less than efficient. It was also time to bring in the specialists in animal health and management, the Army Veterinary Directorate (recently administratively conjoined with the 'Remount Service', the source of Army war horses, as the new 'AV&RS').

At first its officers, members of the Royal Army Veterinary Corps, seemed bemused. Their traditional responsibility was horses, of which the British Army in 1939 had six thousand, a shadow of its former equine glory. The Corps had dwindled to 'a mere handful of officers and men'. Their knowledge of dogs (other than as pets) was minimal; they would prove eager to learn.

On 19 January the new AV&RS Directorate was put on standby to supply a Veterinary Officer for a larger establishment than the 'present Training School at Ickenham capable of handling 350 dogs with the necessary number of handlers and trainers'. A week later, they were asked to consider the 'supply of dogs', something that had 'gone off the rails already because the Directorate of Military Training had been dealing with the matter,' as the new Directorate's War Diary noted. This, presumably, was the public appeal of May 1941 that had brought a barking clamour in response with no means of dealing with it other than Mr Lloyd's strange trip to Leeds.

Brigadier C. A. Murray, the Army's Chief Vet, was now thoroughly awake to the potential of dogs to the war and indeed to the future of his own Corps. Horses were out, but dogs were in. Now he was in charge of somehow getting them and keeping them in fighting form. How to recruit an army of dogs? He wrote at the time:

I was much exercised in my mind as to how this could be done. It was clear that only a very limited number could be purchased in the open market, and then only at a high cost to the state. It was equally plain that owners would be very reluctant, if they could be induced at all, to part with their pets for money. But if an appeal were made to the public for the loan of their dogs for the duration of the war, I felt that it would meet with an overwhelming response.

The misfired appeal of May had proved that already. But 'war dogs' were presumably war stores, like boots or shells.[13] The Quartermaster General, Sir Walter Venning, the man in charge of such things, was acutely sensitive to the politics of asking people for their pets. Already the public had patriotically offered all sorts of things to the government — vehicles, motorboats, houses — but these were living creatures. Were they gifts, or were they loans? Could they really ever be returned? The National Pigeon Service instigated in May 1939 by which patriotic breeders made their birds available (£5 per 10) to the services for message-carrying duties showed it could be done. But dogs? It had been done before — in the days of Colonel Richardson, those with longer memories might have pointed out — but his first recruits had come from lost dogs' homes. Brig Murray's big idea was to draft in the RSPCA, the stateliest of animal welfare charities, whose uniformed inspectors would add order and

---

[13] The War Office body that would have the final say about war dogs would be the Deputy Chief of the Imperial General Staff's 'Policy Committee on Weapons and Equipment' that dealt with 'general and warlike stores'. The School itself (which was about training handlers from the wider Army as much as dogs) with its RAVC staff and ATS kennel maids would be under the Directorate of Military Training until 1945, when it was formally taken over by the DAV&RS.

respectability to the whole bizarre process. General Venning agreed.

Twelve dogs should simply be bought meanwhile from the pet trade to train the trainers, who would shortly be assembling. Food must be considered. It was further reported that these early arrivals at Swakeleys Farm were being fed satisfactorily on 'condemned meat roll', obtained from Messrs Morels of 153 Commercial Street, London E1, for 3s 3d per 3lb tin. An RAVC butchery department might be required to 'ensure a regular and sufficient supply of meat from the carcasses of army animals', to feed potentially thousands of dogs who might be on their way, it was noted.

With no in-house canine expertise, a fashionable Belgravia vet, Mr Denys Danby (lately the Honorary Veterinary Surgeon to Cruft's and eager foot beagler), was commissioned as an Emergency Reserve Officer with the acting rank of Captain to be Veterinary Officer for the new establishment.

Everything was set. On 5 March 1942, a joint Army–MAP–RSPCA panel met at the War Office outstation in Droitwich[14] for a canine summit chaired by Brigadier Murray. Colonel Baldwin was there, so was Herbert Lloyd, Mr Arthur Moss of the RSPCA and representatives from Military Training.

Lieutenant J. H. Clarke, the new commandant of the school, was there, plus an official from the Ministry of Aircraft Production, and Brigadier A. E. Clarke, the 'Vulnerable Points Adviser', who

[14]   The Worcestershire spa town to where a sizable chunk of the WO secretariat including AV&RS had dispersed from London away from the bombing — accommodated in requisitioned hotels and temporary huts. It would function henceforth as War Dog Supreme HQ.

answered both to GHQ Home Forces and to the War Cabinet. His voice would carry the most weight.

To the Army's canine requirements, the MAP could add a further 1,200 for factory defence, making a total of almost 2,500 dogs. Breeding puppies would take fifteen months before they might be useful. The situation needed mature animals now; the whole scheme would only work if a united public appeal for dogs was launched, said the chairman, stirringly. Although nobody mentioned it, the misbegotten press appeal of the previous May had more than shown the public willingness to cooperate.

This time the need for dogs should be released as 'news' in national and provincial newspapers, it was agreed, and by BBC broadcast later, if necessary. The breeds to be accepted should be Alsatians, Collies, Airedales, Bull Terriers and Lurchers — 'plus one or two other which Major [sic] Baldwin considered he could employ usefully'.

The RSPCA and its inspectors would be responsible for recording the dog's particulars and initial selection; the SPCAs of Scotland and Northern Ireland would do the same. The National Canine Defence League would also be consulted.

The meeting got down to detail. Dogs would be transported (and unsuitable ones returned) by railway and in transit they must comply with company regulations regarding muzzles and chains.

The supply of food for Army and MAP dogs should also be a joint responsibility. Biscuits were a 'potential cause of canine hysteria' and should be replaced, if possible, by stale wholemeal bread, it was usefully pointed out. Each dog should be given a number, but Colonel Baldwin observed that 'tattooing the ear flap would be unpopular with owners of Alsatians as it might interfere with the carriage of the ear'. A stamped, numbered collar-plate should suffice, he suggested. In the end it would be both.

A week later, Brig Murray explained the proposed means of obtaining dogs to the Quartermaster General – it would be by a 'system of registration cards', recording name, breed, age, etc., which would be administered by the RSPCA and NCDL, pre-post paid, to be filled in by owners and then assessed in the first instance by the Society's experts. It could be assumed that the Inspector doing so, 'must know something about dogs and thus he would prevent masses of unsuitable applications'. They would need 20,000 such cards, to be ready by 15 April.

A little later Brigadier Murray would explain the process further in the RSPCA's own journal. 'The owner is also requested to state if he wishes the dog to be called up immediately or whether he would be willing to retain it for six months before calling-up,' he said. 'This was designed to obtain, as far as possible, a constant flow of dogs into the school as obviously only a limited number can be trained at one time.' It would turn out to be a shrewd move.

The Quartermaster General noted gloomily in return on 16 March that: 'If [civilian-loaned dogs] are ever to be used in war, the wastage will be very high and even if they survive the war there are bound to be considerable difficulties in returning them to their owners, who may have moved or died in the meantime.'

Loans must be unconditional, he stressed. It was the same with offers of vehicles by the public. There could be no guarantee of return, just an undertaking that if the dogs were 'still there when no longer needed, and the owners could be traced, they will be sent back'. But any way of doing so was looking remote. 'It will be very easy to rub dog owners up the wrong way unless this was clearly understood at the start,' General Venning counselled. Brig Murray agreed. Restoring dogs to their owners was going to be 'exceedingly difficult', he wrote. Both men would turn out to be right.

Who would such dogs actually belong to? The Treasury Solicitor would rule that, once accepted, 'they were the property of the War Department and, as the Crown is not liable to tax, no dog licences are required.' In fact, a clear distinction would be drawn later, for murkier reasons than revenue gathering, between dogs on loan and dogs owned outright 'by the state'.

This was far bigger than Mr Lloyd's suburban kennels could handle. A site at Ashton Keynes, north of Swindon, was considered, but the Quartermaster General preferred something grander — 'the best kennels in the country', as they were described, with accommodation for about six hundred dogs. It belonged to the Greyhound Racing Association at Northaw, near Potters Bar, north of London, set in 'seventy-five acres of beautiful parkland'. On 18 April it was promptly taken over under wartime emergency regulations in spite of 'violent opposition' from its existing owners. Dogs would be moved in by a process of 'gradual infiltration', it was agreed, as racing greyhounds were evacuated to face their own uncertain future.

Thus it was that on 5 May 1942, stories about a new 'Government Appeal to Dog Owners' appeared in the press. Alsatians, Airedales, Collies, Lurchers and crosses between them, Bull Terriers and Bull Mastiffs, of either sex and over nine months old, were required as 'loans', it was stated. Once registered, owners would be asked to 'keep them until they are "called up" for training by the Government department concerned.'

'An undertaking is given that the dogs will be well looked after; and it is proposed that when, on completion of its war service, a dog is returned to its owner, a certificate of such service shall be awarded to it.'

Once again a dog-loving nation stirred. Just as in the great panic of 1939, pet-loving families faced a momentous decision: should they send foodless Bonzo to the Army? But would he ever come home? Stern fathers said it was the best thing to do, mothers soothed and children, no doubt, wept.

'Rex', the peerless columnist for *The Tail-Wagger Magazine*, would write of how it was for him:

> Well, pals, here's how it's started… My mistress was listening to the wireless one day, something about big dogs being needed. She got up all of a sudden and said: 'Rex, you've got to go out and do your duty, you're going to be a "sojer dog".'

There were all sorts of reasons why. Just as in the previous July, food was the first of them. The dangers of the Blitz may have receded but British dogs (not to say cats) on Civvy Street were still having a tough time. In fact the anguish at the Ministries of Food and of Agriculture about how much pets were eating had increased.

It was not the only reason. Mrs B. M. Harrold of Whitecross Farm, Hardingham, Norwich, asked for her dog 'Tito' to be called up because: 'I do not have much time to train him. I have two small children and have to go into a nursing home.'

Whether or not he turned out to be suitable, Mrs Harrold still wished to have Tito home. Mrs Winnie Pearson of Barnsley offered Alsatian 'Jack' via the National Canine Defence League, but for family reasons, 'she could not wait longer than a month for him to be called up'.

In breezy Eastbourne, 'Caesar', an Alsatian, was proving too much for his owner, whose husband was in the forces. He was 'chasing cats and stealing rationed meat from the butcher's shop.' Inspector Winn of the RPSCA suggested the War-Dog Training School and it was the Inspector himself who took him to the railway station for his journey to Potters Bar. 'Now he is a guard dog at an important aerodrome,' it would one day be reported. 'Perhaps he will return home with a medal round his neck.'

In suburban Tolworth, southwest London, 'Khan', a five-year-old Alsatian, might be getting on a bit, but seemed to be what the authorities were looking for. Eight-year-old Barry Railton, with whom Khan had grown up since he was a puppy, thought that the family pet should do his bit. His father, Mr Harry Railton, a clothing-shop manager, agreed.

Off went the prepaid brown cardboard forms to the post box, heading for Droitwich, to await a reply – and if their pet passed the first hurdle, a home visit from the RSPCA Inspector would soon follow. If they were accepted, a modest parcel would arrive with a muzzle, chain and collar, and a paid travel warrant. It was the owner's responsibility to take their pet to the station, where Tex and Rover and the rest of them would travel in the guard's van under the eye of railway staff to arrive at Potters Bar on the LNER main line.

And it was all good for national morale. Two days after the first appeal, there was a photo-call of dogs and donors milling around at RSPCA headquarters in London's fashionable Jermyn Street. It was observed:

A Bull terrier was inclined to pick trouble, it was expected, but one of the soldiers who had come to fetch the dogs said, 'I know how to deal with Sergeant-majors who growl like that,' and he soon quietened the disturber. It was the owners who were the most upset. They were worried lest their pets might not be well looked after, but there is more chance of them being spoilt by too much kindness from the men whom they are to help on guard.

The Canine Press Bureau (the voice of the National Canine Defence League) commented: 'Alsatians are the most numerous among the trainees, but they are not the obedience-trained prodigies that one is used to seeing at shows. These would have too much to unlearn before they could be turned into useful army dogs.

'The Alsatian excels at patrol and reconnaissance work, while Border Collies, who form the next strongest group, make wonderful messenger-dogs.'

Those arriviste Alsatians were in the charmed circle at last, indeed it would be the making of them thereafter in the post-war pantheon of British Dogdom. But what of Airedales, stalwarts of an earlier war, beloved of Colonel Richardson and the Kaiser's army alike? They were yesterday's dogs, it would seem. Northaw veteran Sgt Bill Adams, speaking many years later, could only remember one Airedale at the school: 'Mark', sent in by Lady Muriel, wife of the BBC Director General.

'[He was] already five years, a very good tracking dog,' wrote Adams, 'with good eyesight, but we discovered he was already going deaf. When the wind was against him, we discovered we could walk right up behind him. Obviously he was not fit for active service.'

The RSPCA meanwhile had proposed that 'stray dogs from bombed areas' should find a place at Northaw. The police were obliged to keep them for three days before destruction. Getting them from a dog-pound to the WDTS would take ten days. According to the War Diary, the Society asked, would the Army pay the maintenance cost in the meantime of 1/- per day?

Judging from the number of waifs and strays that would end up at Potters Bar station, it seems the Army agreed. 'Ownerless' dogs would prove very useful one day. Colonel Baldwin, meanwhile, would get recruits from the same pool, visiting Droitwich every month to go through the latest batch of little brown cards and make his selection for Staverton.

That was the dogs. Meanwhile the training staff began to arrive at Northaw, the old guard from Swakeleys Farm, plus more celebrities from the civilian dog world, now in uniform — Mr Holland Buckley, for example, the noted dog trainer and Kennel Club luminary. There was a clear growing rivalry between Mr Lloyd's and Colonel Baldwin's operations. Pte David Cooke recalled the tension over who was top dog in the competitive world of canine training:

I had been a kennel man to Major James Baldwin, who owned the famous 'Picardy' kennels before the war and was the no. 1 breeder of Alsatians in England.

Although I was not aware of it at the time, Major Baldwin was starting up a dog training school for the RAF and was trying to get me demobbed so that I could join him [on call-up he had tried to join the RAVC, but was posted to the RAMC].

Unfortunately before this could happen I was posted to a new unit being set out for the War-Dog Training School at

Aldershot and later moved to H. S. Lloyd's kennels, near Uxbridge. Mr Lloyd and I never saw eye to eye.

Mr Lloyd wanted to send me back to the RAMC because I could not carry a rifle. However the office transferred me to the RAVC and poor Mr Lloyd could not get rid of me, and because of my experience with Mr Baldwin, I was on the training staff for a long time.

Then I had a few words with Mr Lloyd. There was a meeting of officers and Mr Lloyd said he wanted me off training. Major Danby said he would be delighted to have me under him so that was that.

Private Cooke found a very happy berth in the dog school's sanatorium; he would also find himself a wife.

8

Disciplined Pets

The first of Colonel Baldwin's dog trainees were already on active service. On 30 April 1942, the station commander of RAF St Brides in Glamorgan reported: 'The team of eight dogs has been with us for the past ten days, handlers and dogs are in fine fettle. This method of protecting against sabotage leaves nothing to be desired.' He himself had been detected in a parked aircraft, 'while in the act of placing a time bomb.'

After a big scramble to get Northaw ready, the Army's 'Dog Training Centre', as it would be briefly called, opened officially for business on 5 May, with forty dogs taken on from Mr Lloyd's establishments. He would stay civilian technical training adviser, with Lieutenant Clarke as Commandant and former Master of Foxhounds, Capt A. J. Garle, as Chief Instructor. *The Dog World* magazine went over the top at the news. 'The dogs of Britain are going to war!' it trumpeted on 22 May. 'There is delight in the hearts of the dog lovers of Britain. To arms, to arms, you dogs of Britain!'

There followed a eulogy to the work of Colonel James Baldwin, a master self-publicist, and the antics of his aerodrome-guarding

Alsatians at Staverton, Gloucestershire. Herbert Lloyd's style was much more discreet. Northaw was a military establishment with a serious purpose — and let nobody think he was running some kind of village fête canine obedience display.

The move to Hertfordshire meant the Lloyd family could return to Swakeleys farm. Jennifer Lloyd recalled: 'Dad used to come home at the weekends to see us while Mum ran the home and family, including us four children, plus goats, and chickens so we were pretty well self-sufficient. When we left Swakeleys Farm we left the cockers there too until we came back in 1942.'

Getting dogs and trainers for the school was proving straightforward enough, but what about handlers? They were the men who, so it was intended, would come from line infantry battalions, 'the Field Force' of the regular British Army, who would spend six weeks with the dogs, then return to duty with them. Notices went up in Battalion Orders across the UK Home Commands for volunteers who would 'like to work with dogs', and attend a course at the War-Dog Training School. Successful applicants were instructed to arrive at Potters Bar station — 'armed and fully equipped with blankets and (if in possession) gumboots'.

Monty Hunt was a Corporal in 5 Wiltshire Regiment when he saw the notice. He volunteered with two others, Privates Coates and Edgerton. They passed out of the first course in 1942 and returned to their battalions, 'with message and patrol dogs, working them successfully in manoeuvres', as he would recall many years later. Herbert Lloyd was impressed with his evident affinity for dogs and wrote to him personally, inviting him to be a full-time trainer at the school — in fact he would become the

Commandant's driver and would one day end up as the school's unofficial historian.

And so the first dogs on loan from the public began to arrive, big dogs, small dogs, bold dogs, timid dogs, noisy dogs, pedigree dogs, mongrel dogs, posh dogs – heading in furry streams from all over the country for Potters Bar – where they were 'placed in kennels sited along Station Approach and the WDTS notified by telephone [by the station master, apparently] of the number awaiting collection'.

Colonel Edwin Richardson had spoken of his dogs of an earlier war in tones that readers of schoolboy fiction would recognise. Assuredly among the stream of new-bugs arriving with their tuck boxes at the canine academy, there were sneaks, bullies, cads, oiks, cowards and swots. Not every dog could be a hero.

It was always intended that dogs loaned by the public should keep their pet names. Hence all those suburban-sounding 'Brian's, 'Peggy's, 'Sandy's, 'Bruce's and 'Timmy's, who would one day implacably advance towards the Third Reich. The most popular name by far among publicly offered war dogs was 'Rex'. Dogs acquired by purchase, captured or picked up in a theatre of war were given quirkier names. Among them there would be several 'Adolf's and a military police dog guarding an Egyptian prison was called 'Guilty'.

Collected from the station in good boarding school style by kennel orderlies in a utility van, the candidates were driven the two miles to Northaw, then 'admitted to the holding wing and kept separated from the other dogs', as the reception routine would later be described. It was reported:

'Each dog was given a War Office number, a WDTS number [tattooed in the ear] and a Veterinary History Sheet was compiled, giving details of owner, breed, age and distinguishing marks etc. Within 24 hours, each entrant was examined by the Veterinary Officer and, if found suitable, was given an anti-distemper inoculation,' according to Sgt Dennis Hipgrave RAVC, a stalwart of the sick bay from 1942.

School vet, Capt Denys Danby, recorded how: 'Entrants are then confined to isolation unit about a quarter of a mile distant from the main training kennels. Incoming dogs are isolated for a period of eight to ten days and, in the event of any illness developing, or should an inoculation reaction occur, such dogs are detained in isolation until recovery.' Temperatures were taken 'twice daily and faeces tests taken daily for the first week, after which temperatures were taken once daily.' The level of care was exemplary.

The big news at Northaw in the second half of 1942 was the arrival of women. They were members of the 'Auxiliary Territorial Service', established in September 1938 during the 'Munich crisis' as part of the Territorial Army. Its volunteer members were expected to carry out 'domestic and clerical duties'.

From April 1941 it was granted full military status, and members were no longer volunteers, while the National Service Act later in the year called up unmarried women between the ages of twenty and thirty for war work. Some manned searchlights, or anti-aircraft batteries, were mechanics or drivers (like Princess Elizabeth). And some, who considered themselves very lucky ATS-girls indeed, worked with war dogs.

It happened just as it had for Army trainers and dog handlers. One day, on barrack-room notice boards, up went a call for 'kennel maids'. It was better than cleaning or filing.

Private D. M. 'Micky' Pilkington, W/97959, enlisted in the ATS in mid-1941 at Chester. She recalled: 'I moved into camp with two gunners and six ATS-girls, we shared the task of keeping the officers' quarters spick and span. So when volunteers for kennel maids were needed, I quickly offered my services.'

When she got to Northaw, she found it 'a strange place and not at all like a military establishment. Security was almost nil,' she remembered, 'although at night there was always a team doing guard duty and guardroom tea was always welcome before turning in after a long walk home, returning from an evening out.'

There would be all sorts of nocturnal comings and goings, official and unofficial, by both dogs and humans at the spasmodically guarded canine camp.

ATS-girl Gay Agocs (Spackman) was another early arrival, from Warwick in late summer 1942, where she had been working as a clerk. She recalled:

My first location was in the kennels for VP dogs. However due to my small stature it was decided I would be better off working with the smaller dogs. So I was transferred to the liaison kennels [message dogs] where I was more compatible in coping with the likes of Collies, Spaniels, Labs and the like. They were certainly easier to handle than the larger breeds, mainly Alsatians, who were engaged in guard work.

She remembered the 'wonderful time when we were waited on by our officers and NCOs for dinner on Christmas Day, the squeaky door in the canteen leading to the ATS quarters, the news bulletins preceded by classical music. Bill and Frank who ran the canteen and their cheerful cockney banter, which used to cheer me up. I also remember the excitement when the post arrived in the canteen and the disappointment if there was no mail from one of my many boyfriends (I was a terrible flirt!).'

Kay Manning was an assistant cook, then a filing clerk in her first months in the ATS. Delighted at the chance of working with animals, as she had done before the war, she described what she found at Northaw:

> Every building had its wired run on to the grass, where the dogs were allowed to romp at regular times. It always amazed me that there were not more fights, considering the many breeds and personalities that were thrown together.

She was posted to the hospital — which 'with hundreds of dogs coming in and out, infectious disease and injuries [was] nearly always full.' As she recalled:

> There was an isolation bay, the vet's surgery, and the dogs' cookhouse, which you could not fail to find by scent alone. The accommodation for us ATS and the men were long huts with cubicles and bunks. Each had a curtain and a bed with a pillow and Army-issue blanket, which had to be folded neatly and stacked at the bottom of the bed each morning for inspection. This took place regularly with brass buttons and badges, and shoes, which had to shine, plus clean combs and brushes.
>
> Our dining room was furnished with long trestle tables and benches for seats, with always the clatter of large aluminium containers of stodgy food. I especially remember

the trays of strong-tasting liver swimming in gravy, much of which went into a can so I could keep what was left of my ration to tempt the faded appetites of the dog patients in the hospital block.

I became a scrounger for them, in fact, and on occasions it paid off, and was the turning point for many a sick dog.

'It was inevitable that an interest was taken between the sexes,' she added, 'and several long-term romances, and war and peace-time marriages followed in due course, including mine.'

As Kay Manning recalled, the dog-collecting run in the little utility truck to Potters Bar station was now a female responsibility. Micky Pilkington remembered the yapping arrivals in their government-supplied collar and leashes:

> Some dogs were bored and frightened while others were snarling and aggressive. All were treated the same with a cheery word from the kind ATS-girls and swept off in the back of a truck to become doggy recruits.
>
> Intake dogs were housed in a very large place called Central Bay. Early on some recruits were homesick, while others seemed not to mind and all enjoyed large dinners with real meat, lots of biscuits and gravy and greens — things that we were unable to get in Civvy Street. All recruits were given numbers and identity discs, also one stamped in the ear. They also had their inoculations.
>
> Standing orders to dog handlers was no smoking within three yards of the kennels. In case of fire, our instructions were to free all dogs, then try and put out the fire.

After two days the new entrants were paraded by the kennel orderlies and subjected to a 'gun-shy' test. Private Pilkington remembered: 'We ATS-girls walked them around in groups while the head trainer chucked thunderflashes around. It was pretty hairy for the unsuspecting dogs, pretty hairy too for a girl I knew, who had her cap knocked off by one.'

Some dogs passed at the first attempt, others were 'borderline', while some 'cowered and whimpered in terror' at the bangs. The borderline dogs got a second chance test, some days later, before a final decision was reached.

Jennifer Lloyd had a special memory of the bang-makers. She recalled: 'Sometimes when I was a child, Dad would come home with boxes full of the insides of fire-crackers on strings, which I and my brothers would play with, letting off to frighten each other. Dad used these on the dogs so that he could tell which ones would turn out to be too nervous to train as war dogs.'

There was no disgrace in failing entry to the WDTS, not for the dogs anyway. But it could be dangerous. Brig Murray recorded: 'It may be reckoned that only about 50 per cent of the dogs sent to the school prove suitable for training and are retained. Those which are not accepted are returned to their owners.'

Micky Pilkington expressed it more directly: 'Dogs that showed stress were rejects and returned to owners. Sadly not all were reclaimed and had to be put down.'

A Northaw dog was not home and dry yet – there was a lot of family pet still in him. Brig Murray was sensitive to his charges being 'house dogs rather than kennel dogs, and it is this factor which is probably the fundamental cause of a great deal of the sickness which is always present.'

'Fretting is undoubtedly the chief worry,' he observed, 'and it is important to have plenty of staff available so that each dog shall have ample time devoted to it. Personal attention and patience are often all that are required.' And he observed:

> Owing to variations in the feeding of dogs by their owners, it is found that a large percentage of them refuse their food for several days after arrival. This may be due to fretting or to the unaccustomed time of feeding, or again to the nature of the food which they are expected to eat; nevertheless, it is the rule that, once a dog has settled down to the kennels and taken to the food, it thrives remarkably well.

The food was on all accounts not bad – for a dog. According to Brigadier Murray: 'The daily ration for each dog consists of a pound and a half of meat and a pound of biscuits. The meat is usually boiled and mixed with broken biscuit to which is added some cooked vegetable. Certain individual dogs, such as hospital cases, bad feeders and recent intakes, are given a special ration. Scraps from the cookhouse provide some of these with a more palatable diet.' Like kindly Kay Manning and her chunks of overcooked liver for poorly dogs.

After two to three weeks of medical observation and acclimatisation, successful candidates moved from intake into general training to teach 'the dogs to ignore explosions, gunfire, vehicles and any other animals when working'.

As aptitudes were noted, they were selected for specialised training. Noisy, suspicious dogs were going to be better at Vulnerable Point guarding with Corps of Military Police handlers. 'Tactical' dogs were always going to be a bit more difficult, but the same principle applied, training with a single soldier rotated through the school by his line infantry battalion, to make the bond between one man and one dog. 'It must be understood that all this work was silently carried out in the dark,' wrote Mr Lloyd. 'Message' dogs had the added complication of requiring two 'masters'.

Monty Hunt, the school's unofficial historian, would later write of L/Cpl Cyril Plumridge of 'C' Company 6 Battalion Queen's Royal West Kents, who was introduced that summer of 1942 to 'Bob', a Collie-cross with black ear and black cap and big white patches. His background is obscure. It would be said later he 'was sent out from the War Dogs' Training School when almost a puppy'.

Bob's temperament marked him out as a suitable patrol dog, but his colouring made night work problematic. Salvation arrived in the shape of 'Durafur' dark brown patent camouflage-dye for war horses adapted to dogs.[15] It was recorded of Bob and his new friend during their time at Northaw:

> L/Cpl Plumridge had to learn how to groom him, how to give him the right amount of food and when, depending on the training programme of the patrol work. He was allowed one well-balanced meal a day. If it was day work, then he should be fed after work, if it was going to be night work, he should be fed at midday.

Dogs were trained on the system of reward. As soon as they had performed the task correctly, they were given a chunk of meat

---

[15] The DAV&RS War Diary for 15 July 1942 lists experiments at Northaw with 'Durafur dark brown for the camouflage of light coloured dogs.'

'the size of an Oxo cube'. For patrol dogs, the task was to detect at a range of up to 200 yards the presence of a nearby enemy. When the trained dog detected unknown human scent, he must 'freeze' and 'point' and be very, very quiet about it.

Message carrying was a bit more complicated, involving two handlers, one who stayed with the main body of troops, and the other who would take two dogs out on combat patrol. To take a message back to HQ, the message would be placed in a special collar – and 'the dog immediately makes its way to its second master at the base'. If enemy action had caused the base to move, 'the handler will, when moving on, use a drag with a scent the dog has already been accustomed to recognise'.

That was an old Col Edwin Richardson trick from the trenches. Like a patrol dog, sniffing the air for the presence of an unseen enemy, the message dog found its way home by sense of smell.

Bob, the amiable Collie with the big white patches, was by now shaping up as a message dog. It was at this point, it would seem, that he was introduced to his 'second master', Quartermaster Sergeant Robert Cleggett. They got on well. Plucky Bob would soon be starring in a film, and even though it would never get a public showing, he would one day be a very famous dog.

The routine for Bob and his new pals was straightforward enough. A day in the life of a Northaw dog sounds quite jolly:

> 'Reveille' is either at six or half-past, with a roll call at seven, followed by breakfast and a general parade of all kennel staff, trainers, handlers and kennel orderlies at a quarter to eight. Two orderlies are allocated to each block of training kennels (twenty-two kennels to each block). They, with their trainers

and handlers, clean kennels, groom and exercise dogs for one hour, while one man from each block is detailed to go round the paddocks both during and after exercise to clean up faecal matter.

Shortly after nine, trainers and handlers take out dogs for training purposes, and those dogs which are left behind are groomed. All dogs return to kennels at midday, when they are fed and left undisturbed until two o'clock. In the event of night training being held, the trainers and handlers are not expected to work during the afternoon, and thus they do not return to kennels until four o'clock for exercising.

Brigadier Murray could meanwhile publicly reassure donors that their dogs were being trained 'entirely by kindness, and it is simply astounding to see how quickly the dogs react to this, and how rapidly they can be taught the various duties expected of them.

'I feel sure that owners who have loaned their dogs will have every reason to be pleased with the disciplined pets which will be returned to them when the war is over.

'The dogs are handled as far as possible by the same man,' he said. 'And receive every care when with their unit, indeed the difficulty is to keep them from receiving more food and attention than is good for them.'

Within a fortnight no fewer than 1,200 dogs were in residence at Northaw, with six weeks of intense training ahead of them. Operational commands were to be told what to expect when they and their handlers were ready, how to treat them, what to feed them, what to expect (or not) of their canine recruits on guard duties or in combat.

For those former pets graduating as guard dogs, feed and kennelling arrangements had to be made at the isolated 'Vulnerable Points' where they were to be posted. A senior officer noted: 'Any dog debarred from attaching itself to a sizable cookhouse is entitled to a ration of ½lb condemned meat and 1lb of [dog] biscuit.' Spillers Winalot was the officially recommended rusk – if they could be obtained. 'Green vegetables will be obtained from NAAFI for dogs at vulnerable points where the number of men in mess is not sufficient to provide adequate scraps,' said the War Office on the eve of issuing of dogs to 'vulnerable points and battalions'. As for dogs going to the infantry, they were to 'subsist on the cookhouse scraps of the unit'.

Military police duties for dogs were straightforward enough, but how were patrol and messenger dogs to be integrated into a modern, fast-moving army? For this was indeed still the plan, after all the misfired experiments and broken promises of the first years of war. A new army was in the making; dogs would serve with it.

That spring of 1942, preparations had begun for a new British Expeditionary Force to somehow take the war back to the enemy on land. It centred on 'Force 110', an ever-growing command, which, when ready, must make some kind of opposed landing from the sea on an enemy-occupied coastline. Stalin, dictator of the embattled Soviet Union, demanded immediate action – a landing in France, at the least. The new Anglo-American allies looked for a softer option. Units were assigned – including line infantry battalions that had already begun experimental 'combined operations' training featuring seaborne landings, centred on Inverary in Argyllshire, Scotland. Could there really be an opportunity for 'war dogs' in any of this? It turned out there would be.

Force 110's headquarters formed at Largs on the Clyde in
March 1942 with Lt-Gen 'Teddy' Schreiber, the senior officer
so enamoured of James Baldwin's West Country dog
demonstration the year before, as Commander. When the
Anglo-US allies agreed in June to the invasion of the Vichy
French colonies in North Africa, the command became the
nucleus of a whole new Army designated for what would be
called 'Operation Torch'. For a short time it was called '2nd
Expeditionary Force', then on 6 July it became '1st Army'.
Lt-Gen Schreiber was invalided out, to be replaced by General
Sir Kenneth Anderson. As far as can be seen, he had no firm
opinion on dogs either way.

Training went up a gear with a huge exercise called
'Dryshod' conducted over a heathery swathe of southwest
Scotland. It showed among much besides that the newly formed
78 Division, the main British infantry component of 1st Army,
was as yet only capable of mounting an operation against weak
resistance — as might be anticipated around Vichy-controlled
Algiers on the eastern edge of the invasion front. For political
reasons it was all to be portrayed as an American-led operation.

With the Germans in Libya still at the gates of Egypt, the
grand strategic intention was to take the whole Axis (German–
Italian) position in the rear, with an advance eastwards from the
beachheads towards Tunis. It was also clear that Axis airpower
based in Sicily and Sardinia ruled out an opening amphibious
stroke from the sea at Tunis itself. But a bold advance through
the mountains, so it was planned, might capture the strategic
prize within two weeks and transform the war, even if just on this
dusty margin, and open the way somehow to an invasion of
southern Europe.

War dogs were to be part of this — and supposedly in the front line. The sponsor charities, the RSPCA and National Canine Defence League, could hardly object. Sir Ernest Gower, Chairman of the RSPCA, could report from Northaw on the eve of battle, 'It was like raising a regiment, where all had seemed to pal up. I came away happy, knowing the animals were so happy and comfortable.' Mr Charles S. Johns, Secretary of the NCDL, was less sentimental: 'A patrol dog [will be] the means of cutting short the career of many a Hun lurking in copse or cellar,' he declared.

For Jennifer Lloyd, aged six, it meant not seeing her beloved father. 'He had to do lots of night work, coming home in the early hours [he had priority petrol ration],' she recalled, 'although I never knew exactly when as I would have been long in bed myself by then. He had a theory that dogs behave differently at night and that this behaviour alteration was more marked in some breeds than in others.'

Training at Northaw for patrol and message-carrying work was intense. Four dogs per battalion implied at least fifty animals for the Torch operation with a small reserve. The volunteer handlers from the infantry, many with the kind of farm-boy, or hunt-servant doggy experience looked for in the original trawl, duly arrived from their battalions for the six-week course in the mysterious arts of canine warfare. Everyone knew something big was coming; nobody knew what.

'Guard' dog training continued in parallel and by mid-July 1942, the training course at Northaw was complete, and forty so-called 'VP' dogs and their handlers were allotted to UK Home Commands. Dispersed to remote spots around the country, veterinary cover was always going to be rudimentary. 'All men on the short VP course are given a few hints on the care and welfare of their dogs,' said a briefing document. 'Owing to the danger of making [a] wrong diagnosis, or attempting unskilled treatment, it had been considered advisable that no veterinary equipment be provided.' If a guard dog got sick or injured, that was it.

Now it was tactical dogs and their handlers who were being prepared for some mysterious mission. Like the VP dogs, they too would have minimal veterinary cover. No dog field hospital would be sailing to Africa with them, but this time the dogs of Britain really were going to war.

9
Don't Make Friends
with these Dogs

The Northaw dogs might be almost ready for action but was the British Army ready for them? A briefing document, 'The Tactical Employment of War Dogs', was drafted both to reveal the existence of the bizarre-seeming programme to the wider Army and reassure bemused regimental commanders that the War Office had not gone completely mad.

'A dog is not a machine,' it stressed, 'and is not infallible but, when handled with discretion, the dogs will prove of the utmost value in war.' It explained how the handler 'is the person who continually looks after the dog, feeds it and trains it. Handlers are chosen from men who have a natural love for dogs, a sense of country, experience of patrol work, good eyesight and hearing and infinite patience. These men will be given a short course of training at the WDTS and then returned to their units with the dogs.'

Patrol dogs used body scent to locate the enemy, it explained. Wind direction was very important. If it was blowing from the enemy location, then a pick-up at 150–200 yards was possible. 'Suppressed excitement' in the dog was the signal of the enemy's presence, but there must be no sound. Both dog and handler should be five yards ahead of the main patrol, staying in silent contact by 'cord, agreed signals, etc.'

Message dogs could communicate over distances up to 1,200 yards and surmount all kinds of obstacles as they hurtled unstoppably across the battlefield, just as they had done in Colonel Richardson's day. Like then, the technique required two handlers, each regarded as the dog's 'master'. '[The dog] will only move along the same route first taken by his handler on the outward journey. A dog will always find his handler dead or alive, provided the handler stays in the original position,' said the briefing. It was all down to smell.[16]

The briefing stressed the following principles for troops not trained to work with dogs:

DON'T feed any patrol or message-carrying dog at any time.
DON'T ever stop a dog wearing a message-carrying collar.
DON'T make any noise when around working dogs.
DON'T make friends with or pet any of these dogs.

The document was dated 5 August. The file is marked on the next day – 'dogs allocated'. Soon the advanced guard of Northaw graduates would be heading for Scotland to join all those infantry

---

[16] The AV&RS War Diary for 12 August 1942 noted: 'The US Army are to be asked to supply samples of a short-wave radio device for use with dogs for trials at the WDTS.' Newspapers meanwhile had reported experiments where dogs could be 'remote controlled to obey orders under adverse battlefield conditions at ranges of three miles' via headphones wired to a backpack. The outcome of any British experiment with radio-controlled dogs is not recorded.

battalions mustering for their bold expedition. It was vital they should not get turned into pampered pets by all those young men far from home — that was perhaps asking the impossible.

Another canine expeditionary force was being prepared, Lilliputian in scale and unwarlike in intention, but drawing government rations and thus part of this story. At the same time Force 110 was being readied to get to grips with the enemy, even if on the margin 'Force 122' was assembling, intended to boost the tiny self-defence force of the far-off Falkland Islands in the south Atlantic, against any attempt by the Japanese to come round Cape Horn and grab the colony. The Americans could not be involved for diplomatic reasons (they would have brought in the Argentinians).

In May 1942 the Governor in Port Stanley received a 'most secret' telegram. The new officer commanding troops, Colonel William Henry Hynes, a veteran of several distinguished Irish infantry regiments, was 'anxious to make best provision for welfare and wishes to bring sixteen beagles with him. Telegraph whether any objection.'

Hunting the islands' abundant hares and rabbits (introduced long before by early colonists) would provide recreation for troops far from home. The Governor replied: 'Hounds. Suggestion approved.' Quarantine regulations would be waived. War Office instructions were given for 'one kennel man (sergeant) and two other ranks to accompany and embark with ten couple of beagles at No. 2 Remount Depot, Osmaston Manor, near Ashbourne, Derby.'

Thus it was that along with hundreds of tons of warlike stores, vehicles, guns and ammunition and 1,500 men of the West Yorkshire regiment plus supporting services, twenty

hare-hunting hounds were embarked at Avonmouth docks and
sailed 4,000 miles to arrive at this remotest of colonial outposts by
August 1942. The AV&RS War Diary noted: 'Dog food for
beagles sent with Force 122 placed on ship conveying this force.
15 cwt. biscuits and 15 cwt dog meal, which roughly represents a
year's supply.'

Records show the garrison Beagles meeting at 3 p.m. (in
season) every Saturday afternoon at the Port Stanley racecourse.
Faced with this kind of insouciance, how could the Japanese
even think of invading?

There were rations for the Falkland beagles but not for dogs
closer to home. At the same time as the Army was preparing the
nation's pets for war, the Animal Foodstuffs Division of the
Ministry of Agriculture and Fisheries still fretted over greedy
pets gobbling up the food that could be fed to 'economic' animals
like pigs and chickens.

An official noted: 'We can no longer ignore the fact that dogs
consume 280,000 tons of food per annum of which 170,000 consist
of carbohydrate and the rest protein – meat etc. Practically the
whole of this is food which should not have been wasted or fed to
economic animals.' A cull of dogs was moving up the agenda.

There were discreet briefings to journalists about the internal
dog danger – which paid off in a rash of articles and letters to
newspapers from late July, urging: 'Kill all puppies at birth' or
'One Dog per Family!'

Even trainee war dogs were not immune to the squeeze on
food. On 24 August the Ministry of Food rejected a plea from the
War Office that 'rationed foodstuffs, e.g. milk and rice, should be
obtained for sick dogs at the War Dogs Training School'. How
mean was that! The ruling was overturned two weeks later.

The Germans had war dogs, the Japanese had war dogs, and now the British had war dogs. Apart from some sled dogs in Alaska, the US military now roused for war was innocent of canines. But after Pearl Harbor a vocal group of American dog-lovers pointed out how useful they might be. As the foremost historian of the episode put it: 'The parallels with Britain's enthusiastic doggy patriots in trying to convince an initially suspicious military were great.' And through the next two years of war, the Anglo-US canine allies would find all sorts of mutual war-dog bones to chew on.

The American approach to creating a dog army was certainly businesslike. A commercial company, 'Dogs for Defense Inc.', was formed in January 1942. Mrs Milton (Arlene) Erlanger, a prominent Poodle breeder, was its moving spirit, with the aim of first developing interest in 'sentry dogs'. The American Kennel Club, like its UK equivalent, the registration body for all pure-bred dogs, came enthusiastically into the strange project.

The animals themselves were also to be acquired by public appeal. The US Army Quartermaster General quickly approved the arrangement. At first, there was no limit to breeds accepted, the call being for 'any pure-bred dog of either sex, physically sound, between the ages of one and five years, with characteristics of a watch-dog, qualifying under the physical examination and standard inspection of Dogs for Defense', which, like the RSPCA, would review a preliminary questionnaire on the offer of a dog, then go and see those who might be suitable.

Forty per cent passed the first hurdle. Dogs were then placed in quarantine kennels for twenty-one days. Then they were given gun-shy and aptitude tests on the Northaw model – 'After passing muster, the dog was tattooed on the left ear with a serial number'.

Just as in Britain after Dunkirk, the attack on Hawaii caused a saboteur neurosis to grip America. Dogs for Defense enthusiasts were not slow to point out the usefulness of dogs in outfoxing submarine-landed spies. Thus it was that the first 'sentry' dogs went on duty in April 1942 in small numbers around the industrial New York waterfront, their exploits eagerly followed by the press. Hollywood woke up. A stirring feature, *War Dogs*, hit American movie theatres later that year, in which a patriotic youngster, Billy Freeman, donates his pet German Shepherd, 'Ace' the wonder dog. The poster tag-line declared: 'Drama that grips with the force of a steel trap as "man's best friend" joins the army to combat Nazi agents!' It played nationwide in British cinemas from summer 1943.

The training of dogs and handlers would also follow the British experience – with a big input from civilians. The one-man, one-dog principle was also to be strictly followed – 'no one but the master was authorized to feed, pet, or handle the dog on the theory that the animal otherwise would soon regard all persons as friends and become a mere mascot', it was recorded: 'Sentry dogs required less instruction than other types but were required to be moderately intelligent, willing and aggressive.'

But could dogs do more than just guard things or bark at strangers? Might they be used tactically on the battlefield – as British experiments were suggesting? It seemed that they might. On 16 July, the US War Dog Program was instructed to include training for 'roving patrol and messenger work'. That autumn the War Department's Intelligence Department got very excited at the progress made by its new ally's 'Dog Training Center'.

'Throughout the learning period dogs are conditioned to ignore human beings seeking to pet them,' its January 1943 summary noted. A 'US Signal Corps officer' witnessed a demonstration (presumably at Northaw) of a dog detecting the enemy in a wood at a range of 150 yards, the eagerness with which the dogs tugged at their leads showing the approximate distance. 'Once a dog had been trained it only took two weeks to accustom him to work with new masters,' said the report: 'the men who came from army battalions to themselves be trained as handlers.'

On this transatlantic tide of enthusiasm the US Army Quartermaster General's department was ordered to establish schools across America[17] through which, as with the British model, 'units of the various arms and services seeking war dogs' could be channelled through for the necessary training with what would henceforth be unofficially known as the 'K9 Corps'.

Within the wider US Army there was bafflement. Would these sometime suburban pets be of use in the African desert (where from late 1942, US forces would be engaged after the 'Torch' landings) or on sweltering Pacific islands?

It was officially recorded of the first months of trialling K9s for combat: 'The few animals that were trained for tactical work were employed chiefly for tests or demonstration purposes. The instruction of these dogs was seriously handicapped at first by the scarcity of trainers experienced in teaching scout and messenger work; most of the men with foreign experience in schooling war dogs were engaged in other essential work'.

Some swift inter-Allied canine cooperation was called for.

---

[17] The first was established in August 1942 at the Front Royal, Virginia, Quartermaster Remount Depot. Three more were opened late in 1942: Fort Robinson, Nebraska; Camp Rimini, in the Rocky Mountains, Montana; and San Carlos, California; and a fourth in April 1943, on the semi-tropical Cat Island, Gulfport, Mississippi. Temporary centres were set up at Beltsville, Maryland, and Fort Belvoir, Virginia.

Dogs of the Desert

The fighting in North Africa still see-sawed across the great sand-pit of the Western Desert. In October 1942 the British 8th Army began its offensive westwards, decisively winning the Second Battle of El Alamein after breaking into the vast anti-tank minefields that had barred their way forward. The surviving German troops clambered into whatever transport was left and retreated westwards across Libya, in a staged series of disciplined withdrawals — screened by more cunningly laid minefields which hobbled their pursuers. The non-motorised infantry units, particularly the Italians, surrendered with a pathetic entourage of thirsty horses, mules — and dogs. The RSPCA became animated, prompting the War Office to put out a press statement on 'the large number of ownerless dogs' wandering in the desert. It was reported:

Frightened by the noise of the battle, they took refuge in holes, dug-outs, and wadis [dry riverbeds], and did not emerge until too late to retreat. Many of them have collars inscribed in German or Italian, but the owners are either prisoners, dead, or in full retreat.

Whenever a lorry or car stops, one, two, or sometimes a whole pack of hungry Pointers, Setters, Retrievers, and the inevitable pi-dogs come and sit, patiently hoping for some scraps of food and a drink of water. Few of them go away without a meal, and many have found new homes with the advancing forces.

A moving story was told about an RAF squadron going overland in trucks behind the advancing 8th Army. When they passed German corpses in the desert, a flight-sergeant was 'horrified to see a huge, half-starved Alsatian crouch over one of the bodies as though about to start eating it'.

He got out of his jeep to shoot the dog, 'But, as he approached, she neither cringed nor turned tail, but lay down with her paws over the body and growled. Obviously she was guarding her dead master. Neither food nor threats would induce her to move, so eventually she was captured with a net, venting her displeasure by biting two of her captors and howling. Her grief continued for some time, but when she saw her master decently buried it gradually died away.'

There was a huge rash of such canine PoWs. 'Betty', for example, a little Terrier, whose mother was found in a cupboard when the Axis forces departed Castel Benito airfield in Tripolitania, in a hurry in January 1943. And how about 'Benghazi', 'Boozer' and 'Algy', a mongrel bitch who, according to her Mascot Club register, was adopted by a Royal Artillery anti-aircraft unit, having been, 'bought at Algiers from French people in December 1942, went through North Africa, died in landing at Pantelleria [Sicily].'

Then there was 'Tocra', an 'attractive Dachshund terrier cross' attached to a Panzer division, who had been captured near Benghazi in November by L/Sgt K. R. Hurst, who became the mascot of 2nd Army Signals. Tocra would make it all the way back to England.

'Tich', picked up at El Alamein by 1 King's Royal Rifle Corps, was said to always know when a shell was coming over, and to be able to 'smoke a cigarette, nestling in the shade of a jeep, rolling it from one side of her mouth to the other' and to thrive on shaving water, a taste acquired in the desert. She would have fifteen pups in total and survive the war. Tich would also make it to England.

The Tail-Wagger Magazine would tell the story of 'Shoofty', a 'yellow mongrel the size of a small Collie', encountered by the writer with his grizzled 8th Army-veteran owner in a London pub at the war's end. A true shaggy dog story follows, told over several pints of beer:

Shoofty came from the Middle East, a pi-dog, and had originally belonged to the CO, who had 'picked him near Tobruk'. They had become inseparable, particularly as Shoofty delighted in accompanying his master on parade and on weekly inspections, indicating unpolished boots or other examples of sloppy soldiering by lying down and wagging his tail close to evidence of the offence.

'The fellows took a poor view' — and had given the story-teller, the company cook, the job of getting rid of Shoofty with rat poison. But clever Shoofty sniffed it out. The CO was suddenly whisked out to some new command by air and before he departed appointed the cook to be lucky Shoofty's owner. Now the yellow mongrel became the cook's inseparable pal. 'Naturally when I came home, I brought him with me,' he told *The Tail-Wagger* columnist. 'How? Now that would be telling,' he had said. But there were clearly ways to somehow get pets home. In fact, at the end of the war it would be official policy (see p. 261).

An 'RAF Flying Officer' told the same splendid magazine that 'an incredible number of dogs' had been attached to camps and aerodromes in the Middle East, a lot of them originally captured from the Italians. He remembered especially, 'a tiny terrier called "Musso", which was inseparable from its young soldier-master, who promised to take the dog with him when he was posted home.' There were lots of such promises.

The PDSA volunteers from the charity's animal hospital at Abbassia, Cairo, did what they could in traditional animal welfare, mass-destruction style. A ½-ton truck provided by GOC-in-C, British Troops in Egypt, was fitted out as a dispensary caravan with 'operating table, lethal chambers and humane killers' according to the post-war history of the charity. It also told this illuminating story from the Cairo hospital: 'One soldier who was going home the following day brought three large dogs to be destroyed as he could not hand them to anyone else. He sobbed throughout and waited to see they were dead before leaving.'

Shoofti, Tocra, Tich, and thousands like them, were not war dogs. They were accidental combatants, side-switchers, regimental pets and mascots. 'No mascots are so popular as those captured from the enemy,' an Australian observer of animals in war would comment, and he was surely right. Some of these opportunist survivors would become famous.

The fate of *official* British war dogs in North Africa in contrast would be secret then, and has remained completely unreported ever since. Northaw's first patrol and message dog graduates had gone with their handlers into their allocated infantry battalions in late summer 1942. Almost every such battalion with 1st Army forming in Scotland for Operation Torch had its canine component of three handlers with two dogs each.

Other dogs had progressively gone out to Field Force and Home Defence infantry battalions generally around Britain, or rather to those whose commanding officers had responded with curious enthusiasm to the August announcement that such things as war dogs existed. Several had refused outright to have anything to do with military canines. And there was still deep suspicion in the higher reaches of the War Office that dogs had any place at all on the modern battlefield.

'The Tactical Employment of War Dogs' memorandum has spelt out what was to be expected. Two months later, a supplement was added to the 1942 *Infantry Training Manual Part VIII Fieldcraft, Battle Drill, Section and Platoon Tactics.* As well as outlining how to employ these highly motivated animals ('the duty of all war dogs is to function in the dark silently'), it addressed some practical items of housekeeping. Like this:

Large dogs should be fed 1lb of condemned meat, 1lb biscuit and 1½lb of green vegetables, supplied via the RASC [Royal Army Service Corps]. In emergency no doubt scraps will be obtained from the cookhouse. Avoid getting them too fat. The dogs must be fed by their handler only, and not treated as regimental pets.

The words of command, taught at the school, must be strictly adhered to. They are:

HEEL   Dog to walk closely at the left side

SIT   To get the dog sitting, accompany the word
           with an uplifted hand
DOWN   To prone position
LEAVE   When the liaison (messenger) dog is taken
           away from the post by the handler
GET ON   When slipped by the handler sending him on
           his journey.

1st Army, along with the Home Commands, were informed of
the approved scale of equipment for all sub-units with war dogs.
They were:

Each dog
Brushes, Dandy, small   1
Collars, choke (as necessary)   1
Collars, leather (size as necessary)   1
Chain, double swivel; spring hook 6-ft.   1
Comb, Spratt's. No. 3.   1
Bowls, water, dog's   1
Leads, leather, 5-ft.   1

The combat debut of Britain's war dogs, family pets a
few months before, was drawing near. With their Dandy
brushes and feeding bowls, they were heading for the
wintry, fog-shrouded mountains of Tunisia. Outside a few terse
and unpublished wartime reports, their story has never been
told.

Tiger Country

Putting together what really happened when Northaw's Class of '42 was sent to war is difficult, based on a few scrappy documents from diverse sources. It is not recorded in any official history. But it's clear that Sir Walter Venning, the Quartermaster General, was right when he had warned the Army's Chief Vet that the 'wastage' rate of civilian-loaned dogs would be high. In fact it would turn out to be a massacre.

The troops mustered in autumnal Scotland in 1st Army were nearing the end of their training. An extemporised assault fleet of ocean liners and impressed merchant ships was assembling in the Clyde with naval escorts to take them to war. A 'cadre' veterinary attachment would sail with them, to look after pack transport mules that, it was assumed, could be acquired in North Africa after a successful landing. Provision for the care of dogs was rudimentary.

The 'Eastern Task Force' aiming to capture the port of Algiers contained two brigades (the 11th and 36th) from the British 78 Infantry Division, which had been specially formed for the operation. The invasion fleet left the Clyde under a drab autumn drizzle in two huge convoys beginning on 24 October.

News of the opening barrage at El Alamein had been in the Glasgow evening paper just as they sailed, so after weeks of rumours and speculation at least there was a general understanding of where they were heading — even if the division's actual destination was not disclosed until the convoy was well out to sea. On 'D minus 7' (seven days to D-Day, the start of the operation), officers were given a copy of the First Army Information Bulletin in which the object of the operation was revealed — to invade North Africa and attack Rommel's army in the rear.

The transit would take eight days. There was huge seasickness in the Bay of Biscay among the men, and presumably the dogs too.

How the Northaw graduates were loaded and kept on board is unrecorded. Evidence they made the journey at all is fragmentary. And unlike humans, dogs do not leave memoirs. Thus the story of the invasion fleet's progress towards African shores 'in perfect weather and under a Mediterranean blue sky with the snowy tops of the Atlas Mountains in the distance,' and what happened thereafter, must come from more general campaign histories and battalion War Diaries.

The invasion fleet anchored off Algiers on the night of 7/8 November, assault troops scrambling down nets into chugging landing craft pitching in heavy swell. The 2 Lancashire Fusiliers (war dogs 'Tatters', 'Rex', 'Mac' and 'Chum') and 5 Northamptons (war dogs 'Prince', 'Rex', 'Toby' and 'Mark') of 11 Infantry Brigade landed without opposition, west of Algiers. The Northamptons were greeted by 'cheers, boos, glasses of wine and occasional rifle shots'. Vehicles and equipment (and presumably dogs too) were smartly unloaded without incident.

The Lancashires' first task was to take Blida airfield, about twenty miles from the capital. The French at Blida were 'anything but friendly'. 1 East Surrey Regiment (war dogs 'Chum', 'Lady', 'Gyp' and 'Bob') came ashore on beaches west of Algiers.

In a bold, opportunistic move, the 36th Brigade, standing by offshore in floating reserve, were despatched to Bougie, a point on the coast 100 miles closer to Tunis and arrived in a convoy off Cap Carbon in darkness, early on the morning of 11 November. As first light splashed over the mountains, troops of 6 Queen's Royal West Kents (war dogs 'Bobby' with his handler L/Cpl Cyril Plumridge, 'Wolf', 'Judy' and 'Leo'), 'struggling through heavy surf came ashore at a point outside the range of the coastal guns'.

It looked like a walkover.

The assault companies of 8 Argyll and Sutherland Highlanders (war dogs 'George', 'Leo', 'Duke' and 'Rover') clambered down the sides of the big ships into the assault craft going for the shore at Bougie, about three miles away. 'We rushed up the beach expecting bullets but none came,' said one account. Then came disaster. The ships unloading stores were attacked by wave upon wave of Luftwaffe Ju 88 bombers with no air cover to fight them off. It was a shambles. Three ships were sunk in the bay, including the Landing Ship Infantry (a converted merchantman), HMS *Cathay*, which had carried the Argylls from Scotland.

The 1st Army dogs had it tough from the very beginning. Their story is briskly told in a single-page 'summary of war dogs supplied to the Division' and its component infantry battalions. The document was compiled eight months and more after the events described, assigning named dogs to their 'last known unit'. It is both terse and tragic — and of singular importance in canine military history.

In the unopposed seaborne assault around Algiers on 8 November 1942, Airedale dog 'Chum' 'drowned on landing with the 1st Bn East Surrey Regiment', it stated starkly. Two dogs with 8 Argyll and Sutherland Highlanders were 'lost at sea to enemy action', presumably in the sinking of HMS *Cathay*, at Bougie on the 11th. Poor 'Duke' and 'Rover' never even got to the beach. But of the highland regiment's dogs, two survivors, 'George' and 'Leo', seem to have made it ashore to sniff the mysterious smells of Africa.

And there were more dogs being led through the surf by their handlers to the alien shore with emergency supplies of Winalot biscuits to reward them (the troops would subsist on the newly formulated compo-rations for weeks to come). In December more dogs would follow with their handlers for North Africa, with reinforcing battalions from 38 (Irish) Brigade, 1 Royal Irish Fusiliers and 6 Royal Inniskilling Fusiliers (war dogs 'Gyp', 'Ben', 'Glen' and 'Scruff').

Meanwhile, 300 miles to the west, the very first US war dogs to see action, the Virginia-trained 'Chips', 'Watch' and 'Mena', were at the end of their long transatlantic journey in an assault ship that had sailed straight from the US East Coast, heading for French Morocco.

Chips, a German Shepherd cross, had been donated in early 1942 by Mr Edward J. Wren of Pleasantville, New York, under the Dogs for Defense scheme. He had been trained as a 'sentry', not a 'scout', as the US Army designated guard and patrol dogs. With his batallion he landed under fire at Fedala, twelve miles north of Casablanca, on 8 November — as part of the 30th Infantry Bde, 3 Infantry Division, assigned to the 'Western Task Force' under the command of Maj-Gen George S. Patton Jr.

'On board ship, handlers saw their dogs for the first time,' according to the history of the US Quartermaster Corps, and 'fed them C-rations, and engaged in last-minute training. On D-day the dogs proved gun-shy and flinched with fear when the convoy was subjected to aerial bombardment and naval gunfire. Once ashore, each canine sentry carved out his own fox-hole immediately.'

Chips's co-K9, Mena, succumbed quickly to 'fear of artillery fire, making her useless as a war dog', so it was recorded, but of the three pals, bold Chips romped ashore, eager to get to grips with the beastly Vichy French.

After three days of stiff fighting, they were all soon on camp guard duty. Chips and timid Mena were promoted to be part of the security detail round the Anfa Hotel Casablanca, scene of the Roosevelt-Churchill conference held between 14 and 24 January. Mena, meanwhile, produced nine pups — 'Some were sent back to the States, others kept as mascots'. Chips would soon be heading for Sicily and an even bigger adventure.

The relatively modest British forces consolidating ashore around Algiers and at Bougie were ordered to go all out for Tunis. But instead of evacuating a defensive position now about to be assailed from two sides (the advancing 8th Army was pressing in from Libya), the German High Command urgently flew in fighter and bomber aircraft from Sicily and powerful land forces began to arrive in the Vichy French colony by sea. By the end of the month, three German divisions, including 10 Panzer, and two Italian infantry divisions, had been shipped in.

The British 78 Division pushed eastwards into the hills still in high hopes, the 36 Infantry Brigade advancing along the northern route, the faster-moving 'Blade Force' from 6 Armoured Division taking a central route through the mountain passes, and the 11 Infantry Brigade aiming to take a southern route to the railway and road junction at Medjez-el-Bab. The dogs that had survived the perils of the landing bounced cheerfully along the dusty roads with them. It looked like a walkover until the defenders very rapidly, and with clever use of deception, as it would be said, 'transformed a shrunken perimeter into control of practically the whole of northern Tunisia'.

The first real contact with a determined enemy was made at a place called Djebel Abiod on 18 November when 6 QRWK were bested by a small force of German paratroopers. It would get much tougher yet. The Lancashire Fusiliers regimental history of this period recorded: 'The Luftwaffe had complete control of the sky and was strafing and dive-bombing at will. Every day you heard of some vehicle of the brigade being caught on the road and shot up. Above all, there was the feeling that the brilliant dash for Tunis and glory had petered out.'

And it had. This was not a mechanised romp across the desert sand, it had become a slugging match fought with small arms, knives and bayonets among olive groves, dry stone walls, tumbledown farms and fortified hill villages. And it would be fought in darkness. In fact this just might be where patrol and messenger dogs could prove their worth. And the enemy used them. There were excited press reports of a 'white dog' with a German unit which:

As soon as it picked up [an Allied patrol's] scent, it stood at point, [and] immediately rifle and machine-gun fire covered the ground in the direction in which it was pointing. One of the sergeants was shot through the legs and had to be left. That evening the lieutenant returned with stretcher party to bring back the sergeant. Again they saw the dog and as soon as one of them raised his rifle, it did what a well-trained man would do — crouched on the ground and rolled into a gully.

The resistance of the (dog-assisted) German infantry, backed by punishing artillery and tank firepower, was far greater than had ever been anticipated. Infantry of 1 East Surrey Regiment had reached and occupied the lightly defended small town of Tebourba, less than three weeks after they had landed near Algiers. It was about twenty miles north of the strategically placed town of Medjez-el-Bab, on the north side of the steep-banked Medjerda River — and lay astride the only route that German armour could take through the hills from Tunis. The prize of Tunis itself was just fifteen miles beyond, a day's march. Neither side could afford to lose this fight.

The Surreys set up Battalion HQ in a scrubby wood near the railway station. It looked like a brief pause. Then just before midday, on 27 November, the Germans counter-attacked in strength. More than fifty tanks clanked up the road. Dive-bombers pounded the defenders. The bitter struggle for the town went on for seven days. Eventually tanks cut the road south back to Medjez, leaving the defenders virtually surrounded. Ordered to retreat at last, the survivors slipped to the south in darkness from the ruins. Only a single Surrey dog appears to have made it with them.

Each day that passed, the terrain got rougher, the weather worsened and the resistance grew stiffer. The dogs, it would seem, got soppier. In a curious interlude, a cameraman from No. 2 Army Film & Photographic Unit arrived to film some of it. He caught the West Kents with their agreeable-looking dogs doing tactical exercises, the troops in winter battledress, the landscape in early December looking more like Scotland than Africa.

According to the production notes, the film (preserved as rushes in the IWM [Imperial War Museum] film archive, it was never cut into a publicly shown cinema newsreel) shows: 'War dogs attached to the Headquarters Company of the 6th Royal West Kents, who are patrolling a section of the railway line from Djebel Abiod to Sedjenane in Tunisia'.

The dogs are named 'Leo', 'Judy' and 'Wolf', who 'was wounded by mortar fire' — and a mongrel called 'Bobby'. According to the production notes:

> Captain Nixon appears on screen with messenger dogs Leo and Bobby, who is trained to return to HQ from the patrols with a message. A patrol dog scents something and Captain Nixon writes a message, which the dog handler puts on Bobby's collar. The dog goes to HQ and returns to the patrol.

It was all good Edwin Richardson stuff, the kind of clever dog display that had wowed the crowd at the Agricultural Hall military tournament, fifty years before. Was it of any relevance to this war?

By the time the film was made (it is dated 10 December), the 6 Royal West Kents had already distinguished themselves by holding the crossroads at Djebel Abiod for four days against an armoured counter-attack and themselves making an attack with heavy casualties on 30 November at a place called Green Hill (Djebel Azzag), a heavily defended highpoint commanding the Sedjenane to Mateur road on the northern route to Tunis. The dogs, on the evidence of the film, had survived thus far.

By late December, rain, mud and German counter-attacks had brought the whole offensive to a shuddering halt. The battered British infantry withdrew to Medjez and the hills around to regroup. The texture of the fighting settled down to a grim ritual of night patrols and ferocious small-unit action in the hill villages, each side looking for psychological as well as physical dominance. It was described in a report on the combat lessons of the campaign.

> The German method appeared to be confined to setting traps and ambushes for our patrols (a dummy pulled on a string along a wall) or sending out very strong fighting patrols of 30–40 men well armed with automatic weapons. The German has proved himself well at lying low and never disclosing his posn., not interfering with the recce. patrol and then engaging the fighting patrol which followed the next night.

The Lancashire Fusiliers were now fighting hard in the defence of Medjez-el-Bab, the Germans still occupying positions commanding the town, including the formidable feature known as 'Longstop Hill'. A month of small-scale actions followed, when 'really long patrols would go out on one night, lie up all the following day, and return the next night'.

The 6 Royal Inniskilling Fusiliers (war dogs 'Gyp', 'Ben', 'Glen' and 'Scruff') had arrived in North Africa in mid-November as part of the reinforcing 38 (Irish) Brigade. By 9 December, they were holding defensive positions astride the road from Teboursouk to Medjez-el-Bab, 'everyone busy digging in and covered in mud. All ranks living in the open', said the War Diary. The regiment's post-war history described operations in January 1943 in the 'no man's land' around Goubellat, perched in a bowl of hills on the road to Tunis:

'Patrol tactics were, by day, to lie low in farmhouses,' it said, 'by night to go out on missions for the conversion of enemy parties to the belief that surrender was advisable. Patrols operated night and day to try and secure dominance in no man's land.' After two weeks of this, a battalion-scale attack was made by 'battering through the quagmire in stormy rain, any advance proved hopeless with nearly one hundred men killed or wounded.'

At dawn on 5 January 1943, 5 Royal East Kents (5 Buffs), supported by 3 Parachute Battalion, made a renewed assault on Djebel Azzag (Green Hill) on the northern route to Tunis. Once again it proved too tough a nut to crack. Ten days later, 6 QRWK staged a big raid when 'D Coy, under cover of artillery fire, caused many casualties to the enemy and successfully withdrew'.

The West Kents and 5 Buffs (war dogs 'Nipper', 'Grettel', 'Laddie' and 'Raider') were ordered south to the Robaa valley to resist a new German build-up — which would erupt in an assault in the first week of February when the fearsome Tiger tank made its combat debut in Africa.

The resurgent enemy now threatened the area around Bou Arada, supposedly a springboard for an advance by the whole of 78 Division. Instead on 18 January, the Germans attacked first. To meet the crisis, a scratch force was formed to defend the area — to be known as 'Y' Division, an extemporised command made up of the 38 (Irish) Brigade, 1 Parachute Brigade, and a French battalion, which went through a week of very heavy fighting against the Hermann Goering parachute division, plus tanks from 10 Panzer Division in late February 1943.

The German counterblows at last died down and in March the front became comparatively quiet. But as the rains faded out and spring temperatures dried the mud, 78 Division girded itself to advance again on a front of some ten miles wide, with the intention of taking in turn a series of rugged peaks and fortified mountain villages, north of the Beja to Medjez-el-Bab road.

General Sir Kenneth Anderson, GOC First Army, described the terrain as 'a kind of Dartmoor, but with deeper valleys and steeper hills.' A more robust account described it thus: 'Between these villages are tracks, passable to goats, but which could be, and were, bulldozed into tracks for motor transport. To the east and the west of these villages is a jumble of bare rocky hills — with no tracks at all; and north of Heidous, the last northern village — one runs into real tiger country and all civilization is left behind'. That is where the infantry battalions and their surviving dogs were heading.

The general offensive began on the night of 7 April, when the East Surreys began the assault on the mountain village of Toukabeur, joined early the next morning by 2 Lancashires. The men were still in winter battledress, cosy enough for the chilly nights, but in the day, 'it had become very hot. Soldiers who a bare few weeks earlier had felt that anything would be better than to be cold and wet, now began to feel exhausted by the heat and the strenuous climbing,' according to the regimental history.

Again a combat camera team recorded some of it (it was not shown in cinemas). A clip taken on 10 April shows, according to the accompanying 'dope sheet': 'A Vickers machine gun post manned by men of the 2nd Battalion Lancashire Fusiliers. Panning shot up the Medjerda valley to Longstop Hill. The Vickers opens fire on a suspected enemy position. Major Hudson of the Lancashire Fusiliers, Brigadier E E Eden Cass of the 11th Brigade and Captain Austin of the Royal Armoured Corps observe the ground ahead. Major Hudson has his Alsatian dog with him.'

Three days after Major Hudson was filmed with 'his' dog, the Northamptons and the Lancashires together made an assault on Djebel Tanngoucha, described as 'a wicked-looking mountain with a jagged, craggy peak'. The heavily fortified position of Longstop Hill was beyond. The first attempt was beaten off by mortar and machine-gun fire. A renewed attack went in that evening.

'All went well at first, but in the early hours of the morning of 15 April a thick mist descended and contact with "C" Company was lost. It would be subsequently learned that it had been captured more or less complete in the fog. All its officers, including Major J F H Hudson MC were missing,' the Lancashires regimental history recorded. And so was the dog – the first presumed British canine prisoner of the desert war.

The stalled drive on Tunis was renewed. On the 20th, 1 East Surreys took the hill known as Djebel Djaffa. Two days later, at last, the rocky slopes of Djebel Tanngoucha were captured, ensuring the next objective would be Longstop Hill itself. In one spirited account:

All day on 22 April, 1 Surreys, and their fellow 78th Division battalions, 5 Buffs, 6 Royal West Kents and 8 Argylls dug in, using shallow gullies and depressions wherever they could find them in the open ground. They lay up as still as possible in the hot sun, trying not to attract enemy fire. At 8 pm men's hands went up to their ears. The artillery fire of 400 guns, which would last all night, shattered the evening and signalled that the battle for Longstop Hill had begun. At 11.30am the next morning the Surreys and the Argylls got to their feet and began their slow climb.

For two gruelling weeks, the infantry battalions of 78 Division hurled themselves at Longstop Hill, supported by tanks and most of the divisional artillery. The surviving war dogs had no chance in this mincing machine.

With Longstop's summit at last in the hands of 78 Division, the final great natural barrier barring the way to Tunis was taken. On 7 May, British armour rolled into the city. By 15 May, all Axis forces had been cut off and soon surrendered, with more than 250,000 taken prisoner. Of their animals, it would be recorded, 'although the Germans had used pack animals on a considerable scale, most by the end had been lost, stolen or eaten'. The fate of the 1st Army dogs, family pets just a year before, would be only a little better. A few, a very few, would survive to fight on in extraordinary circumstances. Two of them would become famous; no one must know what had happened to the rest.

What about 'Scruff'?

The campaign in the Tunisian mountains was as tough as anything the British Army ever encountered. Gruelling night patrols, hand-to-hand fighting and crushing mortar, artillery and air attacks made a dog's life on the battlefield nasty, brutish and short. How much so is recorded in the brief summary of their fates.

While Airedale 'Chum' had 'drowned on landing 8 Nov. 1942', the 'other three, one of which was believed to have been wounded, were lost at Tebourba approx 1 Dec. 1942'. They were named as Alsatian dogs 'Gyp' and 'Bob' (War-Dog 241/X495) and bitch, 'Lady', of the 1 Surreys. Tebourba was the scene of the ferocious counter-attack by 10 Panzer Division and the week-long siege that followed.

Labrador dog 'Prince' with the 5 Northamptons, 'burned to death in a bombed vehicle', presumably a victim of the lack of air cover when 'every day you heard of some vehicle of the brigade being caught on the road and shot up'. Three more Northamptons dogs, Alsatians 'Toby', 'Rex' and 'Mark', 'all became ill and had to be shot by their handlers'.

Lurcher 'Tatters' and Alsatians 'Rex' and 'Chum' with 2 Lancashire Fusiliers, 'were handed in at a place unknown in N. Africa. All records have been destroyed but are believed that they were handed in to Y Div., a temporary formation,' said the report. That was the scratch force formed in late February 1943 to defend the Bou Arada plain. Tatters and his chums did not seem to have made it.

'Nipper', an Alsatian dog with the 5 Buffs, was recorded as 'destroyed at Robaa', scene of a desperate defence against the German counter-attack in the first week of February. 'Another dog is on record but believed to have become lost,' said the report. It seems to have been the Alsatian bitch, 'Grettel'.

Three dogs out of four with 6 Royal West Kent Regiment were all recorded as lost in April, 'due to enemy action'. They seem to have survived the fighting all the way from the landing at Bougie, through the battle for Green Hill to the final bloody battle for Longstop Hill, where their luck ran out. One seemed to have survived.

Alsatian bitch 'Mac' (War-Dog 98/X433) was 'presumed captured with Major J F H Hudson MC on 15 April,' said the document[18], when C Company, 2 Lancashire Fusiliers, became lost on the mist-shrouded Dejebel Tanngoucha Mountain.

Of the two Argyll and Sutherland dogs, 'George' and 'Leo', who had survived the sinking of HMS *Cathay* at Bougie, one was 'wounded and subsequently destroyed' and another 'lost in Tunis after its capture in May 1943'.

Of thirty-six dogs in total listed, only five seem to have survived. They were Alsatians 'Laddie' and 'Raider' from the

---

[18]   Major Hudson is recorded as being PoW No. 4209, held in Oflag VII-B, Eichstätt, Bavaria, until liberated in May 1945. The fate of 'Mac' is not recorded.

5 Buffs, who were 'handed over to a salvage depot at Hammamet in June'. A single Surrey dog ('name unknown') also seems to have come through. Two dogs, Alsatian 'Rex' and Collie 'Robb' from 1 Royal Irish Fusiliers, were recorded as having been 'handed over in August 1943 to No. 3 Veterinary Corps Evacuation Centre, Souk El Khemis', an improvised unit set up to tend the riding ponies and pack mules acquired locally for the campaign – including many hundreds of 'enemy' animals.

The Irish battalion, assigned to 78 Division in March, had departed Tunisia from the port of Sousse for Sicily on 26 July and for whatever reason the RIF had chosen to leave their surviving dogs behind. As for 'Robb', his epic wartime saga was only just beginning.

Then there was that one dog from the 6 Royal West Kents. It was Collie 'Bobby' (War-Dog 209/53) with the black and white fur coat, who had featured with his pals in the little message-running drama filmed on 10 December after the first battle for Green Hill. What had happened to him? His story would be told in full (perhaps a little *too* full) later.

The 6 Inniskilling dogs were not on the 78 Division list but their fate in the campaign is recorded in a letter from a Northaw-trained handler who wrote directly (it caused quite a stir) from a dusty depot in North Africa – when the action had all long since moved on to the invasion of Sicily. It read:

E Company, 4 Battalion
1 Infantry Reinforcement Training Depot
BNAF
Date 6.9.43

To: Officer Commanding
War-Dog Training School

Sir,

Could you please send me instructions as to what is to happen to my Patrol Dog 'Scruff' No. 582 and myself? He is the only dog left out of the four that was sent to the [6 Battalion] Inniskilling Fusiliers. 'Gyp' was killed in action on patrol. 'Ben' and 'Glen' the two Alsatian dogs have both died within the last two months. The dogs were never used much in the North African campaign. The conditions were seldom of any use to work the dogs but what work they did do was done well. I am at the base now, having been graded unfit for a fighting unit and no-one seems to know what to do about me or the dog so perhaps you could inform me, Sir. If there is any dog training schools out in this country, I would be glad to be sent there: having gained valuable experience under battle conditions with the dogs which can be passed on to other handlers.

I am,
Sir,
Your Obedient Servant,
5335487 Fusilier Winlow, J.

By any reckoning, the debut in action of Britain's war dogs had been a disaster. Nothing about the canine role passed the censor to be reported in the press until late April 1943, when, with the campaign almost over, a photograph appeared in the *Daily Telegraph*. It was of a 'Brigadier waiting for the return of a patrol after the capture of Chaouach, northwest of Medjez-el-Bab, at the start of First Army's offensive earlier this month,' according to the caption. 'With them is an Alsatian dog.'

And there indeed was a handsome Alsatian lying at the feet of several battledressed officers in a dramatic mountainous location. There was immense excitement among British dog-lovers when the photo appeared. Our pets really were at war! But no more newspaper stories would appear of canines at the front — for good reason. The senior officer was Brig E. E. Cass, commanding 11 Brigade. And the dog in the picture was 'Mac', who in fact had been captured with Major J. Hudson (also in the picture), eleven days before the image was published.

What had gone wrong in Tunisia? A War Office committee got down to examining the canine combat record in detail and would report later in the summer (see p. 136). An early American-originated report blamed the sound of gunfire. 'Preliminary reports on the use of scout and messenger dogs in North Africa by the British [have] indicated that their work was unsatisfactory,' it said. 'According to observers, the animals were easily frightened and confused by artillery fire, those doing scout work losing their sense of direction and neglecting to smell out the enemy. While ordinarily giving good service on short patrols, messenger dogs also were affected adversely by heavy gunfire.'

There are clues to another reason in the archives. Herbert Lloyd's frustration overall was clearly reflected in a post-war account when he wrote: 'Patrol dogs were used very effectively by the British Army wherever COs were sufficiently interested to permit them to function. [T]here existed Commanding Officers disinterested in dogs and, in these units, dogs were very infrequently used and no encouragement [was] given [to] their handlers.' The pictorial evidence from Chaouach seemed to show, however, that some senior officers were *too* interested in dogs, but only as some kind of martial fashion accessory.

Major Bill Miskin, commanding B Company, 6 Royal West Kents, recorded his memories many years later of the gruelling campaign in the mist-shrouded mountains around Robaa in February 1943. He said:

> We were sent a message dog. It arrived to great excitement and was promptly sent up to the forward company, everyone was making a noise, and he came rushing back with a message from the company commander, Frank Taylor. 'Testing dog,' it said.

It was all a terrific lark. Officers and men loved it. Such hilarity was good for morale but disastrous for the dogs. The RSPCA knew whom to blame. 'Thinking it was just another of those orders emanating from a higher level, some commanders did not take the matter seriously,' said its post-war history, describing their combat debut. 'The least intelligent men were given care of the animals or they were allowed to become pets of the regiment. Both had a most adverse effect on the usefulness of the dogs.'

It was inevitable perhaps. The ranks of Rex's Army, who just a few months before had been greeting their masters at suburban railway stations or snoozing by the nursery fire, were sloughing off six weeks of training intended to make them canine warriors. Feted and stroked by young soldiers far away from home, they had become an army of pets.

It had been their downfall.

13
'Cowardly, Noisy and Useless'

After the tragedy in Tunisia, the axe hovered over the war dogs of Potters Bar. The first request for some sort of report on their usefulness had been made at the end of 1942. Until that was in, patrol and messenger dog training was suspended on War Office instructions. It was noted that by 5 February 1943, a total of 258 VP guard dogs had passed out of Northaw, with 143 more still required. One hundred and four infantry dogs were 'with Infantry battalions under the control of Home Forces and a number more supplied to First Army or are under War Office control in this country'. Reports on their value in action were awaited. Meanwhile, a little propaganda battle was being fought out in Whitehall and the press. Through the spring, a stirring sketchbook and amusing cartoons of the 'army dog training centre' appeared in the society magazine *The Tatler*, presumably aimed to win fashionable society, including the wives of senior officers, to the military canine cause. If so, it was a failure.

An early verdict was announced on 19 March. 'Dogs are not satisfactory for patrol or message work in the infantry battalion,' announced Lt-Gen Sir Bernard Paget, commanding Home Forces. 'Their training and allocation for this purpose should cease.' The General, once such a war-dog enthusiast, thought it might be worth having 'some anti-sabotage dogs behind the lines of an operational theatre, either at home or overseas'. He suggested a 'small pool of Bloodhounds'. How humiliating. But it was for authority higher even than General Paget to decide the overall fate of Britain's war dogs: it would go to a grand committee of the General Staff.

The misery for the Northaw enthusiasts went on for months. All those happy, enthusiastic dogs waiting to do their bit, what was to become of them? What to tell owners who had volunteered their pets, but had not received their call-up papers? The *Telegraph*'s heroic tableau of the Brigadier and the Alsatian at the gates of Tunis had been a false dawn.

Herbert Lloyd and co., like the staff of an embattled boarding school threatened with closure, sought nightly solace in the village pub, the Two Brewers, with its plain but welcome wartime fare, where, according to his daughter, he became very good at shove ha'penny. Then it was back to work in the dark with the dogs.

Someone, clearly a Whitehall enthusiast for the survival of the project, thought it appropriate to stage a press call at Northaw on 2 June, which might show the school's pupils could do more than guard things. It would be a big day for war dogs all round. The *Manchester Guardian* correspondent noted how 'photographs from Tunisia of patrol dogs with the British forces show how the Army is making increasing use of highly trained dogs lent largely by private households up and down the country.' He also noted that 'an office staff replies to inquiries from anxious owners, but personal visits are discouraged.' Among names of donated dogs, 'Rex', 'Peter' and 'Kim' proved 'extremely popular', noted the Press Association correspondent.

In faraway Algeria, that very same day, war correspondents and a War Office film crew were invited to an extemporised camp to see men of 38 (Irish) Brigade resting and refitting in a dusty French colonial town, two weeks after the fall of Tunis. They found 'an army message dog in action' in Guelma, one of four belonging to the Royal Irish Fusiliers in North Africa — two for patrol and two for messages.

Company Sergeant Major Garrett was filmed 'laying flat, writing a message for his platoon sergeant. He hands the message to Lance-Corporal H Evans, with his dogs, "Rob" and "Boy". Lance-Corporal Evans places the message in a collar around Rob's neck and releases him. Rob heads for his other kennel man, Fusilier Williams, who is on the other side of the field. Rob negotiates a stream. After running a mile, Rob dashes to Fusilier Williams, [who] hands it to Platoon Sergeant M T McHugh, [who] extracts and reads the message and runs off to give orders to his platoon hidden in the undergrowth. Rob is petted and fed by his master.'

The film ends with a: 'Close up of Rob looking as happy as a dog can be that knows his own, not underestimated, importance.'

It would be the first screen appearance of a huge canine star — in wartime and thereafter. He would still be making news almost seventy years later.

Meanwhile, back at Potters Bar that same 2 June, 'experienced kennel-maids' explained the induction process and told the *Manchester Guardian* correspondent how a 'hearth-rug dog, some distant relative of a sheepdog, had ambled quietly during the initial thunderflash test, where more spirited Alsatians were often nervous.' Another visitor reported:

> There is still a lot which is hush-hush about war dog training and although one can guess a good deal about training methods, the authorities frown on publicity of this kind.
>
> Doggy folk too know many of the famous personalities who are intimately connected with the school, but here again, names are officially taboo.
>
> [The ATS kennelmaids] are as keen as mustard, drawn from all classes and walks of life, one even tried her hand at training lions pre war.
>
> When one recalls the value of the feminine influence in the world of dogs, one ceases to wonder at the efficiency of the ATS and the war dog school, but to many, the usefulness of the girls came as somewhat of a surprise.

That was his opinion. In fact it was all a show. The day after reporters were shown round Northaw, and message-carrying Rob was doing his stuff for the film camera in Algeria, the new Director of the AV&RS, Brig George A. Kelly (he had supplanted Brig C. A. Murray at the beginning of March), noted wearily that he was still waiting for a decision from the General Staff, 'in respect of future policy regarding the employment of dogs with Infantry'. The newly appointed Director of that branch at the War Office, the much-decorated career soldier Maj-Gen T. N. F. Wilson (lately on the military staff at the Washington Embassy), found the whole idea of dogs in the Army ridiculous.

Brig Kelly had originally been advised that 920 such dogs were required, and 'this involved securing liens on several thousand'. In fact a mere 260 had been trained and issued to battalions, but with policy under review, 'everything has been at standstill for many weeks,' he wrote. 'Dogs held in the public reserve have still not been called up and there have been numerous complaints.'

There were plenty of families waiting in vain for the arrival of a collar and lead and a travel warrant for their pet's patriotic journey to Potters Bar station. Instead there was silence.

In his War Diary memorandum the Chief Army Vet implied, naturally enough, that the problem was with those 'formations to which dogs had been issued, not their training at the school.' If those standards could be maintained after they had left its gates, they would not 'develop into regimental pets and become *cowardly, noisy and useless*'.

Sentimental soldiery, both in Tunisia and at home, had turned Northaw's finest into that lowest of creatures, a cookhouse dog. It was not the dogs' fault. Nobody should have been that surprised. And nobody seemed immune from temptation for general canine larking around — even brigadiers.

It really did look like the end. No new war dogs (other than guard dogs) were going out to join the British Army's developing campaign in Sicily and Italy, although a handful of survivors from North Africa made the crossing semi-officially. In fact — rather than proving cowardly and useless — some of them would end up winning medals.

'Rob', for example, who had arrived at Northaw in early summer 1942 and been shipped out for the Torch operation.[19] Rob (listed as '471/322 Collie dog Robb' on the 78 Division casualty return with 1 RIF as his 'last known unit'), after his performance for the camera at Guelma in eastern Algeria, was one of the dogs listed as being left behind at the improvised desert veterinary depot at Souk-el-Khemis. Thereafter, as it would be recorded elsewhere, he was 'adopted by a parachute regiment in Tunisia and ended up [in Italy] with the Special Air Service Regiment'. His awfully big adventure was still ahead of him.

And there was 'Bobby', now known as 'Bob', the 6 Royal West Kent message dog who had not just survived the Tunisian turmoil but seemed to have made the crossing to Sicily with his battalion, avoided the general recall order and was now somewhere in the mountains of southern Italy with one or other, or both of his message dog masters. This would prove a matter of some controversy. His days as a front-line tactical dog, however, were over.

Also joining the Italian campaign was US War-Dog 'Chips', late of Allied-summit guard duties Casablanca, who crossed the Strait of Sicily in July 1943 with his infantry unit as a 'sentry' dog. Although supposed to be on static guard duties, Chips clearly had a talent for a fight. While in Sicily he was reported to have 'attacked an enemy machine gun crew in a pillbox after he had broken away from his handler, seizing one man and forcing the entire crew of four to surrender'. Also he was credited by his unit with having been directly responsible for the capture of

[19] Rob's owner, Mrs Edna Bayne, would tell Mr Monty Hunt many years later, researching WDTS history, that Rob had begun his active service career as 'a liaison dog with the Surrey regiment'.

numerous enemy soldiers by 'alerting them to their presence'. Chips had a scalp wound and powder burns on his fur, showing that he had dodged an Italian bullet.

The unit commander, Capt Edward G. Parr, recommended the dog for the Distinguished Service Cross. It went to the Division Commander, who approved. Chips was also awarded the Silver Star and the Purple Heart. Dogs were not meant to be recipients of medals, but Chips somehow managed it.

American newspapers went crazy, Dogs for Defense loved it and there were even laudatory speeches in Congress. But it was all a bit embarrassing: medals were for service personnel and dogs were considered 'equipment'.

Mr William Thomas, past national commander of the Military Order of the Purple Heart, stuffily complained to both President Roosevelt and the War Department, claiming that by so honouring Chips, they were demeaning all those who had been awarded a Purple Heart. Chips's medals were duly revoked. When General Eisenhower met Chips in Italy, the de-honoured dog nipped the General's hand! Plucky Chips was given an honourable discharge and returned to his family in Pleasantville, New York State. His owner, Mr Edward J. Wren, said he would have preferred a pound of hamburger to medals. The British press would report the Chips controversy with some bemusement in January 1944. Medals for war dogs?[20] Now there was an idea, as long as it could be done without upsetting anyone. A British version of Chips would soon follow (see p. 194).

[20] A British intelligence report coincidentally noted in late 1943 that some Japanese Army dogs on patrol duty in Manchuria had won the prestigious bravery award, the 'Order of the Golden Kite'.

Guard dogs, meanwhile, were having a good war. Corps of Military Police canines and their RAF equivalents were in great demand. Victory in the Mediterranean meant there was a vast new archipelago of bases and supply lines to guard against the pesky 'pilfering proclivities of the native inhabitants', as the RAVC Official History would later describe them. More seriously, German saboteurs had targeted railway lines and water plants in Egypt, and been parachuted into Tunisia, it was noted at the time. Vigilance must not cease: dog power was required more than ever.

A dog training school had been opened at Almaza, near Cairo, in February 1943 and its graduates posted direct to CMP dog companies. Although numbers of Northaw-trained VP dogs were shipped to Egypt, according to the school's War Diary, the bulk of the dogs used for guard duties were donated by local civilians or were former regimental pets that had been acquired in the desert from the enemy. War police dogs 'Pixie', 'Willy' and 'Kittie', 'Boozer', 'Bruce' and 'Anchor' are recorded in the War Diary as gifts from passing military units. 'Bob' was a gift from Mrs Michaeliedes of the Zeltoun Kennels, Cairo, while 'Mena' was presented by Sister Price of the No. 1 Mobile Military Hospital. 'Sheila', an Alsatian captured from the Italians in 1941, was still on police duty in Palestine six years later, so *The Soldier* newspaper would one day discover.

'During the first six months in the Suez Canal Zone they made 308 arrests and recovered property worth £3,000,' according to the Official History of the RAVC. And dogs from Egypt went to Italy to guard rear areas and arms dumps with a small military police training section established at Ottaviano on the foothills of Mount Vesuvius. They were accompanied on their duties by a number of captured, de-Nazified dogs, so it would be reported. Although some VP dogs from Northaw would be shipped out ('chewing their way through the wooden kennels on the high seas'), British dog power in the Mediterranean needed little reinforcement by ex-pets from home.

War dogs were quite at home in the scorching desert but could they be useful in colder climes? The efforts of Major Wall to acquire sled dogs in America had produced results. In December 1942, the DAV&RS was messaged that 'forty dogs inoculated against distemper and rabies' were on their way across the Atlantic. '1lb meat and 2lb cornmeal a day' was assessed as an appropriate ration. On 18 February it was recorded 'forty dogs arrived in good condition, sent to Mountain and Arctic Warfare Training Centre.'[21] Three Canadian 'dog management expert' NCOs arrived with them. Quarantine regulations were waived as long as the 'police were warned' lest a dog should escape.

What the Huskies were actually supposed to do, clearly nobody had much of a clue.

Life at Northaw proceeded that spring and summer of 1943 agreeably enough. The emphasis was now exclusively on VP guard dogs for home and abroad. The big excitement in May was when a 'loan dog escaped'. 'The attitude taken by the owner who appears to be of the agitator type is most unreasonable,' noted the War Diary. A bitch in heat was the standard way of luring a Great Escaping dog back inside the wire.

---

[21]   The dogs were kept at Glen Feshie house, Kingussie, Inverness-shire.

The US War Department's work on tactical dogs had pottered on through the previous winter — boosted by the arrival of a delegation from Northaw headed by the former Master of Foxhounds and dog trainer, Captain John B. Garle. With him were two NCO handlers and 'Paddy', a patrol dog loaned for the duration by Mrs E. Corrigan of 76 Croftfoot Road, Glasgow, plus three more dogs, names unknown.

The British invasion was a sensation. US intelligence reports (from Middlesex rather than Tunisia) had paved the way. 'Captain Garle arrived on 1 February 1943, and proceeded to the War Dog Reception and Training Center at Beltsville, Maryland, where he demonstrated his messenger and scout dogs to officers interested,' said a US official history. 'So successful were these demonstrations that Captain Garle was sent on a tour of all Quartermaster War Dog Reception and Training Centers to indoctrinate our trainers in his method.'

The US Army's TM 10-396 *War Dogs Technical Manual*, published on 1 July, would incorporate much Northaw-gained experience in its pages. The introduction made reference to the '7,000 dogs brought forth [from the public] since the [British] War Office invitation of early 1941, of which one in three have been accepted.

'Success in field trials has resulted in the order that four dogs and two trainers be distributed per [infantry] battalion throughout the British army,' it stated cheerfully. But success in field trials and success in combat were different things. Just as the US War Department were deciding in the spring of 1943 to send six scout and two messenger dogs to the Pacific, 'as a test of their value under combat conditions', the British War Office had already judged such animals to be valueless. No war

dogs were employed in the Burma campaign against the
Japanese.[22]

Tunisia had been a disaster. No one could say otherwise. But
with exemplary impartiality, the 'General Staff Policy Committee
on Weapons and Equipment' chaired by the Deputy Chief of the
Imperial General Staff, Lt-Gen Ronald Weeks, had commissioned
a report on 'dogs for war purposes'. Ready by mid-July and
codenamed 'Paper No. BZ', it made grim reading for canine
enthusiasts.

> North Africa reports were to the effect that Messenger and
> Patrol dogs were of little value, the dogs being insufficiently
> accustomed to battle noise and explosions [something the
> WDTS failed to provide] and becoming, while with units,
> cook-house pets.

Patrol dogs meanwhile had 'failed to range or locate enemy posts
merely giving indication when lead past or down wind' of the
enemy. The supply of the 'right strain of dog' from the public
was anyhow dwindling rapidly. Home Forces were uninterested,
General Paget had already said so. The Ministry of Aircraft
Production at home and the RAF in Gibraltar meanwhile had
reported favourably on guard dogs.

[22] Where, rather than dogs donated by posh Tokyo families, the Japanese were reported to
be using 'ordinary village mongrels' as patrol and message dogs. The patrol leader in
charge 'barked' to give them orders, according to an intelligence summary. The
Australian Army used a small number of US-trained dogs in New Guinea, in autumn
1943. A British report on the jungle warfare lessons noted — 'the dogs were rendered
useless by inexperienced handlers or alternatively they were ruined by becoming
regimental pets.' The US Marine Corps trained war dogs for service in the Pacific —
which were used at Bougainville, Peleliu and Guam in 1944, where sixty war dogs went
ashore and twenty were killed or went missing. A memorial was erected, fifty years later.

As to future policy, if battlefield dogs were to be continued, some kind of special dog-handling units would have to be formed — as the German Army were supposed to have — because *'nothing will teach the normal British unit not to make a pet out of a dog.'* Train patrol and messenger dogs to a higher standard? Stop the public loan scheme and breed them specially? (That would take too long.) Form a special Dog Corps? These were all possible ways forward, said the paper. A final decision would have to be taken soon.

The wait was not long. A high-powered meeting in Whitehall on 29 July looked at the facts. Animals loaned by the public were 'volunteer dogs', it was pointed out, but the supply of 'good dogs was nearing exhaustion'. Those available now were only useful as guard dogs. 'If he was convinced of one thing,' the DCIGS [Deputy Chief of the Imperial General Staff] was reported as saying, 'it was quite useless to have dogs in the Army unless they had specialist trained dog-men to look after them. If not, they quickly degenerated into cookhouse pets and were useless.' The Director of Infantry, Maj-Gen T. N. F. Wilson, no friend of Northaw, recoiled at the idea of 'dog-men' — indeed at dogs altogether. The organisation of an infantry battalion was complicated enough, he said.

The meeting's final judgement circulated to all commands on 14 August was terse in the extreme: 'There is a requirement for guard dogs. There is no requirement for any other type of dog, e.g., messenger or patrol dogs.' The tactical dog programme was thus terminated.

There were lots of Home Front dogs, meanwhile, 'distributing' themselves around the British Army in a rather different way. *The Tail-Wagger Magazine* in a clever article affectionately profiled the 'Khaki Mongrels', the 'shaggy-haired tramps drawn by the mess-room smell of yesterday's liver.' The writer meant the innumerable-seeming camp-following dogs, whose barking presence indicated a nearby military base.

The writer told the story of 'Hawkins', who had attached himself to an infantry battalion and saved them early one morning on manoeuvres by locating a lost field kitchen — 'Barking furiously, he ran over the hill, and soon they saw the mess-tins of their mates shining in the sun. As a reward Hawkins was "put on the strength," and received his due ration daily'. It was a familiar story.

Then there was 'Spud', a Wire-haired Terrier with 'a dash of half a dozen other breeds who had a cast-iron stomach. Cookie taught him that favourite trick, dying for the king, and he'd curl up on the ground and pretend to die after swallowing a lump of ancient cook-house cheese'.

And there was 'Jock', a little Scottie who was 'the master-crook of all scroungers' — 'He once stole the entire meat-roll detailed for tea. After that he was run out of the camp, and was last seen being pampered by an RAF unit'.

'Lady Jane', 'Sweeney Todd', 'Tipsy' (who could salute with his front paw), an elegant, unnamed Borzoi owned by 'a very charming young lady', 'Pickles', a 'loyal little Spaniel', and one cat, 'Garbo', a 'tough tabby who all the dogs were scared of' — also featured in *The Tail-Wagger*'s evocative parade of khaki canines.

Recalling Colonel Richardson's dashing war dogs of an earlier conflict, 'it has been said that dogs are not extensively used this time except as guards at aerodromes — because the British soldier spoils them by feeding them too much,' the article's author noted very wisely. He clearly knew his dogs, and he knew his soldiers.

Why not employ these intrepid dogs as during the last war, when thousands were trained as messengers, so the author suggested. 'This article was written before the War Dog Training Scheme was announced,' explained the editor of *The Tail-Wagger*. And that is exactly where camp-following strays (some of them, anyway) were heading.

When American troops began to arrive in Britain in mid-1942, cookhouse dogs hanging round their amply rationed bases thought their day had really come. The little bands of opportunists became heaving herds of strays and wanderers – lost evacuees and survivors of earlier bombing. Already the RSPCA had brought up 'the problem of army camps, which attracted large numbers of dogs which act as pets for transient soldiery but are routinely abandoned when the unit is ordered to move.'

Now, on the Society's urging, 'the Army Council had given instructions that [it] should be informed before such a move', so that it might bring some humane solution to the mass of excitable pets whose masters had suddenly climbed into trucks and disappeared. US and Canadian forces were similarly instructed. General Eisenhower himself, Supreme Allied Commander, issued a stern warning.

Some dogs were not so playful. In the 1943 spring lambing season, there were wildly alarming press stories of '10,000 killer dogs' roaming the countryside, with farmers demanding they be allowed to shoot them on sight.

What to do with this canine plague? While the RSPCA would put them down, the rival PDSA had an inspired idea to make this canine Home Army somehow official. The Dispensary's experience in North Africa dealing with all those desert dogs showed how it could be done.

The British Army had long had 'mascots' defined as an animal formally 'attached for rations' to a military unit, with their food and medical care provided at public expense in return for 'fulfilling their role in keeping the troops amused'. 'Regimental pets' were another matter altogether, animals defined as 'not having War Office authority and fed from government stores when civilian sources are inadequate but only on repayment'. Official or unofficial, military animals had featured in every British colonial adventure and campaign in history, as had the Royal Navy's ship's cats.

It was suggested that a limited number of mascots per unit be somehow 'authorised', the senior officer in charge accepting responsibility for their care. The plucky animal's papers would later be lodged with the Imperial War Museum in London. A badge of membership would be given.

This so-called 'Allied Forces Mascot Club' would have three classes of member. Firstly, the 'thousands of animals adopted by servicemen', then 'animals and birds conscripted into the services for the empire's war effort' and lastly, faithful beasts – described as 'honorary members of outstanding merit'. Club members must be 'serving with the armed forces or civil defence'. It was not for civilians. The first member in January 1943 was 'Barney' – a donkey foal at Hendon Air Station, who had been won in a darts match.

Its original registered address was the Golders Green home of the PDSA's Secretary and master publicist, Edward Bridges Webb. The club's Secretary was PDSA press officer and former opera-singer, Dorothea St Hill Bourne. Later in 1943 the charity would instigate a medal to be awarded to especially brave members of the Mascot Club attached to all the services, named

after Mrs Maria Dickin, founder of the PDSA. The bravery
medal (for animals, not humans) would turn out to be a publicity
masterstroke.[23]

The exotic menagerie of regimental pets in the Middle East
was ideal recruiting ground for the new Mascot Club. 'Bonzo'
was one of the very first, described as an 'Essex hound' who
arrived one day at the PDSA's Cairo hospital with two 'bronzed
and tired-looking soldiers', his eyes 'swollen, inflamed and full
of sand'. Private Leslie Clark of 'a Stores Convoy Unit of which
Bonzo was mascot', enrolled him as a founder member. The
survival of the desert animals beyond the Axis collapse was
going to be tricky. Were they to accompany their masters to
new theatres of war? Would they find new employment in
Egypt or Italy? Would they come to Britain? Some did, many
did not.

Like 'Abdul' and 'Steve', all too briefly members of the Mascot
Club, who attached themselves to an RASC unit, described as
two 'Cairo-born mongrels who advanced with the 8th Army from
Algiers to Tunis, but were destroyed before the invasion of Italy
rather than be left with strangers'.

While the pet propagandists were boosting the cause of dogs all
being in this war together, in secret ministers were again
considering how to get rid of them. A meeting of civil servants
convened at the beginning of March 1943, nominally to prescribe
a production figure for dog biscuits, heard how after the mass
destruction early in the war, dog numbers had come back to

---

[23] The RSPCA had its own 'VC', the Margaret Wheatley Cross (for humans) named for
a '16-year-old serving girl who lost her life saving her employer's dog' on a level crossing
in Lancashire in 1936. Not to be outdone by the PDSA, it would introduce its 'For
Valour' collar medallion in 1945, although it is far less well known than the Dickin
Medal.

pre-war levels. This was a very bad thing. There were four million of them, consuming 300,000 tons of food that could be usefully fed to pigs and poultry. 'There is no doubt that bread, oatmeal, milk and other sound human foods are being illegally fed to dogs. Most of these products are heavily subsidised,' complained the combined civil servants in their final report.

The meeting recommended persistent anti-dog propaganda 'appealing to everyone who can reasonably do so to give up their dogs, especially in excess of one per household, with arrangements for *free painless destruction* of those given up'.

The minister in charge realised it would not work. Just as the legal adviser had considered the year before, an officially sponsored cull of pets would be a disaster for morale and a propaganda gift to the enemy. It was far too controversial and anyway there was 'nothing to stop a dog owner feeding his pet out of his own rations'. The mass dog reduction plan was yet again put on hold.

'There have been singularly few dog heroes in this war,' Mass-Observation had commented, a year earlier. So it was still. The canine sacrifice in Tunisia went officially unmentioned in public.[24] It might have been too distressing anyway, but right now dog heroes were politically inconvenient. But Britain's brave war dogs had another card up their sleeve, or rather their noses. Again it would be played out in secret — and again it would be an epic of canine courage.

---

[24] The authorised history of the RAVC published in 1963, for whatever reason, states that just four war dogs went to North Africa.

Part Three

'FIND!'

'Patience and understanding of the canine mind are the handler's essential qualities, plus a real love for working his four-legged comrade.'

Lieutenant James Davison RA, CO,
No. 2 Dog Platoon Royal Engineers, 1944–5

Beyond a Dog's Instinct

Everything that a dog might usefully do in war depended on his (or her) nose. That astonishing mechanism, millions of evolutionary years in the making, was how a patrol dog scented the enemy or a message dog knew which way to run to find his handler. But such tactical animals were no longer required.

The Times had reported after a visit to Swakeleys Farm in November 1941 about an experimental dog at the school, which 'used to belong to a gas company'. The animal was somehow used, so the reporter had been told, for detecting 'gas leaks'. In fact it was more than that. Ever since that report, Herbert Lloyd had been working to open a new front in the employment of war dogs.

Not long after the end of the war he would tell how, under his pre-war Home Office contract as canine adviser to HMG, he had been requested to investigate problems at a 'BBC receiving station' at Cooling Marshes in Kent.

In fact this was a very secret place, constructed by the Post Office in 1938, nothing to do with the BBC, as the site for a high-powered, shortwave wireless station with a transatlantic range, receiving a signal from its twin in New Jersey. It would be a vital wartime strategic communication link but it was not working properly: it was suspected that pinhole leaks in underground cable that linked the antenna arrays were letting in water.

Digging up four miles of ducting was not possible. There was a simpler way: pump a gas containing 'amyl mercaptan', a foul-smelling sulphur compound, into the transmission lines.[25] On the first test in February 1939, a Post Office employee sniffing the air found a single leak. Problems persisted.

Someone remembered Mr Lloyd and his police dogs. 'Rex of Ware', a jolly Labrador with a keen sense of smell, was familiarised with the unusual odour. Once he could detect the slightest garlicky hint of it in the ground, meat was buried next to the spot and 'Rex induced to dig'. It was simple conditioning, inducing a desired behaviour by association with something pleasurable. A demonstration was held at the Dollis Hill site of the GPO research station in north London (which coincidentally had the shadow Emergency Cabinet War Room codenamed 'Paddock' in its basement).

When the trial was repeated at Cooling, the control room 'became uninhabitable with the smell', it was reported, while clever Rex identified seven pinhole leaks in the dodgy ducting. It was noted that the dog came through 'a four-mile trip without taking any notice of sheep, cattle, dogs or horses. At the end of a

---

[25] After a catastrophic explosion at a school in Texas in 1937, experts from the United States Bureau of Mines concluded that a faulty connection had allowed invisible and odourless natural gas to leak into the school. The Texas Legislature began mandating within weeks of the explosion that mercaptans be added to natural gas. Soon the practice spread worldwide.

tiring day he showed he was a normal dog by joining enthusiastically in a rat hunt.'

Rex had shown something else. Trained by Mr Lloyd on the reward system, he had very quickly become adept at recognising an artificially synthesised (and highly pungent) source of smell. This was something beyond a dog's instinct, like herding sheep or sniffing out game; this was entirely *induced* behaviour. How this might be militarily useful was not clear — but one day it would be.

'Landmines', explosive charges buried in the ground triggered by a tank's track or a soldier's boot, had not figured much in the first two years of war. It was different in the desert fighting. Mass laying of mines was first employed by the British 8th Army in the construction of defensive lines in spring 1942. It proved very effective in holding back Rommel from the gates of Cairo.

As German forces went on the defensive, they employed great energy and deviousness in creating barrier-minefields, laid in random, cluster-shaped patterns at varying depths such that if one mine was lifted, its neighbour would explode. Heavier anti-tank devices such as the German Tellermine could be found by probing with a bayonet but to deter deminers they were now being routinely 'seeded' with anti-personnel ('A/P') devices, like the hated 'S-mine', which jumped out of the ground before detonating.

The 'Schrapnellmine' had been devised before the war. It was the size of a beer can and was activated by a three-pronged push contact device or a pull igniter attached to a tripwire. When triggered by an unfortunate soldier's foot, a canister was launched about one metre in the air by a primary charge — to be detonated by a secondary charge scattering 350 steel balls

outwards, scything down anything in their path to a range of
150 metres. The loathsome thing had a great psychological
effect.

Allied troops would call it the 'Bouncing Betty'. But it was
made of metal and could be found by technical means. Something
far worse was coming — a mine that could not be detected.

To defeat anti-tank mines, the so-called 'Polish Mine
Detector' devised by Lieutenant Józef Kosacki in 1942, which
picked up buried metallic objects electro-magnetically, had
been rushed into production, men trained to use it and sent out
urgently to Egypt. It greatly assisted the 8th Army to get going
again in the great pursuit across Libya. The device, however,
was fragile, could not be used under fire and worked poorly in
wet conditions.

Just as they had done in Libya, the Germans laid vast numbers
of mines to slow down pursuers in their final retreat in Tunisia.
American combat engineers had to quickly learn what they could
from the more experienced British, including devious booby-trap
and deception techniques, like rolling a vehicle tyre over an
anti-tank minefield to make it seem as though others had passed
this way without harm, as well as the intimate horrors of
anti-personnel devices.

There were stories of exploding bars of soap, bottles that
blew up when the cork was pulled, whistles that detonated
when blown, an innocent-looking 'abandoned farmer's cart'
full of grenades. Everything was tripwired; everything was
deadly.

Lieutenant Colonel Paul W. Thompson of the US Army
described the perils of mine clearing in the December 1942 issue
of *The Infantry Journal*:

The first task is to find the mines. The simplest and oldest, but probably the most used and surest, method is the ticklish chore of poking and prodding with a sharp-pointed instrument such as a bayonet.

When the prod encounters anything hard, the engineer crosses his fingers and indulges in a careful little scraping movement to make sure he has really found a mine. If the answer is yes, his troubles are just beginning, for his next task is to remove the mine without allowing it to remove him. The mine must be carefully uncovered and the detonator discovered and disarmed.

There is no certainty that each mine will be exactly like its mates. A mine detector—a metal circle with a long handle, which works on an electro-magnetic circuit and gives a signal, generally a buzz in an earphone, when the antenna passes within range of the steel shell of the mine—is sometimes substituted for the prod-and-poke method. But this is rarely used under fire.

The Polish detector and prod and poke could just about do the job. 'Flail' tanks (such as the British 'Scorpion' used for the El Alamein break-in), with whirling chains beating the ground, and 'Bangalore torpedoes', were more ponderous methods of clearing area minefields. Yet to defeat Nazi Germany, for a 'Second Front' to succeed at all, the fiendish ingenuity of their mine warfare technicians must be overcome. In January 1943, a sub-committee of the British Ministry of Supply was appointed to pursue a scientific approach to doing just that.

In late 1943 Hitler would appoint Erwin Rommel, cultivator of the 'devil's gardens' in the Libyan desert, as inspector of the so-called 'Atlantic Wall', intended to beat off an Anglo-American invasion force. He would call for a colossal mine belt one kilometre deep, starting at the beaches, containing fifty million anti-tank and anti-personnel mines.[26]

But neither the one-time Desert Fox nor his Führer had reckoned on a man in a tweed suit and trilby hat, smelling ever so slightly of damp Cocker Spaniel.

Towards the end of the Tunisia campaign, something entirely new had been encountered — the so-called 'Schu-mine', a small plywood box with a hinged lid containing a rudimentary detonator and a solid block of explosive. It could not be found with a Polish-style mine detector. The bayonet was the only tool for probing it, going into the ground sideways. One brave sapper would describe this terrifying process:

> The accepted manner of finding these Schu-mines was to get down on one's hands and knees and crawl forward, prodding the ground in front of you with a bayonet, hoping against hope that you would prod and find the mine without prodding the top, setting it off. Even when found, these mines had to be lifted with the very greatest care from the surrounding soil without it blowing up 6 inches from your face.

The little boxes could be sown quickly by inexperienced troops, simply covered with leaves or earth. And they did not kill outright. Instead the dreadful things might blow a foot off its victim and leave 'the remainder of the bone split up through like a stick of rhubarb'. That is what its devisers intended — to

---

[26] Around 8.5 million would be laid by June 1944. How to deal with them was a vital concern of pre-D-Day planning.

sow fear and dread – to slow the pursuit by psychological as well as physical means. Two men at least would have to take the cruelly injured man back to a rear area for medical help.

Allied troops began to hate the horrible 'Schu' box especially. More 'undetectable' mines, their casings made of glass, concrete, plastic and wood pulp, would follow.

Herbert Lloyd had begun mine-hunting experiments at Swakeleys Farm in 1941 with his pioneer super-sniffer, Rex. A meaty snack reward had done the trick on the plucky Labrador's eve-of-war search for a gas leak at Cooling Marsh. The same technique, it had rapidly become clear, could be developed to stretch a dog's olfactory talents into completely unknown territory – way beyond anything that might be regarded as 'instinctive'.

The work had continued amid much secrecy at Northaw in a special proving ground sealed off from the rest of the canine camp. Only a small group of trainers knew what was going on. The saloon bar at the nearby pub, the Two Brewers in Northaw High Street, much favoured by Mr Lloyd and his dedicated band, had become a place of secrets – don't mention the mine dogs.[27]

---

[27] Lt James Davison, the Liverpool medical student who would take mine dogs into the field, commissioned a cartoon from a Canadian engineer friend, which was published post-war in Herbert Lloyd's contribution to *The Book of the Dog*. Called a 'New Method of Testing Scent Discrimination of War Dogs', it depicted comic mutts being tempted by sundry smells, including a dirty sock, a block of cheese, a bottle of gin, four mines (including two Bouncing Betties) and a truck exhaust. There are distractions, including a cat (looking out to announce his conclusion that the whole business is 'utter nonsense'), a greyhound, wearing a Greyhound Racing Association vest, chasing a rabbit and itself being chased by a squirrel, a bone suspended from a lamppost, a parcel of dog biscuits that engage a black Terrier, a discarded Spam tin and a drain grating. A bucolic Lloyd in plus-fours beams benignly while a bespectacled officer pronounces 'Jolly good!' In the distance a farmhouse bears the sign 'The Two Brewers'.

After much trial and error, including a short-lived and disastrous try-out of the American 'repulsion' technique using electric shocks (see p. 159–61), the Lloyd approach would emphasise reward alone.

In its definitive form, the production of a fully Northaw-trained mine dog would take three months. There were six stages. First, candidate dogs were put on half-rations of meat and biscuits for a week. Next, a period on dry biscuit only, 'fed in his kennel, but at work he may be given meat, which will be considered by the dog a great luxury'.

Following this, dogs were acclimatised to wearing a four-foot leash and working harness, the putting on of which communicated to the dog that he was now 'on duty'.

Given the command 'Seek', dogs must now explore a predefined area where defused British Mk V landmines (but still containing chemical explosive) had been placed in a pattern requiring that the dog should 'quarter' the ground when approaching. That is, sweep from right to left and back again as in game bird retrieval. And why should they be interested? Because each mine had a piece of horsemeat (or 'Chappie') placed on top.

Next, the mines were buried with only their tops above ground, with the meat reward perched on them. In the third stage landmines were rubbed with meat so as to pick up the scent before they were fully buried. If the dog made a correct 'point' by sitting a few inches short of the danger spot, he would get a meat reward given to him by the handler from a bag slung from his belt.

In the last stage, the mines were buried with no prior exposure to the scent of meat. A correct 'point' would again get a final meat reward from the handler — but an incorrect point would not. By this stage the dog had learned to associate the reward with the buried object's own 'scent' (what that added up to would be subject to much debate), an association that it was presumed would be retained for the dog's career — but which must be reinforced throughout with meat rewards for successful points in a live minefield. 'False points' were not punished.

To begin with, the danger area was tackled methodically, the dog being required to 'quarter' the ground and further cross-check from corner to corner in a technique known as 'union-jacking'. In action much later, the technique would be adapted to the rapid exploration of captured vehicle parks or supply dumps (typically booby-trapped), with dogs 'experimentally' used loose for this purpose, 'leaving the actual mines to be removed by slower methods', as Mr Lloyd would later write. In fact, the whole mine-detecting dog episode would be the most enormous experiment, from beginning to end.

The Cocker Spaniel expert's insight into dog behaviour made him wary, meanwhile, of canine memory, which might be 'used too efficiently instead of his nose,' as Mr Lloyd would write. Every training session had to represent a fresh challenge — and the handler must be acutely aware that his dog was not merely reproducing a learned routine. One of the most dangerous things to later emerge in the field was a dog's tendency to 'stop working without appearing to'. Only the experienced handler, sensitive to the subtle working habits of his individual dog, could know.

Training tips would encourage handlers to consider 'boredom' as a cause for a dog's loss of keenness. They were warned to look out for subtle signs indicating when a dog had lost 'interest', and advised to immediately rest him. Dogs should not be worked longer than a half-hour at a stretch, and should be given fifteen to thirty of rest after each spell of duty.

That human—canine trust was to be the foundation of everything. As an especially intuitive young engineer officer would explain, personnel should have an 'intelligent appreciation of dog's faculties and limitations and understand what the dog works for, how he relies on consistent treatment, being guided not by conversation, but by isolated words spoken in a particular manner and tone, and by actions which, through constant repetition, are associated with various duties.'

'Petting must be rationed and used as a reward for good behaviour by that dog's handler alone,' he would write. 'Reproachful words must be given promptly and justly. A disillusioned dog, unimpressed by apologies and promises, soon becomes a failure for a long time and is sometimes completely ruined for work.'

There would be plenty of disillusioned humans too along the way.

All this was done in twilight or darkness. As training progressed, all sorts of 'noises off — such as Bren guns, heavy explosions at close range and swooping aircraft' were laid on to 'inoculate' the trainees against the sound of battle. And further, as Herbert Lloyd recalled, 'every sort of distraction was introduced — rabbits, sheep, game, lumps of meat, in-season bitches …'

Only one in five dogs of those already chosen for Northaw made the grade as a mine-hunter. But how, in the final stage of indoctrination, did this snuffling elite actually sense a buried, meat-odour-free mine? There was no scientific explanation.

'Several solutions were forthcoming,' wrote Lloyd after the war. But he was personally convinced that it was because a *freshly buried* (his emphasis) mine, be it metal or not, was in the ground that had not yet been sealed by weather or compaction. This 'left enough fissures for scent to ascend' to the surface and for a dog to pick it up.

He would further assert that a mine left for a long time in soil created a 'chemical reaction' that could equally easily be found by the dogs. Associations built up in all those months of training did the rest. The mine's own smell — metal, chemical, wood, plastic, equated to a meat reward. A dog's business end, his nose, could be made master of any minefield. All that was needed was to convince the War Office — and get the right dogs.

15
No Owner But the State

The US Army was also acutely alive to the landmine menace. A development programme had begun in 1940, which resulted in its own version of the Polish type, electro-magnetic anti-tank mine detector. It was called the Detector Set, SCR-625. The same programme found that 'no means existed for detecting non-metallic mines'. Experimental 'geophysical' research contracts were duly given to oil survey and electronics companies and the Massachusetts Institute of Technology (MIT). A lawnmower-like device to find variations in ground electrical resistance was tried out, as was an acoustic-seismic apparatus devised by the Sun Oil Company of Beaumont, Texas, and an ultra high-frequency device by the Radio Corporation of America.

MIT were exploring 'a radio-active ray method' for discovering soil disturbance and buried objects. The famous inventor, Serge A. Scherbatskoy, founder of the Geophysical Measurements Corporation, was retained by the Army as a consultant. This was the best that American science and industry could throw at it. Progress, however, was slow.

Captain John Garle, the Northaw trainer, had mentioned the pioneer British mine-dog trials to his American hosts on his demonstration tour with War-Dog 'Paddy' and his chums in February 1943. Specially trained dogs could find buried objects, so the New Developments Division of the US War Department would be informed. No one was quite sure exactly how. Work was progressing. What Garle did not say was that it was being done completely by trial and error, guided by the instincts of some eccentric British dog enthusiasts.

It was not rocket science.

With the advent of undetectable Schu-mines in Tunisia, and with more of the nasty wooden boxes now being encountered in Sicily, the US Quartermaster Corps urgently embarked on its own canine experiments. Several civilian trainers and one hundred dogs were engaged in a 'crash program' on Cat Island, off the coast of Mississippi – a primitive place 'without electricity or fresh water', where 'bites of venomous snakes' were a hazard for dogs and trainers alike. Trials soon moved to the more convivial Fort Belvoir, Virginia.

If a dog could find a buried bone, he could surely find a wooden box – it was all in the nose.[28] The US tactical dog manual of July 1943 recognised the discrete sensory realm that dogs inhabited:

---

[28] According to the United Nations Mine Action Service (UNMAS), sixty years later: 'Dogs are capable of detecting concentrations that are several magnitudes lower than the detection threshold of the best technological "sniffers." In mathematical terms, a human can smell concentrations of about one part per million, the best chemical analysers can "sniff" concentrations of about one part per billion, but dogs can smell concentrations of about one tenth of one part per trillion, or about ten thousand smaller – the equivalent of detecting the result of pouring twenty bottles of whisky into the Lake of Geneva.'

The dog's world differs from the human in specific ways. His world is predominantly one of odours. His nose tells him countless things about the environment that entirely escapes humans. He is more sensitive to sounds. His vision is considerably inferior to human vision.

For whatever reasons, in exploiting such gifts the US experimenters discarded the 'attraction' technique. Instead they used one based on the 'emotion of fear and instinct of self-preservation', as it would be described. 'Repulsion' would be a direct way of defining it.

Captain John Garle would later witness[29] the favoured training method. It seemed baroquely cruel. He reported how it worked, calling it 'trapping in reverse' — making the analogy with a coyote that once having been caught in a trap (and escaped), would never be caught again. Once was enough to have learned to fear it. He reported:

> The first phase of training is as follows: Place six steel game traps in a pattern. Place the [six foot] leash around dog's neck. Start about ten paces away from the traps and work towards them at normal speed. Handler must assume an alert and searching attitude. When the dog has become ensnared [by the trap pinching his paw] the shock or surprise will make him howl and whine.

[29] Garle saw the experiments for himself at the War Dog Reception and Training Center, San Carlos, California, in spring 1944 — where the chief trainer was William 'Bill' Koehler, who would become very famous in the post-war dog world and chief animal trainer to Walt Disney Studios. His emphasis on punishment would become controversial.

The length of time that traps should be left on dog before removal by handler is eight to ten seconds. When it is time to remove traps, the handler approaches with assumed fear and removes traps hurriedly and throws them aside. The dog then seeks consolation from the handler, and protection. The handler gives this by petting the dog.

The handler himself had also to show fear of the trap, building in the dog 'a fear of metallic objects'. If this did not work, the trap would be wired to a wet cell auto battery and electrified. Too much and the dog 'will become over cautious and man shy'. After that, 'let the dog run and play as a reward'.

Phase two was five days of encountering electrified traps covered in grass or lightly buried in the ground, aiming to make the dog 'check' — that is, sit or lie down from two to four paces in front of the repellent object. By this stage a trainee dog would not eat from a metal bowl.

Phase three was being trained to 'check' when encountering both metallic and non-metallic objects in a simulated minefield of regular pattern. The dog should 'look upon both with equal fear'.

If the dog missed things, 'sharpen him on traps or electrified wire mesh buried under grass'. Inducing fear of tripwires came next in training by stringing them from car batteries. The final phase was doing all this with the sound of heavy-calibre gunfire in the background, all to instil a fear of 'anything foreign to the terrain'. Captain Garle would relay the information dispassionately to Droitwich Spa and Northaw. But this was not the British way of doing things.[30] Mr Lloyd preferred a nice meaty chunk to get results – so, no doubt, did the dogs.

Britain's own home-grown mine-dog trials were looking promising. General C. J. S. King, Engineer-in-Chief at the War Office, was showing interest, prompted by news of the American experiments, which had begun to reach London in early summer 1943 via the technical liaison staff at the Washington Embassy. A top-secret intelligence report came from China that the Japanese Army were using dogs to 'detect and dig out land mines – proving uncanny in their ability to detect metallic mines at a depth of up to two feet.'

But after the canine wipe-out in Tunisia, could animals loaned for the duration by pet-lovers be employed in such an even more dangerous-seeming way?

Brig George Kelly, Director of AV&RS, was distinctly alarmed. His predecessor had cooked up the whole public loan wheeze with the Quartermaster General. Here was something that could politically blow up in all their faces. He told General King directly that 'whilst most people would prefer to sacrifice dogs rather than men this seems not to be the view held by a considerable section of the public and the animal protection societies.'

Already he had received inquiries from welfare busybodies as to whether dogs were being used for work in connection with mines and had replied, 'in the negative'.

'The majority of dogs are loaned by the public,' he explained to General King. 'If it becomes known that dogs in this category

[30] Lloyd admitted after the war that the 'repulsion' method 'was experimented with at the British War-Dog Training School, but was quickly dropped.' The unpleasant technique was described in the post-war British war-dog training manual but was not recommended because it resulted in an 'inaccurate indication' of mines by dogs so-conditioned.

are being used for the detection of mines, I anticipate violent protests,' he wrote on 14 June. 'The public may become antagonistic and offers to send dogs to the Army and other Ministries, on which I am entirely dependent, will cease.'

The 23 July General Staff Weapons Policy 'Paper BZ' would contain a very short outline of the 'dogs as mine detectors' proposal based on rumours from America but its drafters were sensitive enough to conclude: 'The supply of dogs [from the public] would immediately cease if the belief got round that they were to be used for the detection and hence the *detonation* of mines.' It might look to an alarmed public as if suicide dogs were to be driven into minefields to blow the things up with their paws.

But there was a way.

Twenty-five years before, Col Edwin Richardson had begun his canine messenger corps with escapees, as he described, from the 'lethal chamber at Battersea'. The army of death-row strays looked set for comeback.

'Dogs donated from dogs' homes and by purchase at nominal sums however have no owner but the state,' Brigadier Kelly told General King. A certain 'Mr Cape', a dog dealer, had been set to discreetly acquire more animals. There were other sources. When in September 1943, a Mr William Simms was prosecuted at Nottingham Summons Court for not keeping a 'dangerous dog' under control, a two-year-old Alsatian said to have bitten two people, the defence put in a plea that if the Bench deemed it necessary to order the dog's destruction, 'it might be hoped they would give the defendant the option of presenting it to the Army'.

'Dogs of this breed were required for training for certain purposes,' it was stated. Indeed, 'the defendant had *already been approached* in the matter.' But the chairman would have none of it, and said 'they had not the least hesitation in ordering the dog to be destroyed.'

Mrs Adeline Humphries of 111 Beverley Road, Ruislip Manor, was luckier. When she was prosecuted in May 1944 for allowing an allegedly 'ferocious' dog to attack a neighbour's child, she pleaded that 'she [had] heard an appeal on the wireless for dogs and she would like to send the dog to the RAF or the Army rather than have it destroyed.'

The Magistrates' Bench judged the (unnamed) dog to indeed be ferocious — but they accepted the defendant's offer to send the animal to the armed forces. But, 'if they refused to accept it, it must be destroyed.' One can only hope the dog was accepted — even to take its chances in some horrible minefield.

There were also animals at Northaw, which, for various reasons, were already owned outright by the War Department.

'Juno', for example, Army Dog No. 9, a Labrador bitch purchased back in April 1941 from Mr Andersen, an Uxbridge vet for 'one pound'. Juno had been posted from the very first training course to 8 Duke of Wellington Regt (who were evidently not that impressed) and after a brief stay with the 6 Royal Irish Fusiliers, had come back to Potters Bar with the general stand down of tactical dogs.

It would be 'expedient' to use such state-owned dogs for mine-detection experiments, said Brig Kelly. He further suggested they be conducted not at Northaw with all its comings and goings, but at Porton, the Chemical Defence Experimental Establishment in Wiltshire which was notorious among animal-lovers, where a number of 'lost dogs' home animals' were already being held, as he explained. The Porton dogs would need 'preliminary training before this experiment can be carried out, because they are retained there for other reasons.'

Some of them were retained for a very special reason. In fact they were being tested wearing gas masks, should the use of dogs on the battlefield somehow be continued. The strange work had begun with the capture of documents, which showed that German war dogs were equipped with 'gas mask, gas clothing, decontamination outfit, gaiter, eye blinkers and a recognition coverlet'.

Porton was asked to devise an equivalent, despite comments that putting a gas mask on a patrol dog seemed counter-productive. Even when informed that an American report into the US dog gas mask, the M6-12-8, had found that 'some dogs could successfully detect, and indicate the direction of, wind-borne scents while wearing the mask,' the doubts remained.

But production of a British version went ahead and it was to be tested in live trials on animals at Northaw and at the 'Animal Farm', Porton, the breeding centre for experimental animals supervised by the RAVC. Most of the 120 dogs used were reported to have taken readily to wearing a gas mask, although one became 'obstreperous and refused to wear any respirator'. He too was 'eventually persuaded to wear one satisfactorily, i.e. without wanting to bite the handler'. After a year of such experiments, Herbert Lloyd would conclude:

9 patrol dogs completely confused when asked to work. No direct scent can reach the nose and it appears that if it did, the filter would be faulty. 4 liaison dogs just walking around, unable to make sense of it. 4 mine dogs tried were unable to

detect anything on ground. Masks invaluable out of work, walking or sitting, of no value at all for working in.

In Washington, meanwhile, Colonel Benson, the military attaché, and Brigadier Charles Lindemann (elder brother of Fredrick Lindemann, Lord Cherwell, Cabinet member and Churchill's influential personal scientific adviser) were hugely excited by the M-Dog experiments underway at Fort Belvoir. In their communications with the War Office in London, they had discovered, however, that there had been 'little encouragement at home and indeed the DCIGS has minuted' [after the catastrophe in Tunisia] that 'all training of dogs for military purposes in the UK is to be abandoned except for dogs for guard duties'.[31]

On 1 September 1943 they had witnessed a splendid demonstration in which four dogs of four different breeds trained in the space of seven weeks had proven '100 per cent effective over newly laid mines and 70 per cent over an old minefield'. All this had been to show off 'the possibilities rather than demonstrate a polished method'.

A demonstration a week later saw the M-Dogs eagerly 'freezing', 'pointing' and 'pawing the earth' for their combat engineer handler to plant a little flag. 'All the officers that witnessed this demonstration were frankly amazed,' it was reported.

'Of the 48 mines in this field, the dogs located 45 accurately in 1-team hour,' said the report from Washington. 'In three other instances, location flags were planted where no mine was present

---

[31] In fact the August Whitehall meeting referred to that decided to terminate patrol dogs also considered an American report that dogs could 'detect the smell of grease with which mines are smeared, but this is supposition only and may well not be true'.

but where there was definite indication that the earth had been disturbed some time previously.'

The next day, the prototype non-metallic detectors from RCA and the Sun Oil Company were presented to the Engineer Board. Both required physical contact with the terrain and 'could not be used for a sweeping search'. Militarily, they were useless – better stick with the dogs.

The stream of excited dog-praising reports to London continued. Brigadier Lindemann urged that a dog handler be sent out for a week to see for himself (John Garle would be despatched across the Atlantic again). If there was no General Staff requirement for such a dog, this must change.

There were plenty of questions in return. How might this work on a battlefield? 'The trainer is of the opinion that the principle involved was *not* one of pure scent,' came the answer, and was convinced that the 'discharge of guns and smell of cordite would not impair the dog's ability to detect mines.'

General Omar S. Bradley, on leave from Sicily, had seen a demonstration under hot sun 'when scenting conditions were at their worst', using three dogs along a gravel road with a 'hard, beaten surface'. The results were duly relayed from Fort Belvoir via the Washington Embassy to London, with an explanation that 'it was to test the dogs' uncanny, little appreciated sense enabling them to detect earth disturbances'.

On the gravel road test, one mine was missed. But it was 'buried in compacted earth so the conditions of the disturbed earth principle on which the dogs are trained to work did not exist,' said the message. The experiment was going to move on to an artillery range where much earth disturbance other than that caused by the laying of the mines could be expected. It would further involve 'explosions, reeking cordite smells and be done at night.' Then they would see what the dogs were really sensing.

Meanwhile the War Office in London caught the optimistic mood. The Quartermaster General was very excited: could not mine dogs be imported from the US? he asked. Lt-Gen Godwen-Austen, Director of Tactical Investigation, thought it would 'be folly not to follow it up'.

Lt-Col C. E. A. Browning RE, senior engineer on the military liaison staff in Washington, reported General Bradley's impressed reaction. And he could further inform London:

> The dogs are also being trained to carry explosive charges into pill boxes through gun ports and back entrances with electric leads attached so that the charge can be detonated when the dog is inside. They are also being fitted with flexible hoses through which petrol can be pumped. The dog carries it to the pillbox loophole and flame is projected from that point. I have not seen these tests yet but will report immediately when further information is available.[32]

All that previous moral outrage about exploding Soviet dogs looked a little out of place. The reaction at the War Office is not recorded.

---

[32] The suicide dog programme — codenamed 'demolition wolves' — was real. According to the definitive history of US war dogs, 'a small supply of dogs was made available for test around fortified concrete bunkers' with satchel charges. 'These tests used only simulated explosives and no canine deaths occurred.' In action the dogs were pretty hit and miss. Dogs for Defense Inc. was not to be informed, just as the animal charities in Britain were to be kept ignorant of anything other than guard duties for loaned dogs. The US programme was shut down on 17 December 1943 but later revived with the prospect of an invasion of Japan.

Meanwhile the War Dog School awaited its fate. It looked set
to be just a guard dog production line, not even that. Perhaps
mine detecting would keep it at the sharp end of war, exploding
or flame-throwing dogs certainly not. The War Office generally
was extremely interested in ways to defeat mines. The next great
strategic bound of the war, the cross-channel invasion of the
continent of Europe, might depend on it. In October 1943 it was
decided that the Northaw expert, Captain Garle, should go back
to America to see the miraculous-seeming M-Dogs of Fort
Belvoir for himself.

All those ex-Field Force tactical dogs were meanwhile milling
round Northaw, looking pretty miserable. Had they let the school
down? Herbert Lloyd had a new brainwave: the training
technique could be adapted to produce something called a 'police
patrol dog'. He explained how the new system worked: 'The
handler, accompanied by the dog on a short lead, patrols the
perimeter to be guarded after dark, always endeavouring to
negotiate the ground so as to take advantage of wind. These dogs
"indicate" the presence of any intruder they pick up.' Conversely
some of the most interesting (and secret) work Lloyd was
pursuing was finding ways of throwing enemy tracker dogs off
the scent of escapees from German prison camps or Special
Operations Executive (SOE) agents landed in enemy-occupied
territory. It basically came down to lots of aniseed.

But unlike the earlier VP dogs, these new, improved police
dogs were trained *not* to attack an intruder and thus 'may be used
freely on all RAF stations where personnel are legitimately about
night and day.'

The rival MAP Guard Dog School, it was pointed out, used
the one-man, one-dog principle, which meant handlers were not

necessarily policemen — and it took eight weeks to train them. Northaw could do so more efficiently. It was all going splendidly; war dogs had won through. On 8 October there was another press appeal for 'dogs to guard secret installations, for the British and American armies and air force at home and overseas'. No other warlike duties were mentioned.

A delegation of RAF brass rolled into Northaw on 20 December and liked what they saw. The Army dog school had a new customer. By 10 January the first RAF 'police patrol' dog course was complete and a second scheduled — with a further thirty-two RAF airmen requested to arrive at Northaw with 'light kit only in case they return to their station with a dog'.

Which they duly did: at the end of the month, 'thirty war dogs embarked UK 31st Jan [for] North Africa,' as the AV&RS War Diary put it, ready to confront all those thieving natives. Colonel Baldwin had better watch out or he would soon be out of business. In fact he was making new connections all over the place.

The MAP Guard Dog School also had a new customer. In 1942 the Americans had approached the War Office, asking for help in guarding their own ever-growing number of airfields and camps in the UK and been referred to a delighted Colonel Baldwin. A school for sentry dogs within a school was organised late in 1943, considered to be a US Army Quartermaster unit, but 'it would be used by all of the technical services and many combat units,' according to the official history. On 16 March 1944 there was a passing out parade of '50 dogs and US Army handlers'. The 'American' dogs throughout the war were in fact all British-loaned pets whose cards had gone into the Droitwich pool of little brown cards for Colonel Baldwin and Mr Lloyd to divide. For example, a dog who would later become very famous, 'Jet',

loaned for the duration by a prominent Liverpool family, would
be trained at the GDTS and began his dramatic career posted to
the US Army Air Force in Northern Ireland, to work with handler
PFC Elmer Aleksiewicz, patrolling a big airbase on the shores of
Lough Neagh.

Baldwin meanwhile remained a master publicist apparently
immune to the censors' blue pencil. His military-civilian, US–
UK operation seemed ever available to journalists seeking a
good-news war story. *The Dog World* magazine visited in
December 1943.

'Diet is liberal and the best that could be devised,' their
reporter, a clergyman dog-breeder, found. The dogs' condition
was 'excellent, as hard as iron – they are 100 per cent happier
than in the average civilian home of today,' said the Very Revd
Farrar, rector of St Wilfred's and owner of the Ravenscar
Alsatians. The supply of dogs was 'entirely dependent on the
goodwill of the public, any decent size of dog will do.'

There was a 'reception kennel' at Redditch run by Flt-Lt
Ashby, where three weeks of obedience work would be
undertaken, explained the reporter. At Staverton itself, Flt-Lt
Hugh Bathurst-Brown was in charge, aided by 'eight of the best
known civilian trainers in the country', including Mrs Margaret
Griffin of the famed Crumstone kennels and twin sisters the
Misses Marjorie and Dorothy Homan.

'After four weeks they are far above the standard of the average
pre-war dog. On aerodrome guard duty, there are eight per site,
impossible for saboteurs to evade.' There was the obligatory
demonstration of a saboteur in a 'baiting' suit being run down in
the act of trying to nobble some parked aircraft. If German
intelligence officers were reading *The Dog World* magazine in

Berlin, they would know better than to plan any sneak sabotage raids on anywhere guarded by a Colonel Baldwin-trained dog.

At the home of the Burnell family in Harrow, north London, it was time for a hard choice. Many years later Elizabeth A. Burnell, then aged five, recalled what happened just before Christmas 1943:

> We had a lovely Golden Retriever, called Michael, and a black Cocker Spaniel, called Hamlet — and with rationing it was extremely difficult to buy enough suitable food to feed two dogs and a couple of cats. My parents decided to answer the RAF appeal and in December 1943 Michael was called up for training at Staverton Court Guard Dog Training School, near Cheltenham. We did not know exactly what he would be doing and we did not hear much about him from then on.

But Michael was not going anywhere near Staverton. A different fate in this war had been mapped out for him when his little brown card had gone into the pool at Droitwich Spa. Mr Lloyd had plucked it out. Elizabeth and her family would find out the truth later in remarkable circumstances.

The Burnells thought that Michael was going to do his duty as a guard. And indeed Vulnerable Point dogs were more in demand than ever as new camps and installations for Operation Overlord (the code word for the invasion of Europe) sprouted across the country from end to end. In spite of a much-reduced threat of domestic sabotage there was still the country's civil and war-making infrastructure to be given a canine shield — including Bletchley Park, described in a Cabinet Office brief as a

'communications centre for all services and the Foreign office'.
This fantastically secret place was guarded by three Baldwin-
trained dogs, 'Larry', 'Vic' and 'Charlie' of 'RAF detachment
Bletchley, Bucks' (they were inducted into the Mascot Club in
November 1943; Charlie's handler is listed in the AFMC register
as a certain 'Harold Wilson'). What a story they could tell!

And there was Chequers, the Prime Minister's country
residence, which might be attacked by 'a battalion of parachutists,
600 men in fifty aircraft', of which 'a third might reach the
target'.[33] In fighting off that lot, dogs might seem pretty
inconsequential but at least they could bark a warning.

As many as 220 'sabotage and/or insurrection parachutists'
had been dropped by the Germans in North Africa, noted a
Joint Intelligence Committee briefing paper. Similar goings on
were now afoot in Italy, where aviation fuel dumps were being
targeted. 'Thirty more saboteurs are on their way,' it warned.[34]

The pending invasion meant that some very secret places at
home had to be given a bodyguard of dogs. The shipyards
building the prefabricated Mulberry harbour, for example, or the
phantom US 1st Army in eastern England broadcasting dummy
radio signals to fox the Germans as to the real destination of the
invasion. Even non-existent army bases needed shielding from
spies. Would saboteurs go after these domestic targets? 'We have
no information from Most Secret Sources [the Enigma
code-breaking operation] so it is not possible to say,' said the
Joint Intelligence Committee in February 1944. But overall the
JIC thought the risk remote. The Director General of MI5

---

[33] This thriller-plot concern of an attempt to kidnap the Prime Minister would persist
      even after the success of the Overlord landing.
[34] They knew from Enigma code-breaking.

disagreed: vigilance should be greater than ever; those VP dogs must be kept on their toes.

And more were needed. At the beginning of January 1944 yet another appeal appeared in newspapers to swell the ranks of the six thousand owners who had already made their dogs liable to call-up. It declared:

> That even more dogs are required is evidence of their success in the duties for which they are trained... guard and patrol dogs are protecting both Army and Ministry of Aircraft Production installations, many of a secret nature.
>
> The present appeal is for 200 dogs each month. The breeds required are Alsatians and crosses, Airedales, Boxers, working Collies, Bull Terriers, Kerry Blues, and Labradors. And curly coated Retrievers. The dogs should be not less than 10 months and not more than five years of age. Anyone willing to lend a dog for war services should write to the Under-Secretary of State, War Office (V. and R.), Whitehall, S.W.1, endorsing the envelope or post-card with the words 'War Dog'.

No mention was made, naturally enough, of mine-detecting dogs.

The British mine-dogs trials had continued energetically. It was all looking rather promising. 'Experimental training in mine detecting has been entirely successful in this country, confirming the work done in the USA along parallel lines,' so a meeting of all interested parties held at Northaw on 24 January concluded.

In fact the Americans were ahead of everyone. In November the 228th Engineer Mine Detecting Company (Dog) had been declared activated at the Cat Island Dog Center.

But if mine dogs were indeed going to be approved, a projected initial weed-out rate of 80 per cent meant many hundreds of canine candidates would be needed. The Northaw summit could agree that 'the present system of loaning, combing out dogs' homes, [getting them from] Chief Constables etc. – appears unlikely to produce the number of dogs required.' There was also the 'possibility of the RSPCA attempting to interfere with the subsequent use of the dogs.' Politically, that could be very difficult (especially within the RSPCA itself).[35] Secrecy should be absolute.

At the moment small dogs were not required although they might be later, the meeting agreed. It was also noted that a recent delegation from the 51st Highland Division had requested casualty rescue dogs for field ambulance bearer parties (long an ambition of war-dog enthusiasts from the days of Colonel Richardson, but something that was never actually put into practice). The 24 January meeting also agreed that there 'is no question that dogs can be trained for patrol work provided they are handled and administered by trained personnel in *special dog units.*' Tactical dogs were not entirely out of fashion, among the enthusiasts at least, but it was mine dogs that would keep Potters Bar's finest in the front line.

The DCIGS's 'Committee on Weapons and Equipment' (for that is what war dogs were) that had axed tactical canines the

---

[35] The Society's Secretary would admit that he might be censored by sentimentalist members for putting pets in danger – but 'consider the fate of the nation's pets if the Nazis had won,' he would write after the war.

previous August examined the latest Northaw proposals. It decided: 'There is a requirement for mine detecting dogs — until further trials show whether mechanical devices are more effective.' 'Dogs may be trained on live mines,' it decreed. And 'the Secretary of State [the civil-servant-turned-MP, Sir Percy Grigg] has accepted the fact that political repercussions could be expected,' it was minuted. Sending people's pets into such apparent mortal danger was clearly going to be a minefield of its own. But on reviving infantry dogs, the hopes of enthusiasts were dashed.

'There is no requirement for patrol dogs for use in NW Europe, except possibly with units operating in mountainous regions.' Medical rescue dogs were to be examined — while 'patrol dogs might be required in SE Asia, and India and Australia will be invited to examine the possibility,' the committee decided. The next day Brig Kelly was told the news about mine dogs by the Director of Staff Duties — 'and therefore we are free to go ahead'.

And there was timely news very soon afterwards from the Leningrad front, its heroic two-year-long siege lifted at last, that 'girls wearing the Leningrad Defence Medal', helped by specially trained dogs that scratched mines out of the snow, had cleared vast swathes of icy landscape. 'One dog had found as many as 2,000.' It was in the *Daily Telegraph*, so that was all right.

The renewed public appeal of two weeks earlier had meanwhile produced another tidal wave of offers from generous (or desperate) dog owners. Three civil servants were lent to the RSPCA to deal with the deluge of little brown cards. But it is clear there was deep sensitivity about using these new offerings for mine hunting — and training them on *live mines*. Or that is, telling the animal charity, let alone the public about it.

Brigadier Kelly was instructed on 31 January by the War Office to explore the '*secret purchase*' of animals, if necessary. If that did not work, 'requisitioning' with 'payment to follow acceptance' was the only way forward. That seemed to imply conscription for mine dogs.

Meanwhile, the waifs and strays would have to do. After some negotiation, an agreement would be reached in April with the animal welfare society, Our Dumb Friends' League (the 'Blue Cross'), that its Secretary, Mr Keith Robinson, should 'write to its branches asking them to send all stray Alsatians, Collies, Labradors and Retrievers to the WDTS.' The army of outcasts was getting bigger by the day.

Their operational use was now becoming more than a possibility. It was time to make a plan. Men and dogs in the field would be part of the Royal Engineers, it was agreed.

If everything went to plan, the 'Mine Dog Platoons RE' would duly take their place in the order of battle of 21 Army Group, the British headquarters formation established in London in July 1943, commanding the British and Canadian forces assigned to the invasion of Europe. On its formation, 'no veterinary staffs had been assigned because no military animals were included.' It was a little different now — it was decided that an RAVC Sergeant be attached to each dog unit to look after the animals' welfare.

No one was quite sure even at this stage what sort of dog was best. It might turn out that small dogs were exemplary mine-hunters, but if lots of them were rejected in the early stages of selection, they could not be diverted to guard duties. A military police Sealyham would be absurd. Nevertheless in the first months of 1944, twelve 'Cocker, Springer, Lakeland etc.' were purchased for 'special trials' at the WDTS, along with thirteen more small breeds on loan from owners and 'ten purchased at 7/6 each from the Dogs' Home, Battersea'. But the eager little dogs were 'too distracted by game scents'. By March they would be 'surplus to requirements' — their fate is unrecorded.

Early results had shown Labradors, Alsatians, Collies and crosses of the same were all viable mine-hunters — and robust enough to stand up to war conditions. In selecting a mine-detecting dog — 'care should be taken to look for an intelligent expression and one broad across the nostrils should always be quivering, indicating the dog is using his scenting powers unconsciously,' it was noted.

'Dogs with black eyes are surly and erratic while dogs with very light eyes are usefully wilful and inclined to use their sight over their sense of smell.

'A dog with hazel coloured eyes usually has the firmer character and for this reason should be selected.' For now, however, they would have to make do with what they could get.

The prescription that only state-owned dogs should be trained in mine hunting was quietly abandoned, meanwhile. Too many potential mine-hunters were already in the pool or arriving at Potters Bar station each day, loaned by the public. War-Dog 'Ricky', for example, a crossbred Border Collie–Old English sheepdog bought from a 'destitute family' by Mrs Sheila Lichfield of Swanley, Kent (moving later to Bromley) for 7s 6d, aged four months. Ricky (also known at home confusingly but inevitably as 'Rex') had been offered to the War Office in 1943, accepted, and paired with Pte Maurice Yelding, otherwise a member of a famous circus family. His sister, Susan, had a noted dog act. Their relationship was to be eventful.

Suitable dogs in the general pool (still benignly fronted by the brown-card gatherers of the RSPCA and the NCDL) were also switched from going to guard training at Colonel Baldwin's canine academy in Gloucestershire to more exotic duties at Northaw.

Just don't tell their owners.

No one at the WDTS was to whisper anything about the strange trials, with meat rewards and buried wooden boxes going on somewhere in southern England. German spies were not the concern. Owners must not know, nor should the animal welfare charities. Northaw had become a place of secrets, a canine Bletchley Park.

Which meant that ATS Private Winnie Burberry had to watch what she said on the party nights that seemed quite frequent, even in war-straitened Hertfordshire. She remembered:

> The American hospital in South Mimms cheered our lives up as we were given the kind of food we had not seen for ages. They thought we were an odd lot and our dog language was beyond comprehension.
>
> Many a night we spent in the Two Brewers [the nearby pub much favoured by the training staff] listening to Capt Danby's piano recitals. Occasionally dogs would get out of their kennels at night and we'd use a bitch in season to lure strays home, rounding up any other escapee dogs, who were usually rather frightened.
>
> I noticed there were not many fat people at WDTS, although whether that was from the food we ate or the amount of exercise we all took I didn't know.

She remembered especially that: 'during an epidemic we had a great number of VIP visitors at the school to study our training methods, especially the mine dogs.' The War Office was taking a big interest all of a sudden. Was this going to work any better than the tactical dogs that had been sent to North Africa? Sending pets to war looked like a very dangerous business.

On the mine-dog front there was yet more cheering news for the enthusiasts, meanwhile, from Russia via the RSPCA (which adored stories about brave Soviet animals). A mongrel named 'Zhuchka', a graduate of the Red Army's animal training centre, was flying round the front line with his master, ready to demine captured aerodromes and supply dumps, so *Animal World* would report. Sergeant Lagutin and 'Dick', and Private Kutkin and 'Tubik', had between them neutralised over 1,600 booby traps and hidden explosives during the Stalingrad fighting. In Kiev, dogs of a sapper unit commanded by Captain Shishov had cleared hundreds of buildings, while 'mine hunting dogs had discovered two huge bombs buried deep beneath the flagstones of the entrance to the Kiev Pechersky Cathedral'. Clever Red Army dogs! Maybe the RSPCA would not make protests (as some sentimentalist members might be expected to do) about British mine dogs and 'cruelty' after all.

America's M-Dogs were also girding for battle. In early May, seventy-two of them departed Cat Island for shipment across the Atlantic company of four officers and 102 enlisted men attached to the Fifth Army Combat Engineers heading optimistically for Oran, Algeria, for operational training in desert minefields before going into action in Italy. Nazi Germany was facing a canine tide of sniffer dogs advancing on all fronts.

With pre-invasion nerves stretched tight, readers of the *Daily Mail* had further cause for worry at the news that thousands of 'Nazi killer dogs', including 'Alsatians and St Bernards', were ready to give the alarm, 'should anyone approach French beaches from the sea at night'. Each one was 'trained to run to its master, should it hear suspicious noises'. And readers of *The Dog World* magazine were treated on 5 May to a made-up story 'that thousands of [British] dogs have now finished their training and are ready to go with a second front.' There was no mention of mine hunting. A 'War Office dog training expert' was quoted as saying 'pure bred dogs had not been accepted, they were too nervous and have not sufficient stamina for long night guards.'

Colonel Baldwin was asked for his opinion. Pure bred or mongrel did not matter – what did was that 'a dog should have sufficient intelligence and stamina'. Meanwhile he had vacancies for kennel maids and trainers – 'Applicants who love dogs should write to him direct.'

The Allied Forces Mascot Club had been boosting the cause of animals at war meanwhile from summer 1943 onwards, enrolling hundreds of Baldwin-trained RAF guard dogs with official approval (more than fifty of them were called 'Rex') via their handlers. The Royal Air Force seemed most ready of the services to cooperate with the charity. Club Secretary Miss St Hill Bourne had expressed her ambition in a letter to the Air Ministry on 1 November 1943 as being nothing less than 'to enrol *all* animals and birds serving with the Allied Forces'. The War Office stayed aloof.

Then there was the newly instigated 'Dickin Medal', named for the charity's founder, Mrs Maria Dickin, for 'special acts of courage, endurance and fidelity' shown by club members. News would come from across the Atlantic that US Army K9 'Chips' had been awarded (on 19 November 1943) the Purple Heart for bravery in capturing an Italian machine-gun nest. The award would trigger huge controversy in America. In contrast the DM was clearly for animals only. They had to be military animals but it was 'official' only in the sense that the Club's registry would be lodged with the Imperial War Museum. Who could object to that? The RAF was sympathetic. Would British army war dogs win medals? The mine-dog programme was very sensitive and Tunisia not to be spoken of. Giving awards to service animals would not be without difficulty.

The campaign started modestly enough. A Mascot Club wheeze that same month to enrol and award medals to three birds of the RAF pigeon service, already much reported in the press to have summoned help for downed aircrew, was vetoed personally by the C-in-C of Coastal Command. The extra publicity might deleteriously 'bring the matter [of air sea rescue operations] to the attention of the High Command of the Luftwaffe,' he insisted. Air Force pigeons came from the 'National Pigeon Service' formed on the eve of war and, like war dogs, were technically on unconditional lease from owners and breeders.

The Club persisted. There was a brisk argument in the Air Ministry, but not about operational secrecy. Could pigeons be intelligent and brave? Had they really saved lives by flying back to their loft? What about dogs? They *chose* to show courage in the face of danger, pigeons just followed instinct, said the Deputy Director of Signals. The RAF pigeon supremo, Wg Cdr W. D. Lea Rayner, argued back that his birds were intensely courageous, and that dogs might only appear to be more so based on 'the sentiment of a wagging tail or eloquent eye'. Pigeons would die trying to get their message home, he said. Would a dog do that?

The pigeon champions won. Three NPS birds, 'White Vision' (who had saved eleven lives from a downed Coastal Command Catalina by reporting their plight and approximate position northwest of the Shetlands), 'Winkie' and 'Tyke' were awarded medals in December 1943, with little ceremony. A national tour of Home Guard and Police Pigeon Shows would follow, with lots of press coverage. But it was just the beginning. Miss Dorothea St Hill Bourne, the club's energetic propagandist, bluntly expressed her desire to the Permanent Under Secretary at the Air Ministry to get RAF dogs on the medal roster. It would not take long – but the first DM dog was not the animal she, or anyone else, might have been expecting.

There was mournful news from Scotland. For almost a year the Huskies acquired from America with such difficulty in early 1943 had been happily scampering around the Cairngorms with 52 (Lowland) Division, training for some snowbound enterprise in Norway –part of the D-Day deception plan. In April 1944, however, the division's role was switched from mountain warfare to air landing. The assigned infantry battalions, including some Scottish TA units, had managed to keep their original assigned Northaw-trained war dogs – and would keep them still. This would prove significant.

On the 22nd the AV&RS War Diary recorded tersely: '39 Huskies and 8 puppies on the strength of 52 Division were humanely destroyed in the presence of representatives of the

Britain's war dog pioneer was Lt-Col. Edwin Richardson (right, seen far left, about 1905). He raised a dog unit which served on the Western Front. The arrival in Britain of the Canadian Toronto Scottish regiment in December 1939 (below) commanded by an old friend, gave him a chance to show off his favourite Airedale Terriers.

The Home Office was meanwhile experimenting with police dogs – seen here at Balham Police station in 1938. Their trainer, the many times Cruft's winner, Herbert Summers Lloyd, suggested using them for military purposes – the origins of the Army War Dog Training School.

TO BRITISH DOG OWNERS

YOUR COUNTRY NEEDS DOGS FOR DEFENCE!

Alsatians, Collies and Other Large Breeds.

Here is **YOUR GREAT OPPORTUNITY TO ACTIVELY HELP TO WIN THE WAR WILL YOU LOAN ONE?**

For particulars write to the Acting Editor, "Dog World," Idle, Bradford.

IT IS URGENT!

The creation of a military dog unit was agreed by the War Office. In May 1941 press adverts appeared (left) as a test of public reaction. The dogs were gathered at Herbert Lloyd's kennels in west London with the first volunteer handlers (below) while troops posed for the cameras (bottom). In May 1942 a much bigger loan appeal was launched with the RSPCA as intermediary (bottom right).

on _____ at _____

Name of Owner
(BLOCK CAPITALS)
Address of Owner

Dog. Name

Breed

Sex , Age

Inoculated against Distemper ? Yes*/No*

If so, date
As all dogs accepted cannot be called up at once,
is the owner willing to keep   1 month*
      it for a period of up to   3 months*
until it is required ?   6 months*

**TO BE COMPLETED ONLY BY THE
INSPECTOR DISTRIBUTING THIS CARD**

Name and Address of Inspector

Were you able personally to see this dog ?
                                        YES/NO*
If so, do you consider it suitable ?   YES/NO*
        * Strike out whichever is not applicable.

*M11328 4/42 702

ON HIS MAJESTY'S SERVICE.

(PART A—To be retained by owner of dog.)

**GENERAL CONDITIONS UNDER WHICH DOGS MAY BE OFFERED
TO AND ACCEPTED BY H.M. GOVERNMENT ON LOAN FOR
WAR SERVICE.**

1. Dogs are accepted subject to trial. The trial may last for only a few days or for several weeks. If a dog is unsuitable, the owner will be consulted regarding its disposal and may elect to have it returned, carriage paid.

2. During the period of trial and subsequently, if found suitable, the dog will be on loan unconditionally and will continue to be so loaned for the duration of the war or for such less period as it may be required.

3. The owner will not be entitled to any kind of remuneration while it is on loan.

4. An undertaking is given that throughout the period of loan the dog shall receive good care and attention, but no liability will be accepted in respect of sickness, injury, loss or death, from whatever cause, whilst on loan or in transit.

5. The owner will be indemnified against any claim in respect of loss or injury of any kind caused by the dog whilst it is on loan.

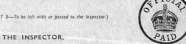
ON HIS MAJESTY'S SERVICE.

(PART B—To be left with or posted to the Inspector.)

THE INSPECTOR,
ROYAL SOCIETY FOR THE
PREVENTION OF CRUELTY TO ANIMALS,

OFFICIAL PAID

Alsatian-fan Lt-Col James Y. Baldwin
meanwhile persuaded the Ministry of
Aircraft Production to trial his dogs as
aerodrome guards (above). The trainers
at his Guard Dog Training School
(top) were mostly civilian and included
several women already famous in the
dog world.

In summer 1942 dogs began to arrive at the WDTS, collected from Potters Bar station each day by Auxiliary Territorial Service kennel maids. Sick or injured dogs were treated in a veterinary hospital (bottom).

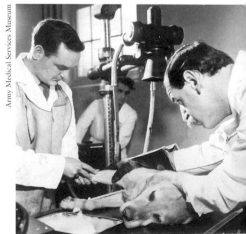

Getty

After acclimatisation, special training began for the dogs and the men who were supposed to go into action with them. Continually being attacked by sceptics, the School made sure it featured in cinema newsreels and society magazines such as Tatler (below).

Jennifer Lloyd Carey

Britain's canine army first went to war in North Africa in November 1942. This movie-still (below) shows message dog 'Rob' (later of SAS-fame) in action with the Royal Irish Fusiliers at Guelma, Algeria. But soldiers made them into pets while senior officers saw dogs as fashion accessories – like 'Mac' caught on camera in Tunisia in April 1943 (above). Dog and master were captured in a German counter-attack a few days later.

The first 'Dog Platoon Royal Engineers' went into action soon after D-Day in Normandy, clearing mines at Carpiquet airfield (below). Lt. James Davison (above) commanded No. 2 Platoon in Holland. His notebook listed dogs including 'Smiler' from the Battersea Dogs' Home and 'Gerry', from Bromley, who was killed by a mine.

2909: 7114 BRUCE.   Mr W. Miles,
                      Windy Ridge, Church Road,
                      Baldon. Tamworth.

2958   S.S. SMILER. Battersea Dogs Home.

2966   4708. BUCK.   L. F. Henbury,
                        114, Hook Lane,
                        Welling. Kent.

2993   7146. JODY   W. B. Brown,
              (NELL'S) Millbank,
                        Western Hill.
                        DURHAM CITY.

3005:   6913. PRINCE.   R. Calderwood,
                        61, Nicholson Street
                        GREENOCK
                        Renfrewshire.

3005: 8488 GERRY.   SULLIVAN
3055   18, IVORY DOWN,
                        DOWNHAM
                        BROMLEY

              killed 29/3/45
              minefield

Heather Bayne

War Dog 'Rob' was adopted by 2 SAS in Africa and accompanied the unit on missions in Italy, so it would be said in a War Office citation. His handler, Cpl. Sam Redhead (in background), proposed him for the Mascot Club in January 1945 and a Dickin Medal soon followed, awarded at a much publicised ceremony in London.

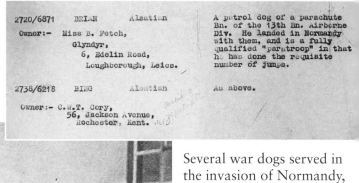

2720/6871	BRIAN	Alsatian	A patrol dog of a parachute Bn. of the 13th Bn. Airborne Div. He landed in Normandy with them, and is a fully qualified "paratroop" in that he has done the requisite number of jumps.
Owner:-	Miss B. Fetch, Glyndyr, 6, Edelin Road, Loughborough, Leics.		
2738/6218	BING	Alsatian	As above.
Owner:-	C.W.T. Cory, 56, Jackson Avenue, Rochester, Kent.		

Soldier magazine

Several war dogs served in the invasion of Normandy, including 'Brian' and 'Bing,' who went into action with 13th Parachute Bn on 6 June 1944. Bing was bought outright by the army – as featured here by Soldier magazine in 1946. Brian came home and was awarded a Dickin Medal. In spite of his War Office citation (above), Bing got no further recognition.

Scottish SPCA. Unfortunately no feasible employment for these fine animals could be envisaged either with British forces or the Allies including Russia.'[36]

36 It was especially sad because in late 1944, twenty-five Husky dogs would be obtained from Labrador, shipped in secret to Liverpool (they could not make a staging landfall in New York for diplomatic reasons) and thence to Port Stanley, capital of the Falkland Islands, in support of 'Operation Tabarin', a semi-militarised expedition to the coast of Graham Land in the Antarctic, supposedly to confound German U-Boats but really to deter Argentine territorial ambitions.

16

Airborne Dogs

Mines were just one concern of the D-Day planners. Just as problematic was how to secure the flanks of the invasion beach-heads in the vulnerable opening phase against armoured counter-attack. Airborne troops (which had been used to a limited extent in Tunisia) were the answer. The Americans would drop on the westward flank, the British in the east, astride the River Orne. Detailed planning began in late 1943. It would turn out that the British would have war dogs with them.

It happened almost by accident. In December 1943 the story of 'Tess' appeared in the London papers, a morale-boosting tale from the Middle East concerning a 'parachuting Alsatian', origin unknown, who was the mascot of 190 Transit Camp MEF, set in a seaside suburb of Alexandria, Egypt, through which troops from the Italian campaign were rotated for leave. Tess was described by the *Evening Standard* as 'the only dog in the British army who has made a live parachute jump.' She had been adopted by an 'unnamed parachute battalion as a pup', it was said. She had been taken up in the dropping aeroplane and watched the men go out — then had her own harness made, 'a canvas coat with four holes for the legs'. And 'when her master jumped he whistled and she followed and slightly injured one of her hind legs on the first jump,' ran the remarkably detailed report. Then, when the unit moved out, poor Tess, like so many others, had been simply 'left behind'.

'For days she wandered, off her food, looking for her battalion, every time she saw a man in a beret she went up expecting to find an old friend,' went the yarn. How Tess ended up in Egypt was not explained.

Tess's story featured prominently in *The Dog World* magazine. Very soon thereafter, a dog-loving officer of the Parachute Regiment would recruit a tiny but significant force, which would turn out to be the last (excluding mine dogs) British tactical war-dog unit of the war. But first, its canine members would have to learn how to jump out of an aircraft.

Lt-Col Peter Luard, commanding 13 Parachute Battalion, was a gentleman farmer and all-round dog enthusiast. He would famously rally his men in the drop zone with a hunting horn. It was a bit of showing off, but it worked. Colonel Luard was happy to discover an early recruit under his command was Lance Corporal Kenneth Bailey, late of the Royal Army Veterinary Corps. Six years after the great canine adventure, Bailey would write a unique account of parachuting dogs for the *RAVC Journal* under the pen name 'Pegasus'. There, he explained something of how it had begun:

'In January 1944, I received instructions from the CO to investigate the possibility of parachuting war dogs into action,' he wrote. 'The dogs were required to be already trained patrol dogs supplied by the War-Dog Training School and I went there to select suitable dogs.'

Although the War Office had ordered tactical dogs to be pulled out of infantry battalions the summer before, and directly restated the decree on 1 March, Herbert Lloyd's new improved 'police patrol' training programme was clearly still producing canine candidates up to snuff for the testing demands of airborne warfare. The Parachute Regiment had had a way of getting round War-Office orthodoxy from the beginning. This really was going to be some sort of war-dog elite — if it could be made to work and higher authorities turned a blind eye. Accidental combatant 'Tess' had shown the way that it might.

'They should be absolutely fearless and if anything of an aggressive nature,' the account by 'Pegasus' continued. That the dogs should be able to exit an aircraft unassisted was a further stipulation. 'The Commandant and Chief Instructor [at Northaw] gave me a free hand to select those I thought most suitable, and after a fortnight's testing and casting, four dogs were eventually selected as possible.'

They were Alsatian-Collie-cross dog 'Brian', Alsatian dogs 'Monty', 'Bing' and Alsatian bitch 'Ranee', this last apparently his own pet from home in Liverpool.

Colonel Luard's brigade commander was sympathetic to the canine wheeze — if for different reasons. Brigadier James Hill (commanding 3 Parachute Brigade) would record many years later:

From January 1943 until D-Day, we had to keep the chaps interested and on top form. One of the things I introduced in order to do that was parachuting dogs. A team of paratroops were trained in handling Alsatian messenger dogs. The dogs were given bicycle parachutes, as they were roughly the same weight as bicycles. The first time we took one of the dogs up he didn't want to jump, so we shoved him out. It turns out he enjoyed himself so much that the next time he couldn't wait to go! The dogs were trained to be messengers, but they were really just a sideshow to keep the men amused.

Amusing diversion or not, two months of experimental training at Netheravon airfield in Wiltshire began with 'battle inoculation', loud bangs and crackling small-arms fire. With his four trainees, Cpl Bailey started jumping in and out of a Dakota transport aircraft on the ground (which also acted as the dogs' kennel), rewarding desired behaviours, Herbert Lloyd-style, with meaty 'tit-bits'. Now it was done with engines revving and the fuselage vibrating mightily on high-speed taxiing runs. Army doctor Capt David Tibbs RAMC of the 225 Parachute Field Ambulance was enlisted (there being no veterinary cover) to attend the dogs' medical needs.

'The dogs salivated considerably but there was no vomiting,' noted 'Pegasus' (Bailey), writing five years after the event, and the author also noted that they got excited when the engines throttled back at the very end of the run — when it was climactic meaty-chunk-reward time. This would be very significant.

A parachute harness was devised by the packing-shed technicians at Netheravon and tried on a wooden dummy dog. Each one had to be tailored to fit an individual animal. The 'chute itself would be opened by a static line as the dog exited the aircraft.

This was the next big test to come. To begin with, handler and dog jumped from a Dakota on the ground, spinning props providing a slipstream. But the Dakota's side door meant the animal's eyes, nose and ears got a big blast of air and he would be slammed against the door-jamb when trying to get out, even at a low airspeed. And a dog must be last in the 'stick' to avoid tangling up the static lines. It would not work.

Salvation appeared in the shape of the Armstrong-Whitworth Albemarle, a twin-engine bomber converted into a transport, which paratroopers exited via a rear hatch in the fuselage floor. It was, said Bailey, the ideal type for dog parachuting. Lots of acclimatisation trials later (one of which was so bumpy all the dogs and men vomited) and the 'para-dogs' were judged to be almost ready for a live jump.

'Around midday on 2 April, the Met people forecast ideal conditions for the next two days,' Ken Bailey recalled: 'The jump was therefore arranged for late the following afternoon. At 1600 hours on 3 April (normal feeding time), the writer along with Ranee took off from Netheravon airfield for the DZ, two miles away. I carried with me the bitch's feed consisting of a two-pound piece of meat, of which she was readily aware.'

The 'chute was clipped to Ranee's harness. The pilot throttled down for the run in and 'the bitch began to get excited. When the red light came on (45 seconds to go), she followed the writer excitedly down to the Action Stations position.'

At the green light, Ranee sat at his feet, eagerly watching as the eight men at the front of the line, including Colonel Luard, jumped out.

'After my 'chute developed, I turned to face the line of flight,' recalled Bailey. 'The dog was 30 yards away and slightly above. The 'chute had opened and was oscillating slightly about ten degrees. [Ranee] looked somewhat bewildered, but showed no sign of fear.

'She hung below the 'chute with her spine curved, four legs extended, [her] feet almost touching the belly.

'I called out and she immediately turned in my direction and wagged her tail vigorously,' he recalled. 'The rest of the way to the ground, the writer "talked her down".

'The dog touched down 80 feet before I landed. She was completely relaxed, making no attempt to anticipate or resist the landing, rolled over once, scrambled to her feet and stood, looking round. I landed 40 feet from her and immediately ran to her, released her and gave her the feed, which she bolted down with great gusto. Then she was left to play, parachute experts from the RAF were waiting on the ground.'

They were evidently convinced.

Ranee had hit the earth just fourteen seconds after exiting the aircraft at four hundred feet. It was too fast; a 'human parachutist would have probably broken his neck,' according to Bailey. And the handler should hit the ground first, to release the dog and stop it being dragged by its parachute. Bigger 'chutes were prescribed, which were ready a week later.

The dogs jumped, landed and ate. Then they did so again — they were really getting the hang of it now. There were no failures, according to Bailey: 'With each training jump, the dogs started enjoying their job more. In fact, the dogs sometimes allowed themselves to be thrown out of the planes or leapt out without coaxing. Each dog made four descents, after which they resumed a normal existence.'

17

'Not to be Returned'

As Ranee and her fellow para-dogs were jumping out of aircraft over Wiltshire, Britain's pioneer force of mine dogs were also getting ready for their big day. First, there would be a provincial try-out. It was a twenty-two-strong rag-tag army, 'most of which have come from dogs' homes or been secretly purchased,' so Brigadier Kelly confessed on the eve of the performance. Only six had 'come from owners'.

They arrived from Northaw in a barking convoy of trucks at Malta Barracks, Aldershot on 24 March 1944 to take their turn at mocked-up minefields in the obstacle assault course at Claycart Bottom.

'Kay' from the Grimsby Police (marked as 'not to be returned'), 'Smiler' from the Dogs' Home, Battersea[37], 'Chappie' from the Hatfield Police and 'Tich', another Battersea outcast, more ex-strays from the ODFL's North

[37] There is no original actual cast list for the day. Names of state-owned dogs come from the roster of No. 2 Mine Dog Platoon RE, raised three months later. Of the pool of fifty 'M-Dogs' put together in the spring, twenty-four came from dogs' homes and twenty-six were 'procured through owners'. Fourteen of these had died or been destroyed. The balance was 'found useless and given homes or otherwise disposed of'.

London Dogs' Home — all of whom were animals, as Brigadier Kelly put it, who had 'no owner but the state'. It was convenient that way for who would mourn them, should they be killed in action? Who would cause a fuss if their pet should not be returned?

A fleet of staff cars bore bemused senior officers of 21 Army Group to see the show. What was all this about dogs? Spectators were requested to keep 'at a distance so as not to distract them' — and of course, 'dogs must not be handled or petted and feeding is strictly forbidden'. Score-cards were issued, to note down mines found or missed, and time taken. The whole thing was supposed to take two hours of a chilly afternoon. Spectators were invited to draw their own conclusions and relay their thoughts to higher commanders.

It was all rather clever. Test one was a mocked-up one hundred yards of roadway, with mines laid twenty-four hours before in undergrowth and mounds of leaves along the verges. Mines concealed included captured (and defused) S-mines, Tellermines, Schu-mines and Bakelite (plastic) mines.

'Smiler' was first on stage, running into the little arena in his harness, sweeping from side to side as he had been taught to on the command, 'Seek!'. Suddenly he lay down. The handler poked away with his prodder. It was a Schu-mine (or rather a mock-up made by a furniture company in east London). Smiler wagged his tail and looked rather pleased with himself.

Then came a minefield laid eight days previously in a 'cart track of dry, friable soil'. All the dogs did well. Next on the race-card was an 'abandoned enemy vehicle park' — 'Petrol and oil foul the ground. Scraps of food have been scattered and men have urinated on the site'. The dogs did not seem to mind.

The fourth act in the drama was a barrier-minefield. 'An officer's patrol will go out to obtain information while the dog's duty is to give notice of the forward line of the mine belt,' said the brief. 'It must be assumed that this is night-time.'

This 'forward area' trial was conducted again with loud explosions and small-arms fire recreating battle conditions. The finale was a comparative trial, with dogs versus sappers using poke and prod and Polish pattern detectors. The electro-magnetic sweep missed all the non-metallic A/P mines; the dogs missed none. It was a bit hit and miss (the dogs were not good on S-Mines) but, on any reckoning, the dogs had won. Clever mine dogs! There were meaty rewards all round.

Brig Kelly was delighted. 'Although the dogs were not 100% successful they proved very satisfactory even under battle noise conditions,' he wrote. Results with the wood and plastic mines were exemplary. The War Office was convinced. The strange programme, for so long the preserve of a few cranks, was now blazingly urgent.

War dogs were in good books all round. Two days after the triumph at Claycart Bottom, a signal was on its way through Army channels to an infantry battalion in Italy, the 6 Royal West Kents. It concerned Bobby – or 'Bob' the brave Collie-cross (War-Dog 209/53), with black and white patches, who somehow, against all orders, Quartermaster Cleggett had managed to hang onto.

L/Cpl Plumridge, who took him to Africa, seemed to have been left far behind. The account by Dorothea St Hill Bourne in a book published soon after the war told how Bob Cleggett, registered by the AFMC as Bobby's 'owner', had corresponded from Italy with the Mascot Club. He had relayed a stirring tale of events at Green Hill in January 1943 involving Bob.

The Collie had been trained as a message dog but he had turned out to be an exemplary patrol dog. The story concerned 'a patrol out into enemy lines on that well-known place called Green Hill in North Africa. Bob went with [us] as a message carrier. It was a very dark and cold night and Bob, who is white, had to be camouflaged':

> The patrol was soon in the enemy lines. Shortly after, Bob stopped and gave the warning of a near enemy. The patrol leader waited for a period to try and find how near he was. As he could not hear anything he decided to go on but Bob would not move.

Bob's warning had saved 'one or two of the patrol from being taken prisoner or perhaps wounded, or indeed being killed'. This was confirmed by an officer of the unit, who added: 'Bob, our Company dog, has been a true and faithful servant, landing with the assault troops in North Africa, and taking part in the Sicilian and Italian campaigns.'

Brave Bob was described as the best pal of his master CQMS Cleggett; indeed so worn out was he with patting and praise that he was taking a nap on a blanket by his master's bed. It was perhaps not the point of all that Herbert Lloyd training, but never mind — Bob the morale booster was doing his bit.

The Green Hill story and the CO's confirmation inspired the Mascot Club to award its first animal bravery medal to a non-pigeon. It had bagged a Northaw-trained war dog. On 24 March 1944, the battalion was signalled in Italy with the good news. A 'special menu' was prepared in the mess as 'congratulations poured in'.

Lots more news of Bob continued to arrive by letter from Italy at the Mascot Club's Golders Green HQ in north London — he was guarding stores, sleeping under a fly-net by night and standing up to the summer heat as well as he had stood up to shellfire. With the onset of Apennine snows, Bob Cleggett had fashioned a winter coat out of a battledress blouse, upon which Bob 'wore with his rank and decorations', whatever they were. The Dickin Medal was despatched but never awarded, it was recorded, 'because the unit was engaged in almost continuous fighting'.

Bob seemed to be much more of a regimental pet than a combat canine, but never mind, there were plenty more hard-working war dogs being made ready for action. On 21 April it was agreed at the War Office — four platoons each of thirty 'Dogs (Mine Detecting)' and ten men should be raised and trained ready to go to war. The WDTS itself would undergo a crash expansion — one hundred Other Rank handlers and fifty kennel men, the rejection rate of 80 per cent and the one-man, one-dog principle necessitated it. Suitable candidate dogs would come from the joint Northaw—Staverton pool of public offerings. It was all suddenly terribly urgent — the first such platoon should be trained ready for action by 1 May. That was a little ambitious.

A war establishment and outline training doctrine was urgently codified with a new 'trade' of RE Dog Handler. The Treasury was consulted about the implications of a special pay rate (three pence extra a day). 'Neither skill nor responsibility in anything like the same degree is required of soldiers whose duties are concerned with watch dogs,' it was noted.

Men who had hitherto had an agreeable enough war would find themselves at its most dangerous end. Like Pte Donald May, for example, who would recall: 'I was actually in the Highland Light Infantry when they wanted volunteers to work with dogs. So because my dad was a gamekeeper, I put my hand up. I liked the idea of training dogs but they didn't tell me they were for mine detection until it was too late.'

'There have been dogs in the Army hitherto and we have got by without a trade grading,' a mean-spirited official would note. He was over-ruled. So secret were mine dogs meanwhile (the whole operation would be graded 'Top Secret' until well after D-Day), 'the proposed test for candidates should however contain no mention of the specific type of work.'

Each platoon would have one corporal, three handlers and nine dogs, made mobile with a 3-ton GS 'kennel-truck'. Three dogs plus one handler formed the reserve. It was noted – 'the platoon is a mine detection and marking unit only. It is not able to undertake the lifting of mines.' And further, 'it is unlikely that special dog food will be available on active service. It is recommended the dogs are included in the human ration strength.' Special facilities for 'holding rejects pending disposal' would be required.

'The dogs will be totally ruined if all and sundry try and make friends with them,' the document stressed. 'They must not be petted or even spoken to except by trained handlers. Any attempt to do so should be treated as a serious military offence.'

A consignment of practice 'Schu-mines' was commissioned (in some secrecy) from Footman Bower & Co., an east London furniture manufacturer, with a brief to get the type of wood and varnish as close to the original as possible.

A renewed appeal for the public to lend their dogs (with no mention of what they would be up to) was to be made on the 'Home Service after the 6 pm news'. Clerical staff would be lent to the RSPCA to cope with the expected new deluge. Home Counties chief constables were requested to put suitable 'stray dogs' on the train for Potters Bar.

Although nobody knew the exact date, everyone knew a cross-channel invasion was coming. In fact D-Day was just six weeks away. Would Britain's mine dogs be first out of the landing craft, bounding up the invasion beaches? Would America's M-Dogs turn up on time? Or would the airborne dogs of war beat them all to it?

18
The D-Day Dogs

D-Day had come, 6 June 1944. In the whole Allied invasion force, 'Brian', 'Bing' and co., the animals of 13 Parachute Battalion, were the only war dogs to go into action on the day itself[38] – plus a dog called 'Glen', an Alsatian, origin unknown, assigned to 'A' Company, 9 Parachute Battalion, on a mission that would be equally full of tragedy and drama. There were plenty of Wehrmacht dogs waiting on the ground to meet them.

The converted Albemarle bombers carrying 13 Parachute Battalion (South Lancs.), HQ Company, took off half an hour before midnight from Brize Norton in Oxfordshire, heading for France. The Scout Platoon was split around four machines, each carrying ten men, three of them carrying one dog, Brian, Bing and Monty, with their handlers. Ranee was left behind.[39]

[38] Two US semi-official war dogs, German Shepherd 'Jaint de Montmorency' of the 506 Parachute Infantry Regiment and a Doberman, name unknown, with the 463 Parachute Field Artillery, made drops into France later in 1944. Both were killed in action.

[39] According to Ken Bailey's brother, Norman, writing in July 1997, Ranee was his brother's own pet, a pedigree Alsatian with the registered Kennel Club name 'Maid of Kethley'. Although an important part of the parachuting dog trials at Netheravon, she was not taken on the Normandy mission but instead 'sent home to Liverpool'.

At 1.10 a.m. the lead aircraft crossed the French coast. The battalion's objective was to clear and hold Ranville, a small village a few miles inland, which guarded the approaches to the Orne River crossing from the east — and secondly to clear a lane in the air-landing obstacles (mines atop wired-together poles) north of the village for the second wave of gliders to bring in reinforcements. The twenty-minutes-to-go warning had already brought everyone to readiness. Dropping from an Albemarle involved much shuffling and squeezing down the narrow fuselage to the rear hatch but the dogs seemed happy enough. The report on the operation of No. 296 Squadron tells the story:

> Considerable light flak was encountered and several [aircraft] suffered minor damage. These aircraft dropped without mishap with the exception of Flight Lieutenant Scott, whose stick also had adventures in the back of the machine. Three men dropped on the first run in and then the doors collapsed. On the second run, the stick were not ready to jump and a third run was made. At the end of this the wireless operator reported from the fuselage that there was still one man and a dog left. A fourth run was made. On the approach to the D.Z. the W/Op. tried to encourage the dog to jump but [it] finally took refuge near the gun turret. The man and dog [it seems to have been War-Dog 'Bing'] jumped on the last run in.

Everyone was out, but the drop was a shambles. No one was that surprised. More than a third of the battalion's strength did not reach the rendezvous point; many had been caught up in trees and those not killed outright by the Germans had to be somehow cut down. The battalion assembled as they might, guided in by the sound of Lt-Col Peter Luard's hunting horn.

Poor Bing was snagged in branches; Monty was wounded. On the RSPCA's account of Bing's adventures, published in 1947, 'he was caught in a tree and was then mortared by the enemy until he was found the next morning. Although wounded in the neck and eye he was completely undaunted and at once took his place with his handler in the line, his presence affording great comfort to the troops, especially at night.'

On an account from sixty years later to accompany the sale of his medal, War-Dog Brian reported to his post on the edge of the Bois de Bavent — and thereafter was said to have 'endured heavy mortar and shellfire, during which he was slightly wounded, but, with the provision of his own slit trench, survived'.

The next morning Lieutenant Jack Sharples, commanding the Scout Platoon, was dug in on the right of the road leading to Caen in a little orchard by the Ranville village crossroads. He recalled:

> Private Lloyd Neale, one of the dog handlers, was in his slit trench with a dog and I said to him, 'That's not your dog' and he replied, 'No, I lost him on the drop, this is one the Germans left behind.' A few days later Neale called out: 'We're going to be shelled, sir.' I asked him how he knew. 'Because the dog's trembling and he was like this last time.' Sure enough, over came the shells, all airburst.

A fourth airborne war dog, 'Glen', was in action that night. The story would be told of how a nineteen-year-old Private Emile Corteil of 'A' Company, 9 (Essex) Parachute Battalion was on a charge for a minor misdemeanour and as 'punishment' was ordered to collect two dogs (origin unknown – but it may be assumed WDTS-trained) and bring them to the training depot at Bulford Camp. The allocation of the dogs had been requested by the Battalion Commander, Lt-Col Martin Lindsay, according to a diligent researcher into the story.

'From that day he [Emile] loved that dog. It was a beautiful animal and he called it Glen,' recalled Pte James Baty of the 9th Battalion, 'and he trained it and they were inseparable. You weren't allowed to say good dog or lovely fella, he wasn't allowed to get too friendly with anybody.' There is a famous Company photograph of smiling young paratroopers with handsome Glen front and centre. The fate of the second dog with the battalion is unrecorded.

It was all very experimental. Glen was fitted with a parachute harness designed for folding bicycles, adjusted so the animal's rear legs should hit the ground first and absorb the shock of landing. Trial jumps were made for a tethered balloon at eight hundred feet, in which Glen, 'when he was given the order by Emile would give a yelp and jump straight through the hole in the basket. His 'chute was opened by a static line. When he landed, he had been trained to run in circles and lie on his parachute to prevent being dragged by the wind. This he did and waited for Emile to come up and release his harness.'

Of Glen, Pte Baty said, 'he loved to jump', equipped with a parachute harness and a little red light on his back as a guiding light for his handler – 'Everybody loved him, he was the pet of the battalion.'

Pte Corteil and Glen had boarded their aircraft, a Dakota, late on the night of 5 June to jump in darkness over Normandy. The objective was a German Army artillery battery at Merville-

Franceville, whose guns menaced Sword Beach, where British 3rd Division were due to come ashore at dawn. On the approach to the jump the ground-fire alarmed Glen, who, 'for the first time was not keen to jump. Emile eventually got him to jump and followed himself'.

The drop was another shambles — many of the assault force drowned in the flooded Dives River, but enough rallied to make a brave attempt on the battery. At 0600 hours, Private Corteil and his dog had reached their RV-point near Varaville and joined a group of strays led by Brigadier James Hill, Commanding Officer of 3 Parachute Brigade.

They began making their way from the drop zone towards the objective. Hill later described how, at the village of Gonneville-en-Auge, the group came under fire: 'I had with me one of our parachute dogs, together with some thirty-five good chaps. We were walking down a lane when I suddenly heard a horrible staccato sound approaching from the seaward side of the hedge. I shouted to everyone to fling themselves down and then we were caught in the middle of a pattern of bombs dropped by a large group of aircraft which appeared to be our own. The lane had no ditches [and was] littered for many yards with bodies of groaning and badly injured men.'

Months later, the dead were found, having been hurriedly shovelled into a bomb crater. Among them were Private Corteil and Glen. 'When found, Emile and Glen were linked together by the dog lead,' it would be reported. Eventually their bodies would be moved to Ranville War Cemetery. At the request of Major Allen Parry, Corteil's company commander, who had led the assault force of just fifty men against the Merville Battery on the early morning of the 6th, Private Corteil and his dog were buried together. Private Corteil's mother wrote the epitaph for his Commonwealth War Grave headstone in Ranville cemetery. Very unusual in its personal detail, not to say poignancy, it still has the power to bring old warriors to tears:

> Had you known our son,
> You would have loved him too.
> Glen, his Paratroop Dog
> Was killed with him.

Glen was once someone's pet. Like his young master, he would not be returning to a loving family.

13 Parachute Battalion had recruited a Wehrmacht dog (it seems to have been renamed 'Bob') in their fight for Ranville. More enemy dogs had switched sides. 'Fritz', a St Bernard, was captured by men of the Hampshire Regiment on 7 June, at Arromanches: 'Somehow or other he got aboard the landing craft while the prisoners were embarking for Southampton.'

And 'Sailor', another St Bernard, was spotted running around Gold Beach at La Rivière on 6 June. According to an account in *The Tail-Wagger Magazine* that summer, Able Seaman Curtis stayed on the beach for five days with the dog in a shelter, before taking him back to England on a warship. The local branch of the RSPCA took him on and now 'Sailor' was being offered to the public when his quarantine was complete by the 'Dogs of Britain Red Cross Appeal, care of the Kennel Club'.

And there was 'a smooth-haired black bitch of uncertain breed,' taken on D-Day from a German Flak ship in Port-en-Bessin, the fortified fishing harbour flanking Omaha Beach, by the crew of the RN destroyer HMS *Ursa*. She was 'very nervy, three of her Nazi masters had been killed by a grenade' in the piratical boarding party action, which meant hand-to-hand fighting below decks, and did not respond to a string of likely German names, so she was given the codename of the port in the Allied planning — 'Sappho'. 'Even when *Ursa* went east, she kept well in spite of the tropical conditions,' it was recorded.

The *Daily Mail* told the story of another 'enemy dog' wounded in action with a German patrol at Roubville, southeast of Caen. Yet another 'Fritz' had been flown back to England with 'a Major from a parachute battalion' — and was set to be interrogated at 'a British war-dogs training school where the tricks he has learned and the kind of training he has received will give us the information we want before going back into action on the British side'. He had apparently been trained 'to attack anyone with a firearm', making a lunge at the RAAF photographer's camera. It would later be reported: 'For a long time he proved morose and intractable but at length his new master gained his confidence. Now he has enlisted in the British service.'

But some dogs were not so lucky. On 2 July the US guards of the PoW camp at Portland, Dorset, handed over to baffled local police a 'black and tan Alsatian bitch'. It had a US Medical Department label: 'Name: Harry Hollmer Line of duty: G.P.W. [German prisoner of war] Location where tagged: D-V-POW A.P.O. 155 [The US Army field post office, Dorchester]'.

Now a 'stray' on police hands, technically it had three days to live. It was a bitch. That night the prisoner had a litter of puppies. On being informed of the development, the Chief Constable in Dorchester told the Ministry of Agriculture in London — in charge of anti-rabies measures. The dog had been landed from

LST 520 (a tank-landing ship) of the US Navy in the possession of a prisoner listed as 'unknown, ex-Normandy beachhead'. It was the third such dog brought back from France; two of its predecessors had been destroyed.

For a further twenty-five days, mother and pups awaited their fate at Portland police station. It was referred to Colonel Curley, the US Army's Chief Vet in the country. With the quarantine option still open for mother, pups, or indeed the whole family, it would be necessary to know who would pay — but the Americans insisted they were now a British problem. On 27 July the ministry's inspector reported: 'The dog appears healthy but is restless. It should either be destroyed or removed to approved quarantine kennels.' It was suggested they be offered to Eastern Command to see if the War Office would take them.

The Command's head vet, Major Bridgeman, was keen and contacted the War Dog Training School. Capt Denys Danby, the Chief Vet, telephoned the police at Portland and told them it was not a British Army dog that had somehow been waylaid. The WDTS commandant, Maj Lindsay Leigh, had furthermore decided that if they took them, it would somehow 'impinge on the French authorities' right to ownership'.

The matter evidently went all the way up to Brig George Kelly — he might want them for his squad of ownerless mine dogs. On 30 July instructions were sent to Northaw 'for the quarantine and subsequent isolation of captured enemy dogs arriving from overseas'.

But it was too late. The death notice on the Weymouth refugees was terse: 'Destroyed by shooting on 1 August and carcass cremated at local gas works. Three pups destroyed by gassing and similarly disposed of'.

19

'Too kind and trusting'

No. 1 Dog Platoon Royal Engineers was judged to be ready for its debut in the field. It was all still wildly experimental. The dogs had performed well enough in trials but joint training with the men who would actually lift the mines had been non-existent. It would have to be done in France, where seasoned sappers were only dimly aware that a new kind of mine detector was on its way: it had four legs and a tail. They would react at first with bemusement, then, some of them, with growing anger that they should be ordered to risk their lives with this motley assortment of dogs' home strays and one-time pets.

At first it would be done in rear areas from where the fighting had moved on. It was never intended to use dogs to make a 'mine gap' in a combat assault but an undetected mine was deadly, wherever it was. And there were millions of them.

In command was twenty-six-year-old 2/Lt John Pritchard. On 10 June 1944 they had clambered into their 3-ton Bedford GS trucks and driven with their dogs from Northaw to the sandy creeks of West Wittering on the Hampshire coast, supposedly to demonstrate to Southern Command their unusual skills. But the parade had moved on. D-Day had come and Allied forces were already ashore in Normandy — including the surviving para-dogs.

Platoon member Sapper Les Coates left a remarkable memoir of the unit's progress:

> We were sent to Southampton in convoy one evening and boarded an invasion barge. It was American, where the food was fantastic, it seemed nothing was rationed. I was lucky, most of the boys were very seasick.
>
> At the time we had very bad storms just after the start of the invasion, they kept us on the barge at sea for 2 days. All the time the dogs were in their kennels, in our 3-ton truck, though they did not seem to suffer too much, they were unable to get much exercise, only a walk round the top deck in ones and twos.
>
> We got to Jig Beach [Arromanches], not far from the Mulberry harbour. The first off the barge was a Jeep, which disappeared into a shell crater [the platoon comes ashore in its vehicles, three 3-ton trucks, one 15-cwt truck plus two motorcycles].
>
> I palled up with Jack Smith, our dogs usually ran together although 'Laddie' (his dog) and my dog 'Wolf' hated each other. It was now very hot, the weather up in the 90s in July. The dogs were fed once a day before a job.
>
> [The platoon starts out for Bayeux]. We slept on one side of the truck and the dogs on the other. The first and second nights were very noisy with gunfire in the distance, then everything opened up.

Poor Laddie hated every minute. 'He just kept howling, Jack sleeping next to me repeatedly had to get up to reassure him. The other dogs were good, but Laddie began to upset them. But when all was quiet, Laddie would start howling again for Jack's attention,' recorded Les Coates.

'While exercising the dogs, a reporter spotted us and the result was the photos were in the Sunday newspapers. My parents had quite a shock — they thought their son was at Northaw.'

The first public hint at the truth was when reporters and official War Office photographers met the mine dogs in action near Bayeux in early July. The seasoned American radio reporter William 'Bill' Downs (he had covered Stalingrad), reporting from the front, told startled CBS listeners on 3 July that 'British engineers have been training dogs to sniff out mines'. London-bound reports were more circumspect.

'Thirty French mongrels have become experts in scenting mines,' it was reported on the 4th with more than a nod to the censor. 'You simply cannot keep them away from the mines and, quite unofficially of course, they have been given the status of a platoon.'

The day before, this scratch force had 'lost all sense of discipline' and 'scampered all over the place, chasing an Army lorry down the road,' it was reported. More truthful accounts soon followed, with pictures of handlers and dogs, 'Pedro' and 'Rover', described as 'pets at British homes until recently, trained at a school for four months where mines lie alongside a juicy steak'. The press loved it. No. 1 Platoon dogs 'Jasper', 'Monty' and 'Peggy' soon featured in a rash of good-news mine-detecting dog stories. The Army Film Unit turned up to record their sniff-find-and-reward routine on celluloid.

'A secret panel of government experts including famous masters of foxhounds is behind the training,' it could be revealed, while *The Times* got into the tabloid style by pointing out that 'Heinz Hounds, 57 varieties of mongrel lent by the public,' had proven their worth in this strange new form of warfare, because 'being lighter than men [they] can move around among mines without setting them off.'

Mindful of the public reaction to sending pets into harm's way like this, the AV&RS Directorate drafted a formal casualty notice. It had the formalised compassion of that for a human soldier and read:

> It is with deep regret that I have to inform you that ... (number, name, breed) ... was killed in action while serving with the British armed forces.
>
> I hope that the knowledge that this brave dog was killed in the service of our country may in some sense mitigate the regret occasioned by the news of his death.
>
> I am directed to express our appreciation of your generosity and patriotism and our whole-hearted sympathy in your sad loss.
>
> .... War Office

When the animal welfare pioneer Maria Dickin heard the news that the authorities were going to issue death notices for conscripted pets she declared it to be 'progress, one up to the animals'. Quite soon these notices would be arriving through bereaved dog owners' letterboxes.

But the mine dogs were not just in France for show. The platoon was heading for a place called Douvres-la-Délivrande, five kilometres north of Caen, the site of a massive fortified radar station which had resisted capture on D-Day and had held out for twelve days thereafter. Its mine defences were still intact. This was the place for the first test of the mine dogs in as near to a live minefield under combat conditions as could be imagined.

Les Coates recalled: 'I was waiting my turn with three dogs, 'Wolf', an Alsatian, 'Nigger', a cross Labrador, and a Labrador called 'Rover'. We were, I believe, the first handlers to work in a live minefield under war conditions with dogs.' His account continued:

> We were in an orchard behind a farm building, which blocked our vision. There was an explosion. The Sergeant came back with his motorcycle crash helmet OK on his head but his goggles smashed and there was a piece of metal sticking out his neck. Jack Smith removed it.
>
> We took the dogs away and learned that our officer, Lieutenant Pritchard, was wounded. We never heard at the time what had happened to him although we asked enough. The handler who became shell-shocked was sent back with the officer. He also never returned to the platoon.

The official report on what happened is brief: 'A lane 30 yards wide and 66 yards deep was to be made, the dogs to be used in detecting the mines and sappers from I Corps to neutralise any mines so detected'. The dog teams and the mine-lifters (commanded by Lt Taylor RE) seem never to have worked together before. The operation was more a demonstration than a live operation, with spectators invited to witness what the platoon could do.

The dogs went in. Nine mines were duly discovered and marked with little cones. The dogs were withdrawn and the sappers sent in to neutralise their finds. A French light anti-tank mine (stock captured in 1940, used in enormous numbers by the Germans) was discovered with a damaged igniter – and the sapper asked for instructions. 'Lieutenants Pritchard and Taylor entered the minefield, inspected the mine and decided it would have to be blown in situ.

'Lt Pritchard walked two paces when there was an explosion and he was next seen lying on the ground with his left foot blown off and a wound in his right thigh,' said the report on the incident. The platoon sergeant was slightly injured. The unfortunate Pritchard had evidently trodden on a Schu-mine – the crater was 18 inches in diameter and 4 inches deep, whereas the anti-tank mine blown later made a 38-inch crater.

Lieutenant Taylor, the RE officer commanding at the site, in spite of having been 'blown backwards twenty feet', recovered enough to order that the lane be swept again with Polish-type detectors. 'A further nine mines were discovered, none of which had been detected by the dogs.'

It was a disaster. This mix of training and live operation was still a very dangerous experiment. On 22 July, No. 1 Platoon tried again at Carpiquet, a much-fought-over Luftwaffe airfield astride the Caen–Bayeux road, finally captured by the Canadians on 5 July. It must be assumed to be mined, and had to be made safe to get it operational.

'There was much gunfire near at hand and a strong smell of dead bodies,' wrote the acting platoon commander. The Germans were still shelling intermittently. Work was laborious and very slow, owing 'to the dogs continually pointing at buried shrapnel'. A day of training followed and the dogs seemed relieved to be back to real, if still practice, mines. Restarting at Carpiquet, the dogs gave up as the summer temperature rose. Many dogs just refused to start work at all. No mines were found by the dogs who did — instead a mass of shrapnel, bullet cases and unexploded ordnance in the smashed metal hangars.

Switched to clearing verges on the tank- and truck-choked Villers Bocages—Caen road, dog after dog refused to even start work. They were pulled out, then tried again in a different location. 'They have been kept short of meat in an attempt to restore their keenness,' it was messaged on 11 August. 'So far this seems to be working,' wrote Royal Engineer Lieutenant T. J. S. Morgan, brought in to replace the wounded Pritchard. Morgan had no previous experience of working with dogs. He was clearly suspicious of the whole venture.

'Bitches in season' were proving a problem due to the attentions of 'vagrant French curs abounding in the area', wrote Morgan. 'The proportion of bitches is too high, but they work as well as dogs. Handlers are far too kind and trusting,' he wrote. 'On the job [the dogs] must be handled very strictly.' But the approach of Morgan was a little too peppery for some. The principal Northaw mine-dog trainer, Lt John Ladbury, would be flown in to bring proceedings back to the proper way of doing things.

One of the 'too kind' handlers was Les Coates, who would write: 'After Normandy our luck held as we went through France and Holland, where we cleared many demolished canal crossings, for the bridging company to bring in a Bailey Bridge. On one occasion we were in front of the Royal Ulster Rifles and could see Jerry [on the other side], watching no doubt the dogs, at that time a novelty to them.'

The Germans must have been astonished.

In Eindhoven, the first major Dutch city to be liberated, Sapper Coates watched the sky fill with gliders and transport aircraft as the airborne forces fighting to seize the bridge at Arnhem were reinforced. It was to be, famously, a bridge too far. When the Germans counter-attacked, the dog unit was trapped in an abandoned barracks. 'Exercising the dogs was restricted,' he wrote. They would stay holed up through the freezing winter to come.

No. 2 Dog Platoon RE, working up at Northaw, was six weeks behind the pioneers of the unfortunate John Pritchard's command. Its equally youthful CO was Lieutenant James Davison, a twenty-three-year-old medical student from Liverpool, who had joined the Royal Artillery and applied to train as a spotter aircraft pilot. Instead he had pitched up at the WDTS in July 1944 for a week-long course in 'war dogs'. Herbert Lloyd would later pay tribute to him as a 'particularly observant officer [and] a great dog lover'.

Davison's despatches from the front would be both insightful and hugely respectful of the dogs and the men. His unit's War Diary is blunter, of necessity. It begins on 24 August with: 'Mobilisation completed, left Potters Bar by road'. A rough passage of the channel in a Landing Ship Tank follows, with half the men and 25 per cent of dogs seasick in the crossing to Juno Beach. One account from a young infantry officer, Lt Basil Tarrant, on the beach described his surprise 'at hearing barking in the distance, out to sea,' as the LST, laden with twenty-nine eager dogs and the twelve men of Davison's platoon, came through the breakers. But the dogs soon recovered from their sea journey — indeed they seemed to be loving it.

As Lt Davison wrote:

> The dogs look forward to riding in lorries and are trained in mounting and dismounting, as well as elementary obedience. Each has his personality and his pet names but officially the dogs are documented by numbers tattooed inside their ears, each handler must know the idiosyncrasies and mannerism of his three dogs, reading these signals as if it were a delicate instrument, not animals. Backward dogs, perhaps becoming sluggish through working too long on mineless fields, may be encouraged by baiting practice mines with meat.

Northaw-trained handler Don May, a member of the platoon, later recalled: 'I had sausages for breakfast. Then we were in action. My dog "Roy" found a French light anti-tank mine. It had been [on the beach] for ages. This really put my trust in Roy. If they were all metal mines, we left them to the REs and their detectors. If the dogs found non-metallic mines, we put a marker on it and left it for the sapper mine-lifters to deal with.'

In fact Roy's adventures were only beginning (see p. 257).

By September they were at a place called Bretteville-sur-Laize, attached to 25 Bomb Disposal Group RE, for operational training in a live minefield. But there was 'too much sweet grass, and sappers with whom we were to work were sceptical due to scratching dogs being liable to set off Schu-mines and S-mines but mainly due to the carelessness of the handlers,' wrote Davison. The dogs found one hand grenade, an unexploded 105mm shell, plus '1 tin of Spam and 1 Jerry helmet'.

'The dogs work 8 yard strips,' he explained later, 'in staggered formation for safety and seeks from side to side in the manner of a Polish mine detector sweep. On finding a mine, the dog lies down and will listen keenly for the tap of the handler's prodder on a solid object, then wag his tail in anticipation of the reward, a friendly pat and a word of encouragement.'

Results at Riva Bella on the 18th were equally disappointing, with 'several dogs off from mole, mouse and rabbit pollution of ground plus water-logging causing problems'. Davison thought the dogs were being 'guided by hand scent [from those who had laid the mines] and fresh distribution of ground ...'

That is what the Americans had thought from the beginning, as Captain Garle had reported from California. Just what it was telling the dogs that there was something buried close by was still unresolved. It would be debated for the months, and years, to come.

The smallest observation in the field must be sent back to Northaw for a tweak in the training. 'Make sure no mines are contaminated with the smell of meat,' messaged Lt Davison. 'Use new mines that only have their natural odour.' Collating the reports at Northaw, someone (almost certainly Herbert Lloyd) wrote: 'The best trained dog is the one who has *never* been allowed to find mines purely by spotting earth disturbance.' In training, 'the earth must be perfectly camouflaged.' Almost everyone was coming to the view that the dogs could sense *something in the mine itself*.

Working in the field, Lt Davison would soon be completely convinced. He could report: 'Capt Garle once explained that a dog might be guided by earth disturbance, but a dog finding a Schu-mine in long grass above the ground refutes this. A Schu-mine does smell of wood, even to human nostrils, especially when the box is new. The explosive, when examined separately, smells of wood. Perhaps the dog smells the mine and the earth disturbance too.'

By early November, No. 2 Platoon was in Brussels — where poor Mine-Dog 'Mick' was found dead in his kennels (from an internal injury somehow sustained in transit), and War-Dog 'Judy' one day wandered off from a road-run exercise session. The Belgian police were informed, the Brussels lost dogs' home contacted, but Judy had vanished into thin air.

Lieutenant Davison made his report for the month of October past to Northaw. Of the mines encountered, the igniters of many were faulty due to long periods of burial and submersion — two or three years in some cases, as part of the anti-invasion defences. That they had failed to explode had been fortuitous: Don May had triggered an S-Mine, which miraculously had chosen not to 'bounce'.

Of the dogs he could report — 'a few apparently in good health have not been satisfactory workers since disembarking.' And 'fighting dogs give more trouble than sickness, they create trouble in the minefields when working and bark at night and in vehicles.'

'Some good dogs are being kept off work with bites. Bitches in season when properly segregated have not been troublesome. Prodders, kennels and bowls he found all satisfactory, but 'a few spare chains, leads and collars are desirable.'

The men were tired and dirty (their one change of clothing was still in England after six weeks) but morale was high. 'A well-disciplined soldier, who is interested in his dogs, makes a better and safer team in the minefields, than a "dog-man" who is not well-disciplined,' Lt Davison reported.

There were further poignant observations of his strange unit in action. 'Bitches in season had worked very successfully on [practice mines especially laid for them].' And a dog whose kennelmate, a bitch, had been removed to the 'season bay', 'had fretted for a while and refused to work. Then escaped and broke his way into the bay, but the attraction was purely platonic'. Camouflaging dogs with Durafur was a waste of time as the marks were disappearing, as the dogs, where they could, delighted in romping in the sea.

And dogs 'responded to the tone of a handler's command, not the actual words,' he noted. Davison's dogs, he insisted, 'regarded sarcasm as the lowest form of wit, while abusive words spoken loudly, even in fun were invariably misconstrued by the dog who would greet them with the bland querying expression which they deserved.'

Much equipment had to be improvised — leads made out of balloon cable, for example, and metal containers to carry the meat rewards, otherwise the flies would swarm all over them. 'My platoon is using captured German respirator [gas-mask] canisters,' it was reported. By such means did the British Liberation Army (as forces in northwest Europe were designated since soon after D-Day) make its way forward to the frontiers of the Reich.

The mine dogs were a brave experiment, everyone knew it. Much more proven were the guard dogs that had crossed to France that late summer with Corps of Military Police VP units to guard the beachhead supply dumps and ever-extended Lines of Communication. It would seem, remarkably, that a number of infantry battalions had dogs with them that had survived the recall order.

A senior 21st Army Group Vet, for example, recorded inspecting dogs of the 6 Beds and Herts Regiment and 7 East

Yorks Regiment in August 1944, plus the animals of 606 CMP (VP) guarding base supply dumps before their shipment to the beachhead. On the 'farshore' he found dogs of 1 Bn Leicester Regiment guarding a petrol dump. One of them was 'sick', another was 'gun-shy and very nervous'. 'The location of War Dogs is proving very difficult owing to the number of moves the unit are making,' Major Hickman RAVC wrote in the War Diary. At Bayeux he inoculated thirty dogs of No. 1 Mine Platoon RE against rabies. Six months of hard campaigning lay ahead of them but unlike the dogs sent to Tunisia two years before, these animals might have an expectation of one day coming home.

Battalions of 52 (Lowland) Division, the former mountain warfare specialists, would also have tactical dogs with them when they arrived in the theatre of operations via Ostend in October 1944 destined for action in the Netherlands. The Scottish dogs would actually go into battle. One of them (in fact from suburban southwest London) would become a very famous dog.

20

Good Dogs

The British Liberation Army was slogging through Holland for urgent reason. In June 1944 the Germans had launched the bombardment of London using 'flying bombs' (otherwise known as V1s or 'doodlebugs'). Pets were once again barred from public air-raid shelters — and there was a new wave of destruction and abandonment of cats and dogs.[40] Doodlebugs fell on grimy terraces and leafy suburbs alike. Several chugged as far as Potters Bar, where one fell in fields close to the War Dog School without exploding. ATS-girl Kay Manning recalled the newly reinforced blackout and anxious trips to London now under bombardment by the horrible things.

---

[40] The Dogs' Home, Battersea, was once more stretched to the limit in destroying abandoned and injured dogs. The renderers, Messrs Harrison & Barber, to whom the carcasses were sold, could not cope with the numbers. The Ministry of Supply was informed that the supply of high-quality glycerine thus obtained (used in explosives) would be cut off unless 'their staff difficulties were overcome'. The amount was judged to be too small to be of concern. Unfortunate strays were evidently either being trained to hunt mines or turned into explosives themselves.

Black out was the rule and no lights allowed after dark in camp. Sometimes when I was on time off, and on trains to London from Potters Bar, it could become noisy and quite terrifying. I remember too once being late having missed a train and then a bus, stumbling across a field in the dark, falling over sleeping cattle and getting covered in mud, eventually getting into my bunk via the back door, rather late and giggling thankfully.

The dogs did not bark in the night. Good dogs!

ATS-girl Gay Agocs (Spackman) remembered 'the many times the sirens would wail whilst we were exercising the dogs, and the nights when we became too lazy to respond to Sgt Allen's frantic calls to rush to the air raid shelter on her side of the barracks. The trouble was that at the beginning there were so many alarms without anything appearing. Little did we realise that they were the beginnings of the "doodlebug" attacks, and one of the first fell a few miles from Northaw. I believe it was then that I realised how much I valued the friendship of my colleagues.'

The flying bombs could be shot down in flight and, after three months, the Allied armies' breakout from Normandy had pushed their launch sites out of range. But in September, the first V2 rockets (long predicted by Intelligence) had hit the capital – against which there was no defence. To prevent panic, for over two months the government would not admit the mysterious explosions were anything but 'exploding gas mains'.

The German Army rockets' mobile launch sites were in Holland, on the island of Walcheren, and latterly in parks and woods of the Dutch capital, The Hague. The brave, doomed

Arnhem venture, intending to 'bounce the Rhine' bridges with an airborne army, was inspired by the urgent need to 'rope off' the launch sites. Mine dogs were doing their bit in Holland. Higher canine abilities would also be employed in extraordinary circumstances in London itself. It happened like this.

There had been lots of times in the 1940–41 Blitz when it seemed that dogs (and sometimes cats) were natural rescuers but they were not official. One little east London mongrel called 'Rip' became famous for finding casualties trapped under the rubble. In this new time of trial it was thought by some that if dogs could smell out a Schu-mine, they could surely find a buried body. Yet no official rescue animals had been used in the flying-bomb summer of 1944. In fact Northaw's only interest in 'sniffer dogs' centred on the very secret programme (see p. 168) conducted by Herbert Lloyd to find ways that Special Operations Executive parachutists and escaping PoWs might throw enemy tracker dogs off the scent (and the obverse for patriotic British guard dogs to better track escapee prisoners and saboteurs). These experiments would go on long after the end of the war.

There had been a bit of a shake-up at Baldwin Towers meanwhile. Having lost his patron, John Moore-Brabazon, in a political scandal, the Colonel's craving for publicity had caused some eyebrows to be raised in Whitehall. There was a BBC Home Service outside broadcast in which a well-known wireless personality had been pursued by Alsatians named as 'Lady Paula', 'Boy' and 'Thorn'.

A chorus of barking punctuated the show. But Thorn's celebrity career was just beginning.

Two weeks after these Radio Fun shenanigans, the MAP Guard Dog School was quietly taken over by the RAF Police. On

24 March 1944, the first intake of RAF Police NCOs had
commenced their training at Woodfold as dog handlers at what was
now to be called the 'RAF Police Dog Training School'. Colonel
Baldwin remained as the Chief Training Officer; Flight Lieutenant
Bathurst-Brown went back to being a solicitor and for the first time
the school was commanded by an RAF 'provost' officer, Flight
Lieutenant R. D. Cooper. The militarised operation, however,
kept its civilian trainers. In fact something quite unmilitary was
about to come out of Gloucestershire — which would more than
match the Army's mine dogs as an epic of canine bravery.

There is a story that Colonel Baldwin was watching a Soviet
film in a Cheltenham cinema, *The Siege of Stalingrad*, which
gave him the idea that dogs could be trained to 'point' to the
whereabouts of snipers. That idea soon developed into finding
buried casualties. A stalwart Staverton trainer, the famous
Alsatian breeder, Mrs Margaret Griffin, was especially
convinced it could be done. Two MAP guard dogs were recalled
to Gloucestershire for experimental retraining, including a dog
called 'Jet', an Alsatian subsidised by government rations since
he was a Liverpool pup. Plucked from guarding a USAAF
airbase in Ulster, he would soon be doing something very
different.

After some crash experimental training, there was a
demonstration in Birmingham on 7 October in 1940-era ruins,
where volunteers hid themselves deep under 'rubble and burning
rags'. Herbert Morrison, the Minister of Home Security, saw it in
person. It was reported: 'The four dogs were released from 20
yards away and given the command Find! In less than two
minutes, each dog had fought its way through the flames and
discovered its man.'

Jet had led the way. After that, it would be said, 'when Jet was satisfied that he had a find, then he would indicate it by starting to dig. He was never known to give a wrong indication, but frequently burnt his feet by the attempted digging.'

Unlike the London Blitz (which had roughly targeted the docks), rockets fell arbitrarily on the giant dartboard of the capital. Posh suburbs were taking a pounding. The first Staverton dog, Jet, and his RAF handler, Cpl Wardle, arrived on 16 October 1944 to be based at Civil Defence Depot 1, Cranmer Court, an art-deco block of flats in Whiteheads Grove, Chelsea. Cpl Wardle's first act was to take Jet to the mortuary at St Stephen's Hospital — 'He sniffed, stepped over the bodies and took no further notice.' This was good; he was supposed to be interested in living survivors! The next night in Norwood, he found two.

On the 19th, 'Thorn' and trainer, Mr M. Russell, and 'Storm' with his trainer, Mrs Griffin of the famous Crumstone kennels, all arrived in London, driven urgently from Gloucester by Colonel Baldwin. Canine history was truly in the making.

The Royal Engineer dogs sniffed on, their noses tested ever harder as winter began to grip the dykes and polders of the Scheldt Estuary in southwest Holland. By mid-November No. 2 Mine Platoon was in the ruined town of Middelburg on the fortified Dutch island of Walcheren, captured only two weeks before after very heavy fighting. Die-hard snipers were supposed to be holding out in ruined villages. The sea wall had been breached by RAF bombing and large tracts were underwater. British, Germans and Dutch civilians alike were trapped, and much of the 'island's vermin had taken refuge on higher ground', according to a report by the platoon commander. It was a horrible place. A horse had triggered a mine and as it careered off, desperately wounded, it left a trail of blood, which confused the dogs. 'PMD' detectors were being baffled by 'quartz in pebbles and steel railway lines'. The mine dogs' chance to show their special skills had come.

'We found nine Tellermines in the ballast along the Middelburg-Flushing railway which the PMDs had missed,' Lt Davison noted triumphantly.

It was a start.

No. 3 Platoon had been declared operational on 26 November. The Burnell family had a very unofficial glimpse of their dog's progress with it to the front line. Elizabeth Burnell recalled:

> Quite by chance, my father was travelling to Eastbourne to visit a patient and had to change trains at Lewes. As he stood waiting, a group of twelve dogs appeared on the opposite platform with their RAF [sic] handlers and amongst the twelve, Daddy recognised Michael and quickly went over to speak to the group. The handlers said: 'You cannot talk to these dogs, they are in transit with the Army.' Daddy said: 'Yes, but that Golden Retriever happens to be mine, where are they going?' To his surprise he was told they were en route for France to search for mines.

The platoon suffered a serious incident on 3 December when a sapper Section Commander was injured and Mine-Dog 'Ricky', the Collie-sheepdog cross from Bromley, Kent, was wounded in the head on operations along the Nederweert canal. Plucky Ricky kept working 'calmly and steadily'. He was 'like the Rock of Gibraltar,' his handler would later write to his owners. 'I think it was his coolness that brought us out of a sticky patch safely.'

Ricky would soon become famous.

The platoon was pulled out for intensive training on disarmed Schu-mines. On 18 December, they were back in the field at a place called Stokershurst. On the afternoon of the second day, there was the dreadful soft crump of an exploding Schu-mine, and a khaki-uniformed figure down. It was the platoon CO, Lieutenant David Saunders, whose foot was blown off. The report was dispassionate, in the way these things had to be: Dog and handler had gone first into the suspected area when 'the dog pulled hard by the canal bank indicating mines.' Lt Saunders followed with his prodder when, a few moments later, there was an explosion which shattered his right foot. The handler was injured in the buttocks; the dog was unhurt. 'This was human error which should not throw discredit on the concept and training of the dog platoon,' wrote Lt-Col Gardiner, 12 Corps Chief Engineer.

During the Walcheren operation, a Northaw war dog came back from the mists of the past. It was 'Khan', the Railton family's Alsatian from Tolworth, who was now 'Rifleman Khan', having passed out of Northaw as a patrol dog in 1942 and been posted with his assigned handler, Lance-Cpl Jimmy Muldoon, to 6 Cameronians, the famous Scottish infantry regiment. When patrol dogs had been stood down and recalled to Northaw in late 1943, Rifleman Khan had soldiered on in his War Office-approved 'mountain warfare' role. The 52 (Lowland) Division had arrived in France, in September, with a small number of tactical dogs. Now they were about to go to war below sea level.[41]

On the night of 2 November he and his handler, L/Cpl Muldoon, were fighting their way onto the Dutch island when shellfire hit their assault craft. Dog and handler were pitched into the icy dark waters. After a desperate search, the fearless Khan grabbed his struggling master by the collar and paddled to the mud-flat shore — 'Man and dog collapsed on the bank'. The story of Khan's bravery was soon in the newspapers.

Patrol dogs were suddenly back in fashion. Davison was asked to investigate. Could mine- or guard dogs revert to the 'tactical' ideal? He concluded: 'A patrol dog is trained to scent with his nose in the air, not like a tracking dog. He must point silently and is a high grade specially selected animal, not easily come by in large numbers …

'And he has a quarry, which to him is an instinctive natural attraction. The mine dog is encouraged to keep his nose to ground and has to seek an object which is not naturally attractive to him …'

An all-purpose war dog was not possible.

Even after six months in the field, Britain's mine dogs were still on probation. Sapper Brian Guy, toiling in the Scheldt Estuary, recalled many years later:

---

[41] When the Animals in War monument in Park Lane, London, was being subscribed in 2002, as well as publicity-seeking corporate sponsors, according to IWM records, a number of elderly war-dog donors sent sums of cash, including Mr S. Hillson of Woodford, Essex, who sent £10 in memory of 'Rex', who had gone to war in the Battle of the Scheldt with the Glasgow Highlanders. He had gone to Northaw aged six months, he wrote. 'It was heartbreaking giving him up.'

Every day, men were coming in injured on Schu mines. Holland seemed to be infested with them. There was a lot of talk about mine dogs, some units thought they were wonderful, my experience was quite different; we found that the poor dog, when hearing the violent explosion of a mortar or shell nearby, would disappear, with its tail between its legs, never to be seen again!

Why should weary, battle-hardened men in the mine-lifting squads trust these animals at all? They looked like something their auntie would take for a walk in the park. Just too many Schu-mines were being missed.

A later report would condemn shortcomings in training and a rush to get the dogs into action. Very few Schu-mines had been used in the training fields of Hertfordshire, it concluded, and 'those that were used were nailed up'. No training had been given with mixed anti-tank and anti-personnel minefields, the kind that were being operationally encountered all the time. 'A certain number of dogs have been trained to the very high standards required for Schu-mines,' said the report, 'the rest of the dogs, probably the majority, are passengers.'

Winter's grip on Holland was retreating; the great experiment could continue. 'Dogs do not like working in sand,' reported Lt Davison, while battle noise and parachute flares dropped by aircraft disturbed some dogs. 'V1 bombs [aimed at Antwerp] and AA fire had combined to unnerve them and on hearing rifle fire, some of them seemed to cringe in anticipation of the big explosion,' he wrote.

Although disturbed momentarily, they continued to work but with limited concentrations. Their sense of frustration at being unable to course a hare which successfully negotiated the Schu minefield was apparent for many minutes.

On 19 February, No. 1 Platoon was working with an airborne engineer unit, near Venlo, in a specially 'dirty area, mines buried for four months'. 'A good dog, working well, found an R[iegel]⁴² mine but missed six Schu-mines all in his track,' said the War Diary. 'This resulted in an injury to an RE working with us.'

The dog was unhurt.

The platoon was up in 6 Airborne's area in Panningen when there was conference with the commanders of Nos. 3 and 4 Platoons (No. 4 had left Northaw and begun its field training in Normandy, the November before). They agreed that the present 'work confirming suspect areas and establishing limits of the field' was the dogs' most valuable contribution. A US Army engineer captain was there to witness a 'satisfactory demonstration'.

It was a bit late — the Americans had already given up on mine dogs. The 228th Engineer Mine Detecting Company (Dog), raised in such high hopes towards the end of 1943, had been sent from its desert try-out to Italy and been set to probing live minefields — on the Fort Belvoir orthodoxy that the dogs would associate turned earth with electric shocks. The results in the field were disastrous — 'Further testing showed dogs

---

42 A German anti-tank bar mine, notoriously difficult to deal with because a corroded fuse made it extremely sensitive to the smallest disturbance. The injured Sapper, Lance Sergeant Mills, lost a leg. The RE account of the incident described the dog as the 'duffer of the party and had been chained to the lorry daily and not employed. For the last shift of this day, however, he was brought on and took part in the proving of the last few hundred yards of a track.'

detecting only about 30% of planted mines.' After a few weeks, they were returned to the Naples Quartermaster Depot in disgrace, then shipped ignominiously back to the US. By the New Year, as it was reported from Washington to Northaw: 'The only activity is a small group of dogs and trainers working on experimental lines.'

A history of the M-Dog episode quotes the unit's Veterinary Officer's observation in January 1945 that dogs '[u]nder fire are absolutely worthless as sentries, messengers or mine detectors, because they become neurotic very quickly, and shellfire can drive them crazy with fear.' Or perhaps it was all those metal traps connected to auto batteries. British dogs, trained by reward, sniffed on.

British mine dogs in wintry Holland, for the most part, were not so frightened of gunfire (although they did not like the sound of nearby tank tracks). They were just having a very hard time finding mines that had been in waterlogged ground, sometimes for two years. And a new kind of mine was also being encountered, the horrible little 'A-200', with a simple contact fuse, an aluminium tube which when crushed by 35 pounds of pressure detonated the explosive charge of powdered picric acid and granulated TNT, 'fatal in most cases, but enough to take off both legs'. Sappers called it the 'Picric Pot'.

Front-line combat units respected the mine-dog teams' special kind of courage. On Walcheren, an RM Commando unit enlisted their help in clearing a fortified church. 'The mine dogs went first,' recalled dog platoon handler Don May. 'The RMs said they would not have our job for anything. In January we moved to Breda. It was so cold. Lots of snow and ice and no mine detecting.'

They met some Dutch children with a sledge on an icy canal bank — 'There were no hills for them to slide down so we tied our dogs to the sledge and the dogs pulled them along. The children loved it.' It seemed the no-petting rule could be broken sometimes. Some of the children were killed when a V1 'flying bomb' aimed at Antwerp crashed into the village the next day.

The worst job, according to Don May, was clearing mines so that the 'Padre and his men could collect the dead for burial'. Bodies were routinely booby-trapped. James Davison would recall the 'shock at finding the body of a [four months dead] British glider pilot near Arnhem, with his parachute [harness] strapped to a Schu-mine with a Teller mine under it.' He seemed to sense the platoon's luck was being pushed to the limit. On 11 January he could report: 'There have been no casualties among dogs or men — yet.'

No. 1 Dog Platoon had lost their CO in the first week in the field, with both legs blown off. No. 3's commander, Lt David Saunders, lost a foot on 19 December. No. 4, operational since December around Geleen in southern Holland, had had no casualties apart from 'Darkie', who sustained a 'nasty rip on the ear'. And No. 2 Platoon's luck still held. After months of slogging through Holland without further casualties, the platoon had reached closer to the Dutch–German border, the landscape strewn with grisly relics of the doomed airborne bid to capture the bridge at Arnhem, the September before. They found British- and American-laid anti-tank mines, plus an abundance of Schu- and Tellermines laid on the surface under now-melted snow. 'The first of the thirty-six grenades, which were tied to a concertina fence in tin cans, was found by the leading dog and was a quite unexpected find,' Lt Davison reported on 3 April 1945. The War Diary is evocative:

20 March '45   Groesbeeks-Wyler: Scene of airborne landing and heavy fighting, many grenades,
mortar bombs, equipment, dozens of dead
Germans and cattle etc. did not distract dogs.
Evidently the scent of decomposition was
repulsive rather than attractive and was very
strong on warm days.

30 March '45   Groesbeeks-Wyler: 0945 hrs Dog killed
'Gerry' 3055/9458 Spr. Pitkin injured. V&R
informed. Dog killed instantaneously by
blast. After finding several mines he missed
the last one, turned round and stood on it.
Handler slightly injured by splinters in face
and eyes. Drill was normal.

According to Don May, Gerry had activated the fuse on a horrid
little Picric Pot, 'which was under water so the dog missed it' .

For whatever reason, the dogs were missing the Pot mines too
often.

The death of Gerry clearly affected Davison deeply for the
mood of his reports grew bleaker — and very frank about the
mines the dogs were missing.[43] In a display of his empathy for the
animals, Lt Davison could report that the dogs were 'browned
off' when there were no mines. 'They seem to feel their work is

---

[43] Many years later, James Davison said in a letter to Sapper Pitkin: 'I blush, but every
year when we watch the armistice ceremony from Whitehall on the TV my thoughts
always turn to Gerry as the last post is played ...'

His short history of No. 2 Platoon is dedicated to 'Gerry'. After the war he qualified
as a doctor and practised as a GP in Balham, southwest London. His 1997 obituary
stated: 'His love of animals was legendary and he would often rescue stray dogs and
cats, find homes for them and generally give advice on animal health and welfare'.

useless when they do not receive praise,' he messaged, 'an indication that war-dogs are also soldiers. Even if no mines are found in a barren field, it is not an indication that the work has NOT been well done.'

There was barely hidden disdain meanwhile for the new CO at Northaw, Major Lindsay Leigh, who insisted, almost comically in the circumstances, that he send only optimistic reports.

'What I have heard from the chief engineers in the BLA is that the mine dog is invaluable and those Coys which are fortunate enough to have a dog platoon would hate to lose them,' wrote the Major. That was how it looked from Hertfordshire. On the mine-strewn frontier of Germany it looked different. Were the dogs really doing anything worthwhile – or should the mission just be quietly abandoned before anyone else got killed? No. 4 Dog Platoon commanded by 2/Lt Peter Norbury, the last mine-dog unit to have been made operational, were meanwhile picking their way through the mine-infested Reichswald Forest on the west bank of the Rhine. On 5 March they were engaged around the town of Goch in the Siegfried Line on 'mine clearance check prior to the visit of Mr Churchill,' according to the War Diary (when the Prime Minister and F-M Montgomery arrived at the front line). The next day, War-Dog 'Bill' was found 'shot dead by person or persons unknown'. They were getting deep into enemy territory.

The Chief Engineer 1 British Corps concluded on 20 March that dogs were useful in 'proving a suspect area soon after occupation' – but they were not to be trusted in the deliberate clearance of every suspect object. 'Small short-haired dogs were not robust enough and too excitable,' he added.

How did he know?

Major Leigh seemed more concerned with what to tell Major H. H. Fleming of Great Barton, Suffolk, owner of 'Judy', the dog who had vanished in Brussels. 'HQ V & R who are responsible for dogs lost will write to the owner – do not act till you hear from them,' he told Davison somewhat sniffily. Major Fleming, presumably, got a 'we regret your dog is missing' letter from Droitwich Spa.

Even James Davison was losing faith in his beloved mongrel army. Though very useful in quickly identifying the dimensions of a large minefield, they were not efficient enough in methodically 'pointing' individual Schu-mines. They could be trained to do one or the other to the optimum, he suggested in a despatch of 8 March. Doing both was too much of a challenge to their 'simplex' minds.

But on the morning of the 24th the dogs of No. 4 Platoon showed just what they were made of, when very remarkably, they were part of a live, mine-breaching assault in the epic Rhine crossing codenamed 'Operation Plunder'. The great amphibious operation had begun at midnight on the 23rd. According to the platoon's War Diary, at 1100 hours the next morning, the dogs were ferried across the river 'in a storm boat' to clear mines in the straggling villages of Rees and Groin on the enemy-held side – where in house to house fighting, infantry of the 51st Highland Division were fighting one of the toughest actions of the whole campaign.

After a few minutes, 'heavy mortar fire' started and the unit's Veterinary Sergeant and a driver were wounded. Dogs and handlers kept working under fire until 'the task was completed, two "S" mines [Bouncing Betties] found'.

One dog proved truly exceptional – 'Texas', a Golden Labrador from Sussex, who 'worked under continuous gunfire, detecting mines with complete disregard to the shelling and mortar fire,' wrote Lt Peter Norbury. 'Through his devotion to duty he contributed greatly to the successful conclusion of the task set, that of clearing the approaches for the bridging of the Rhine on both banks.'[44] But Texas would earn no official recognition for his courage.

After two more hours, the unit 'returned to the near bank, dogs very shaken,' wrote Lt Norbury. There had been no further casualties. After a day of 'complete rest', the dogs 'were back to normal', he recorded.

And ready for more.

[44] Royal Engineers began building the first pontoon bridge over the Rhine, codenamed 'London', at Rees, the next morning.

The Dog with the
Magic Nose

The three dogs from Staverton, 'Jet', 'Storm' and 'Thorn', had arrived in rocket-tormented autumnal London for a month-long trial in 1944. Like the mine dogs in Holland, it was a huge experiment. Whether they were of any use would have to be found out in action. And old hands were deeply sceptical that these one-time pets and their female handlers were up to it, as they pulled the living and the dead, men, women and children, from the rubble. There was 'strong language' at one incident. At another, 'Mrs Griffin was approached by a senior warden' and gruffly told how none of them believed in the dogs.

The Staverton trainer Mr Russell complained of 'very poor cooperation' at an incident at Hazelhurst Road, Tooting, on 19 November, where the bodies of two adult males, a child and 'particles of flesh' were found (bodies blown to bits were a common occurrence, something the dogs found difficult to deal with). But by the time the dogs were back in their little utility van, veteran rescuers were 'apologetic and extremely grateful for the dog's assistance'. Mr Russell predicted, 'It is only a matter of time before there is complete harmony at every incident.'

Four more dogs had arrived by early November, posted to depots in Hendon and Lewisham, expected to learn on the job. It would take a month. Mr Russell and Mrs Griffin were enrolled as part-timers in the CD organisation and given uniforms. Margaret Griffin set up an extemporised kennel in Station Road, Loughton, to cover northeast London with six dogs, including two rather special ones, 'Crumstone Irma' and 'Crumstone Psyche'.

They would become very famous dogs.

The reports of the dogs in action, sent into the London Civil Defence Region headquarters in the bomb-proof basement of the Geological Museum in Exhibition Road, Kensington, make for harrowing reading. Bodies in a workers' canteen at Erith hit by a rocket were so fragmented, it was impossible to number the casualties. In Epping, the dog discovered 'blood marks in a garden hut and later, small portions of a human body. This accounts for the missing child.' An incident in East Ham obliterated a backyard stable full of lowly animals — costers' ponies and chickens. But the dogs managed to keep calm and carry on.

By 14 December, Irma and Psyche were ready for work. In Southgate, northeast London, working together, they found a large mound of rubble in a ruined row of houses, whereupon Irma became excited. 'A call for silence was sufficient for a rescue officer to hear a cry from a woman saying she and her sister were in a Morrison shelter,' said the incident report. They were dug out, although the sister was dead.

Rescue dog 'Peter' found three more bodies in the rubble.

The story of Miss Hilda Harvey, a schoolmistress, appeared in a newspaper the next day about a 'V-Bomb incident in southern

England'. In very dramatic terms she told how she had been buried in rubble but could hear the 'jumbled cries of rescuers in the darkness'. Then she heard a dog sniff. 'A woman's voice said, "Leave him alone, he'll find somebody alive down there."' She heard 'the sniff again and then the bark, then the rescuers broke through the debris and lifted her out.'

From West Ham came an account of a blazing street of houses. 'While Jet would not go into the smoke, Thorn went slowly step by step through the thickest of it. He repeatedly flinched but was encouraged forward until he reached a spot approximately over the seat of the fire and gave positive indication there. In my opinion the work of Thorn at this spot was the best I have ever seen from a rescue dog.'

But just as with the mine dogs, there were those who thought technology would work better than a dog's nose. Experimental 'sound location apparatus' was rushed into the fray by the Home Office. On its first outing, on 4 January, the team were unlucky enough to find Mrs Griffin, 'Irma', 'Psyche', 'Dawkin' and 'Bruce' already on the site. Her account of what happened would be hilarious if it was not so serious.

Irma and Bruce had given live indications but just then the 'sound location van backed on to the site and a party of men overran it, placing large metal cones here and there with intervening wires,' she wrote. One radio-rescuer was bitten in the leg by Bruce and the dog's legs became wrapped up in the wires. 'Could they not wait?' asked Mrs Griffin, only to be told that these sound men would now come 'to every incident automatically'. Soon they were picking up the sound of someone under the rubble 'swearing like a trooper', but soon, 'the voice lapsed into unconsciousness'. Mrs Griffin reported that dogs and sound location might each have a role, but not both together.

Nobody needed further convincing. More dogs were sent to live training in the ruins and the Misses Marjorie and Dorothy Homan went into action with 'Rex', 'Silva' and 'Quella' on 21 March at a very serious incident at the Packard car factory, Brentford, just southwest of London.

Mrs Griffin, now with eight dogs at the Loughton kennels, required 60lb of meat a week to feed them and proposed getting it from the local butcher. She was informed instead that she must get condemned meat from the Caledonian cattle market in Islington since the Waste of Food Order still applied. Rescue dogs or not, they were civilians.

Photographs show Margaret Griffin at rescue sites with her dogs, wearing a swaddling blue-serge, Civil Defence greatcoat, leather gauntlets and a floppy beret with an Alsatian's head badge. She is utterly magnificent.

Her own accounts are full of admiration for her animals. Irma 'had a special bark when she located someone she sensed to be alive' (her 'living indication'). In one incident she refused to leave a scene for two days until two young girls were found alive in the rubble. Psyche could also find pets, as well as people, including 'a nice red setter', badly injured but alive in a ruined house.

Mrs Griffin wrote, 'I feared his heart would give out and he could not stand up by himself. We gave him some hot tea and wrapped him in a blanket, left him quiet and telephoned for the PDSA van ...'

Psyche and Irma would regularly work together. At one incident, the dogs dug around two and a half feet down and found 'a lovely cat'. Irma kept giving her 'live' signal. Digging further down, rescuers 'found an old lady, her daughter and her sailor fiancé, all dead.'

But it was not all Alsatians. 'Peter' was a four-year-old Collie-cross who had been offered by his Birmingham owner, Mrs Audrey Stable, in 1943 for training as a guard dog. In spring 1945 he was in the charge of the 'Rescue Man' Archie Knight, based at the Chelsea depot. He was known as 'Rescue Dog No. 2664/9288 Peter'. The Imperial War Museum archives have the record sheet of Peter's big day, 27 March, when early in the morning one of the last rockets fired from Holland fell on Hughes Mansions, a block of working-class flats in Vallance Road, Stepney, inflicting severe casualties – 134 dead, 49 seriously injured. It reads:

> Report of the working dogs, Peter and Rascal [who was there for training]. This was a very big incident and the indications given were many and various. During this long period of duty Peter worked hard and well, and never once refused to do all I asked of him. At the end of this day Peter was very tired.

Dog and handler were recalled to the scene the next morning. 'Peter worked very hard for two hours but was obviously affected by his exertions,' wrote Rescue Man Knight on 29 March. A second dog, 'Tailor', was not very interested – 'This was probably due to the unavoidable lack of proper food for the previous two days. Peter was completely played out and took 24 hours to recover his spirits. He is only a small dog and I consider his efforts very praiseworthy.'

22

'Jump!'

Britain's war dogs had one last brave stunt to pull. The 13th Parachute Battalion, after its hard fight in Normandy, had been withdrawn in September 1944 for rest and refit in England – as part of 6th Airborne Division, and a major component of the Allied strategic reserve. The surviving War-Dogs 'Bing', 'Brian' and 'Monty', had come with them and 'gone into quarantine for six months,' according to an RSPCA report. At the end of 1944 the battalion was back in the line as infantry in Belgium, under the same hard-charging commander, Lt-Col Peter Luard, who had inspired the whole airborne-canine venture which had taken a handful of dogs into action on the eve of D-Day in the first place. The battalion had been urgently shipped across the Channel on Christmas Eve and rushed to the front in open lorries to bolster the defence against the German offensive launched in mid-December through the Ardennes that had pushed a menacing 'bulge' into the Allied front. This time the paratroopers were entirely dogless.

The Ardennes thrust faltered and died. There would be no more German offensives – although the Wehrmacht would take a lot of beating yet. By the end of January, after much hard fighting, the battalion was across the Dutch frontier on the River Maas. It was so cold, ice floes bobbed in the river.

The commander of the Scout and Sniper Platoon was Lt Peter Downward, aged twenty-one. He recalled the sight of a V2 rocket rising from its mobile launch platform, hidden by woods in the distance, heading for London. 'Our artillery was quick to put down two or three salvos in the area of the launch site but there was nothing we could do to stop it,' he would write, many years later. He also remembered an 'enemy' dog which would set out 'from a barn about 600 yards away from us and then make its way round the fields to another building, obviously trained to do some duty.' He thought the dog, an Alsatian, was 'clearly a war dog, but none of our soldiers would ever dream of firing at it. I trust he or she survived the war,' he would write. The young officer's evident deep empathy with dogs (sustained all his long life) would prove significant.

Once again the parachute battalion was pulled out of the front line and returned to training in England for a new airborne operation. It would be almost the finale of the war in Europe, 'Operation Varsity', the air-delivered component of the Rhine crossing. The Normandy veterans Bing (who, according to ATS kennel maid Vee Swan, now 'wore wings on his collar') and Monty were back with the battalion after their stay in quarantine, and had been put back into intensive retraining 'mainly after dark' as patrol dogs by their handlers, Kenneth Bailey and Wally Walton. They would make the jump from one of the American C-47 transport aircraft carrying the 6th Airborne Division. As they got aboard at an airfield in Essex on the night of 23/24 March, 'the only individuals who did not show any tension were [the dogs] already in their harnesses less their chutes,' wrote Peter Downward. He recalled the handlers, Sgts Bailey and Walton, being somewhere inside the aircraft, 'at the rear of the stick, [he was at the front] to avoid any disruption to our soldiers should one of our canine friends suddenly decide to throw a wobbly as happened on one of the Normandy sticks.' The drop would be made in full daylight (too many drop zones had been missed in the dark in Normandy), *after* the amphibious assault had been launched.

The aircraft reached the drop zone on the far side of the Rhine at around 1000 hours, just as Lt Norbury's Royal Engineer mine dogs were getting into their storm boats for their astonishing cross-river assault on the village of Groin, a few miles downstream to the west.

Amid the bone-crunching 'mayhem' of the parachute landing, there was Peter Luard blowing his hunting horn, shouting at Downward: 'For God's sake, there's your objective, take it!' It was a modest farm near the small town of Hamminkeln, earmarked from aerial photographs as a suitable battalion HQ.

'The dogs got out alright on the command JUMP!' Downward recalled, after almost seventy years, and they landed safely with the rest of the battalion, which then endured twenty-four hours of high-intensity fighting as glider-borne reinforcements arrived (taking fearsome casualties from ground-fire in the air) and the Germans tried to overwhelm their position — before the first armour (amphibious Sherman tanks) reached them on the hot side of the Rhine. Then followed a rapid advance, most of it on foot, urged on by the hard-charging Luard to reach the sprawling Luftwaffe airfield at Wunstorf. The German defenders, many of them teenage boys, could still be very dangerous. 'We moved so fast to join up with Russians on the Baltic, there was not much chance to employ the dogs,' recalled Peter Downward. 'Only once do I remember my dogs, Bing and Flash, being up alongside me while I was reconnoitring a route through the enemy line in the dark.'

'They sniffed the air for the presence of the enemy, in which case Bing would come to a standstill and point without barking, just as he had been trained to. I know it was wrong, but everywhere along the way, the men just petted him.'

'And I did too,' he confessed, almost 70 years later. 'I tried not to, but would say "Good Dog", give him a pat, that sort of thing and reward him with a piece of Mars bar, if we had it. He did not exactly spit it out.'

A photograph of the Scout Platoon taken at Wismar on the Baltic in early May at the end of their long, hard-fought trail shows Lt Downward, the men of his Scout Platoon and the dog handlers, plus four Alsatians, named as 'Bing', 'Monty', 'Bob' and 'Adolf', the last two apparently side-switching Wehrmacht dogs. There was a vodka-infused celebratory encounter with the Red Army, 'which included women soldiers who spoke a bit of English,' recalled Peter Downward. What they made of Bing and Monty is not recorded.

The war was tangibly close to being won. No more rockets came London's way. The last V2, launched from The Hague, fell near Orpington on 27 March, killing one. German surrender was surely imminent. But buried Schu-mines did not come out of the ground with their hands up. Mine clearing must go on for months, years, and a defeated country must be policed, prisoners of war corralled and the bases of its occupiers guarded.

It was not a difficult decision to take by the War Office to move the dog school physically from Hertfordshire to the continent and put it formally under the command of 21st Army Group. On Denys Danby's urging and with the agreement of the higher formation's Chief Vet, Lt-Col R. W. Stalker, it would at last become a unit of the Royal Army Veterinary Corps — after five years of administrative obscurity under the War Office Directorate of Military Training. War dogs had become respectable; Bash Street Dogs' School had become Canine Staff College.

On Easter Sunday, 1945, dogs and humans boarded a large number of trucks at Northaw and set off in a barking convoy for an unknown destination. It would turn out to be a suburb of the Belgian capital, Brussels, liberated six months before. ATS Private Vera Cooke recalled the great upheaval:

> I remember leaving the kennels at Northaw in an army truck. We didn't know it at the time but we were bound for Tilbury Docks. We had sausages for breakfast that morning and after being thrown about in the trucks for an hour or two began to feel considerably the worse for wear [they board their troop-ship, the *Ulster Monarch*].
>
> When we arrived at Ostend harbour the next morning we could see a wreck burning just outside the harbour. We eventually disembarked and marched along the cobbled streets to our hotel. I shared a double bed with Noreen, another ATS-girl, that night.
>
> Next morning we were marched to the railway station and boarded a train for Brussels on wooden seats. Arriving at the Gare du Nord, we were met by Sgt Allen and Captain Danby, and then marshalled into trucks and driven to Zellick [Hippodrome in the northwest suburbs]. We were billeted in a château outside the camp and slept in bunk beds. I

remember one night sleeping out on the veranda as it was too hot in the bedroom. We also had to go down into the cellar and pump water to wash ourselves.

ATS-girl Kay Manning recalled the 'day when we were due to go to Belgium. We went over by boat, dogs as well, stopping one night on the coast and then by truck to Zellick, where an advance party had opened up a former race course, and therefore had some loose boxes to house the dogs. The rest were tied by chains to tubs and moveable box kennels in a half circle. There was also an office and a surgery.' With the girls in the château, 'the men were billeted in what had been the village school.'

It all sounds a bit of a hoot!

Over the next few weeks, along with the Northaw dogs, numerous ex-Wehrmacht Schäferhunde swelled the ranks, along with sundry Belgian Bouviers de Flandres and Malinois in German Army service that had been liberated along the way. Evidently 'enemy' dogs proved eager to please their new masters and mistresses. ATS Private Chris Montgomery from Preston told her local paper (hero Rob's medal had inspired a wave of war-dog interest) that she had 'made a pet of one of the small mine-dogs – while many of the dogs are German and have to be taught to obey English commands'.

Gillian Eager had been an eighteen-year-old 'runner' to the British film star Leslie Howard, working on the set of the romantic comedy-drama war film, *The Gentle Sex*, at Denham Studios, west of London, when she decided to join the ATS in 1943. After requesting work with dogs and horses, Gill was sent to the WDTS at Northaw – and following a jolly time as a kennel maid, went with it on the great move to Brussels. She recalled:

I was always out long after lights out and creeping back to the château on moonlit nights, the silence broken only by the hooting of owls was a beautiful and eerie experience. In order to reach our rooms we had to ascend a very long staircase. The orderly Sergeant's room was at the top and she was always listening out for latecomers to return.

It sometimes took us nearly half an hour to creep up to the top, sitting on each stair and nudging up slowly, one stair at a time in complete darkness. When you put out a hand to feel for the next stair and you touched something soft, or saw the occasional glow of a cigarette, you realised you were just one of many other girls making their way up.

We were never caught — but all this just to avoid being put on a day's charge.

The end of the war in Europe was close — everyone could sense it — but no one dared hope that it would be tomorrow or the next day. There had been false dawns before. At the War-Dog Training School in Zellick, it was business as usual.

On 23 April Soviet troops penetrated the outskirts of Berlin and the British 2nd Army reached the River Elbe, near Hamburg. At home, the government lifted the blackout restrictions that had vexed urban pet owners for six long years. On the 28th, in Holland, an unofficial truce began, allowing Allied convoys through German lines to deliver food to the starving civilian population.

On the afternoon of the 29th in the Berlin bunker, Hitler sought to test the cyanide capsules he had been provided with by the SS. He reportedly ordered his physician to give one to Blondi, the German Shepherd bitch he had acquired as a puppy, three years before. She munched it eagerly, whimpered, rolled over and died. After midnight, Hitler married his mistress (and Scottie owner), Eva Braun.

The next day the newly-weds committed suicide. Hitler's personal dog handler rounded up Blondi's puppies and shot them in the garden of the Reichs Chancellery. He also killed the Scotties, the dogs of the Führer's Secretary, Frau Gerda Christian, and his own Dachshund. The charred remains of Mr and Mrs Hitler, and two dogs (thought to be Blondi and her puppy, 'Wulf') were discovered three days later in a shell crater in the devastated garden.

On Friday, 8 May Germany surrendered unconditionally. The London rescue dogs got an extra meat ration, as did the mine dogs still clearing railway lines in Holland. At the War Dog School in Zellick, Brussels, everyone, dogs included, had the most enormous party. By the Baltic Sea, the airborne warriors Bing, Monty, Bob and Adolf shared a Mars bar.

Good dogs!

Once they had all been family pets, now they could be again. From the mountains of Tunisia to the flanks of the D-Day beaches, from the frozen polders of Holland to the Rhine crossing, Rex's Army had done their bit.

Part Four

COMING HOME

'And this he knew; for, honours done
And ceremonials complete,
He sighed like one who'd travelled far
Down endless centuries of war
And slept across my feet.'

Arms and the Dog, Robert Chaloner, 1952

23
'On VE Day we all went mad ...'

Victory in Europe had come. The end of the war in the Far East was in sight. For non-state-owned dogs, the lend-your-dog-to-the-army-for-the-duration contract seemed to be over. All those militarised pets must be returned to their owners, surely? But the wording on the little brown cards said '[your dog] will continue to be so loaned for the duration of the war or for such less period as may be required'. No one yet had formally said the war was over for pets — although the RSPCA as the intermediary agency was anxious for a statement. Even after the surrender of Japan in August 1945 there was no ruling. Owners were pestering the charity. Could the authorities in Droitwich Spa please make up their minds whether the hostilities had ended or not?

It was clear, however, even to the most penny-pinching Whitehall official that the wartime contract was indeed over and some kind of payment would soon have to be offered for those trained animals that the Army wished to retain — especially for guard duties in former 'enemy' territory. And there were plenty of mines still to clear. Some people would readily accept the money; others did not care either way or there were circumstances where there was no home for the pet to return to. And there were conversely those who could not wait to have their pets back by their side and had begun to write cross letters to the War Office and generally make a fuss.

Twenty-one-year-old Miss Betty Fetch, for example, reacted with huge indignation when the DAV&RS offered to buy War-Dog 2720/6871 'Brian'. 'Your feelings are appreciated and the action of this department in circulating owners with a view to purchase their War Dogs is due to the fact that a large number of dogs will be required to carry out anti-sabotage and guard duties for some considerable time,' wrote a shamefaced official on behalf of Brigadier Kelly. Meanwhile, 'Brian's health is good and he is doing exceptionally good work.'

And there was Mr J. Lacey of Edgware, north London, who had offered his Alsatian, 'Bruce', to the Army in October 1942 and henceforth heard nothing more of him, so *The Tail-Wagger Magazine* reported. At war's end, Mr Lacey gently sought news — to be told that Bruce was a VP guard dog with No. 702 Coy, Corps of Military Police. Mr Lacey inquired further, to be told in a letter from the unit's commander that brave Bruce had been stationed in the liberated port of Antwerp and had endured the bombardment of the city by V-weapons through the winter of 1944–5, an ordeal 'he had come through with flying colours'. Bruce had then been posted to Norway (where British forces had the task of disarming and corralling the surrendered Wehrmacht). Mr Lacey pursued his quest through the British Liberation Army's post office system to be told Bruce was 'in fine fettle' — indeed proving so useful guarding ration stores and vehicle parks that the Army wished to buy him outright. But Mr Lacey only had thoughts of Bruce's return from the fjords to suburban Edgware — and so it was to be. Bruce was demobbed, wearing his commemorative war-dog collar, to 'enjoy a reunion the happiness of which,' said the editor of *The Tail-Wagger*, 'could only leave to the magazine's readers to imagine'.

Just as in Norway, there was still much military canine work to be done. And old dogs could be taught new tricks. For example, the London rescue dog 'Thorn', 'and several other dogs went to Europe from 8 May to 14 August 1945 to guard German PoWs and not one prisoner was known to have escaped or even attempted to,' so it would be proudly reported.

In fact it went on much longer than that. Lt-Col Baldwin would tell his local paper in January 1946 that hundreds of former MAP dogs from Staverton were patrolling prison camps, both in Britain and Germany, and no fewer than ninety were on duty at Nuremberg, guarding top Nazis on trial for war crimes. 'De-mob for dogs would have to be delayed,' he said — indeed dogs were still needed from the public although the RAF was now breeding its own.

The defeated forces of the Reich needed lots of guarding, wherever they were. So too did millions more 'Displaced Persons' — and stockpiles of fuel, food and vehicles had to be protected from the hungry and desperate. War dogs would not all be going home quite yet. But for those in charge of them it was time for some rest and relaxation. Gill Eager remembered party time in Brussels:

On VE Day we all went mad and after not having had any sleep for days, Pauline Binns and I wandered into a deserted hotel, found a room and collapsed on the bed. I am sure we slept the clock round before finally waking, having a bath and making our way back to camp to find half of the others still missing. No one seemed to mind and only asked whether we were hungry.

She remembered 'walking through the woods at dusk with the dogs as the days were so hot. After crossing the railway line at Zellick I used to walk on, listening to the silence and the loud clear song of the nightingale, and intrigued by the little religious figures of wood nailed at intervals to the trees.'

But there were also sad memories for the kennel maid, like 'the beautiful horses slaughtered to feed the dogs,' and 'the DPs [Displaced Persons] sitting around the edge of a rubbish tip where, while working with the "mine hunting" dogs, I used to throw away the empty biscuit tins. As soon as I turned away, they would scramble down to search for scraps.'

The mine-dog platoons indeed would keep up their dangerous work for months to come. Handlers and mine-lifters, toiling among the Schu-mines and Picric Pots of Holland, were joined by squads of German prisoners of war. Eighty-seven miles of 10-yards-wide railway line between Flushing-Amersfoort-Enschede were cleared in summer 1945, although 'the ballast caused foot soreness' among the dogs and 'plenty of road work was required to harden the pads'. Smaller dogs were the most sensitive, reported the ever-concerned Lt Davison (operationally now under Canadian 1st Army command). 'The chief difficulty is maintaining the interest of dogs and men,' he wrote.

It was perhaps better that way. There were no casualties in No. 2 Platoon until it was demobilised in October – although

War-Dog 2760/6939 'Roy' had vanished one day while mine-clearing electricity pylons near S'Hertogenbosch. Weeks later, with the platoon having moved far down the power-line in its task, a formal court of inquiry was set up into his loss. Just as it was due to report, the war dog suddenly appeared, 'Seven weeks after loss and 40 miles from where lost, having picked up the scent of the dogs working there daily,' noted Davison. He was in 'bad health' but made a full recovery. Clever Roy had shown the higher powers of canines in which certain people were taking a deepening interest.

There were arrivals at No. 2 Platoon of a different sort – a number of puppies. Lt-Col C. J. Bermingham, Canadian Royal Engineers, thanked James Davison on 29 May, 'for the presentation of my pup, which is now lying at my feet and has the makings of a good friend.' And Lt-Col T. D. Oborne, 1 Corps Chief Engineer, thanked him on 5 August, having collected, 'a sweet little beast, who is very popular everywhere – my chief concern is that she should not become a cook-house dog.'

Another encounter recorded by Sapper Pitkin that summer was when they met a 'Major Domman, who had been in charge of German war dogs, at his home near Bielefeld, who was very interested in our mine-hunting dogs.'

You can be sure that he was!

Meanwhile, life in Brussels for the War Dog School staff was turning into a bit of a canine St Trinian's. ATS-girl Irene Cornish was working with a Royal Artillery anti-V2 radio location unit in Antwerp. She recalled:

Following VE Day, when we were disbanded, a group of us were transferred to the WDTS at Zellick. We were billeted in a lovely château and I was put to work in the stables at Berkus. We began to take in captured German dogs and horses. One dog I remember was a Great Dane called 'Wally', which was used for demonstration purposes.

There was plenty of entertainment in Brussels and I enjoyed myself at the Montgomery Club and visited the Mannekin Pis [the famous urinating statue].

I bred several puppies at Sennelager and two German boys used to love coming in to see them. I had to hold a horse while it was killed and then skin and carve it up to boil for food for the hounds. I had a few flirtations.

Gill Eager would tell how she loved her days with the WDTS, 'and, when off duty in Brussels, made my way to the Canadian Club to start the evening off with a large tomato juice and ice cream with maple syrup and nuts. Then I went to the dance hall in the Boulevard Adolphe Max, where it seemed the whole of the United Nations forces queued to get in, or I would visit the cafes and get on their stages and sing French and English songs, and people bought me so many drinks it was impossible to accept them all.'

Vera Cooke (Goldsmith) remembered 'most of all going to Brussels with David [Cooke, her fiancé] on VJ day (15 August) in an empty coal lorry, and having to walk back as the trains had stopped running. Some didn't get back at all that night and we had to lump up their beds with pillows or anything we could find.' Through the late summer the Zellick dogs entertained the locals at gymkhanas and obedience displays in Antwerp and Breda.

The school was set to move into the British-occupied zone of Germany. It was time, perhaps, to get a little more serious.

In November 1945, dogs and staff travelled by rail to training grounds now at Sennelager, once a Wehrmacht tank range, now the sprawling headquarters of the British Army of the Rhine. 'The move caused a certain amount of amusement and great interest at the stations at which the train halted,' said the RAVC historian. 'In addition to 150 soldiers and 200 dogs, the party included fifty ATS and fourteen (ex-Wehrmacht) horses.' ATS-girl Irene Cornish remembered it well. She recalled:

> On our arrival at the school, we took over a pack of foxhounds and Captain ['Tommy'] Russell [the new commandant] became huntsman of the pack [all mongrel, ex-mine dogs, according to another memoir]. I became whipper-in for the Major.

Kay Manning found 'transferring to Sennelager in Germany from Zellick was like going from warmth to extreme cold. I was never so cold in my life as I was in this camp. We had long wooden huts with a pot-bellied stove. The girls were not supposed to go out without a male escort at all times.'

Perhaps it was the benign regime, maybe a mutual love of dogs, but romance blossomed among the doggy staff at the WDTS, both in England and on its wartime odyssey. As Kay Manning put it: 'It was inevitable that an interest was taken between the sexes and several long-term romances, and war- and peace-time marriages followed in due course, including mine.' (She married Jack Grainger.) 'It was a lovely hot summer and we used to go to the village dances and drink strong beer. Jack bought my engagement ring in Brussels. Afterwards I remember going to eat cake and ice-cream at our favourite cafe, a taste I can still recall to this day.'

Eve Lowery, the former insurance clerk, remembered meeting her husband-to-be, Jack Forest. 'Jack had joined War Dogs after a short posting with the Royal West Kents. I, myself, was in the original batch of ATS-girls in April 1942,' she recalled. 'Jack and I were very happy there, working together outdoors. I was then transferred to the dog hospital, working with my friend, Kay Manning. After demob, Jack and I married and settled to live in Kingston, in Surrey.'

ATS Private Vee Sergeant married trainer Bob Swann in Ilford in 1946. Vera Goldmsith married David Cooke in November 1945 in Suffolk. The wedding of Lt John Pritchard (who had lost his legs to a Schu-mine) to 2/Lt Evans was celebrated at Potters Bar Church in spring 1945. The marriages of Pte M. R. House, RAVC, and Pte C. K. Moore, ATS, were celebrated in summer 1946 at the Garrison Church, Lippespringe, Germany, with flanking war dogs forming a splendid guard of honour.

It was reported: 'on each occasion the wedding dress was made by an ATS corporal in the unit and both couples spent very enjoyable honeymoons at the Möhne See Rest Camp'.

24
Demob Dogs

The end of war in Europe and the Far East meant many happy reunions for demobbed servicemen returning home to the family pets they had left behind. But Whitehall officials, working hard to get human beings home, were distinctly alarmed at the prospect of a global zoo of overseas mascots and adopted pets also heading for British shores. Shrewdly and humanely, a 'Special Services Scheme' for the quarantine of pets began to be discussed between the War Office, Admiralty and Air Ministry in autumn 1944, by which 'a limited number of dogs' might be imported under special licence from the Army veterinary authorities. There was to be no repeat of 1918 when unchecked movements of soldiers' pets led to serious outbreaks of rabies. This was first of all about pets — although war dogs would be following behind since they were progressively demobbed from their overseas duties. For those on home VP guard duty, it would be simpler. But for war dogs wherever they were, some would be going home to loving families, others would not.

And it was about dogs. Cats ('and other felines') were not part of the scheme, but could be imported under special licence and quarantine paid for privately. 'Sheep, goats, other ruminative animals and swine' were banned outright.

Northaw, now just a transit and admin centre, was to become 'No. 1 Dog Holding Section' to corral a small number of canine oddments before going back to being greyhound kennels. A dedicated quarantine centre with individual pens for five hundred dogs was to be created at a former RAF airfield at Chilbolton Down, near Andover, Hants, to be ready by mid-August 1945. Fees for servicemen would be subsidised depending on rank — £20 for senior officers, £5 for other ranks. The RSPCA offered to provide box kennels at the Channel ports and Southampton.

'Commanding officers must verify that the dog in question is a genuine pet and not acquired recently,' said the rules of the scheme. 'Dog Holding Units' were established at Antwerp and Milan to process service pets on the way homewards. An overland route from southern Europe by rail and WD cross-channel transport was sanctioned, while seaborne dogs ('not more than four per ship') will 'be confined to the upper deck in specially constructed kennels and will on no account be taken into saloons or cabins. Dogs will be in charge of the ship's butcher, who will be responsible for the care and feeding of the animals during the voyage,' said the rules of the scheme.

Dogs in the Mediterranean made it home by train. An RAVC Lieutenant noted his three-day journey clanking through the Alps from Milan to Calais with a ragbag of eleven British ex-pat pets and mascots, all trying to get home. The mission was: 'Accomplished with very few difficulties,' he reported. 'Dogs proved very adverse to relieve themselves in the kennels and only did so when they could contain themselves no longer. All dogs travelled well. Ladies' dogs least well behaved, ex-Navy dogs settled down best.'

Not everyone was happy. When canine commentator Huldine V. Beamish expressed 'her horror' in *Country Life* magazine at the prospect of a mass of 'canine oddments' arriving from overseas to add to the already overlarge mongrel population, readers of *The Dogs Bulletin* roared back. A little dog with a unit in Italy had been with them all the way since being adopted in the desert. 'The service departments should be congratulated on their undertaking of fighting men's feeling about the pets who have kept them cheerful through their long ordeal,' said the letter writer. A Royal Engineer captain commented: 'I myself have brought home a dog of high intelligence. She smells mines, has courage and is very faithful. She is a Siberian type of wild dog and now has a litter of puppies. Soldiers' dogs need your help, keep it up!'

The manpower and accommodation were in place. So too was plenty of goodwill. In terms of wartime military operations, how difficult was moving a small army of canines going to be? It would prove enormously so. According to the history of the RAVC: 'Nothing gave more trouble than the repatriation of dogs, both the pets of returning soldiers and the hundreds of dogs loaned by the public for war service.' The difficulty, it seems, was with the dogs. The first releases of home-based war dogs had already begun in January 1945, when it was reported:

> About 200 have been returned to their owners. Release does not depend on either age or length of service, but on the fact that the dog has become surplus to military requirements. When this happens he is sent with his handler to the Dog Holding Section of the R.A.V.C. [Northaw]. An experienced

veterinary surgeon gives him a thorough overhaul and if he proves fit, a letter is sent to his owner and he is sent by passenger train to the nearest station. In the letter the owner is told what sort of work his dog has been doing.

If it was mine detection, it may be put to good use pointing game. If he has been doing guard duty, the dog may have become very fierce. In any case he is likely to be very different from the animal that went away to join up and will not immediately accustom himself to civilian life.

First at Zellick, then at Sennelager, attention turned to this very issue. It was noted: 'Now that hostilities have ceased, the War Office has no authority to hold these dogs. They have no further training but are handled and exercised to make them more amenable as pets on return to their owners.'[45] For dogs abroad that joyful event must be preceded by a somewhat bleak stay at Chilbolton Down, where 'two officers and seventy other ranks, all volunteers and dog-lovers to a man,' so it was reported, were no doubt ready to continue rehabilitation. How difficult was that going to be? For some dogs it would prove impossible.

It was already recognised that guard dogs might be a problem. A meeting at Droitwich Spa in July decided there should be three categories:

---

[45] A process called 'extinction' by modern dog trainers, unlearning a previously desired behaviour, such as barking at strangers. The US Quartermaster Corps' 'demilitarizing' technique was to get the dog gradually used to several people through play, within which the animal 'would be encouraged to consider everyone his friend'. If the dog tried to 'make friends' with a man jumping out with a stick and shouting at him, he was ready to be returned to civil life. Only a few dogs could not be detrained and had to be destroyed, so it was reported. Fifteen thousand homes were offered by the public via Dogs for Defense for K9 veterans, many more than there were dogs. Preference was given to war-veteran handlers.

(A) Those too savage to be transferred to owners (original or otherwise) in any circumstances. (B) Those sufficiently uncertain in temperament to warrant warning owners. (C) Those sufficiently friendly to be returned to civilian life.[46]

The Treasury Solicitor should be consulted on the wording of letters sent to the owners of the first two categories and draft a form of indemnity for the government against owners who insisted on the return of category B dogs in spite of the warning given.

Judgement would be made after some basic tests by a vet at Northaw. If a dog was 'too savage', it was despatched with a humane-killer bolt action pistol. For 'friendly' dogs it was simple enough: after their years of wartime adventures, they would be going home.

Like War-Dog 'Jim', for example, one of the very first to be demobbed, he was an Airedale-Alsatian cross, bought from a Fulham pet shop as a pup in 1937. His owner, Pte J. Barringer of Upper Norwood, was informed by Northaw in late 1944 that his dog, on overseas and latterly on home VP guard duties, was one of 'a small number [of surplus dogs] about to be released from service'. If he was agreeable, Jim would be despatched to him in

---

[46] The film, *The Courage of Lassie*, released in Britain in July 1946, featured Collie 'Bill' accidentally being recruited as a US Army war dog – where he is known as 'Duke'. At war's end Bill/Duke escapes and tracks back to his young owner, Kathie (Elizabeth Taylor), but is suffering 'a canine form of shell-shock' which makes him aggressive. About to be put down on the neighbours' insistence, an Army tattoo is discovered in Bill's ear and a quick investigation reveals him to be a war hero. All then realise that the dog who served heroically on the battlefield will need time to adjust to civilian life. Bill is freed and joyfully reunited with Kathie.

The film stirred up much popular sentiment about the fate of real-life demobbed dogs.

seven days' time. School vet Denys Danby advised in a pro-forma letter that he should be 'kept under careful control until he/she had adapted to civilian surroundings'.

It was also time to say goodbye to the loan scheme. 'In future all dogs required for the army will be purchased,' the July meeting agreed. The Quartermaster General set a price of £25 (£750+ today). Some owners asked for just one pound for their dog, one asked for an astonishing £200, according to the AV&RS War Diary. The Treasury meanwhile agreed to pay £50 (a considerable sum) for unreturnable-to-civilian-life dogs which still had military utility. Their final fate however would be bleak. After some brisk correspondence with their owners, a significant number of loaned animals at Zellick and on duty across Europe were purchased outright for continuing guard duties, their ranks swelled by ex-Wehrmacht animals. It was policy to rename them — with terse, suitably martial names.[47]

In fact the public was still offering dogs. On 26 June Miss L. C. Anderson of Oldmeldrum, Aberdeenshire, was told her Golden Labrador 'Cockabendie' was unwelcome because the 'Training School is full'. The door was barred to the Bull Terrier offered by Major Holmstrom of Ashford, Kent, never mind his owner's plea that he was 'too big for my wife and children to manage'. This really was the end of pets at war.

[47] Which would mean the end of the endearingly domestic pet names that public dogs arrived with — all those 'Timmy's and 'Pixie's and 'Sheila's. Of the ex-Wehrmacht dogs, 'if the name was too difficult to pronounce it is given a new one from a list kept in the training office.' A post-war document on naming WD-owned dogs advised: 'The name should be short, no more than two syllables, and reflect the dog's character. "Fury", for example, for a particularly aggressive animal.' New intakes (bought from the public) would 'produce a multitude of Rexes which, if retained in military kennels, would cause confusion. A simple solution is to change the first letters so that Rex becomes Tex, Shane becomes Wayne, and so on.'

Most 'soldiers' dogs' were accidental adoptees but in a number of cases, handlers of official war dogs could not bear to be parted from their wartime companion, with whom a special bond had been actively encouraged, after years of friendship in adversity. This would lead to much anguish – especially when guard dogs, otherwise responsive and docile with their handler, were deemed too 'savage' to be returned to a family.

Former handler Mr H. Wilson, for example, told the Allied Forces Mascot Club in December 1945:

> I am now demobbed and have had to leave Rex behind. I did my best to get possession of him from his owner but he would not part with him. The parting was very hard as I had grown to love him as my own.
>
> I still think of him and wonder how he is. To have him with me would have made me very happy. And I'm sure he would have been too. Three years together takes some forgetting after working, sleeping and playing together.

It was altogether heartbreaking.

The great dog demobbing epic was meanwhile rumbling into barking life, with first a stream of mascots, adopted strays and regimental pets – to be followed by veteran war dogs – heading by air, land and sea for No. 1 Military Quarantine Station, as it was now called, in Hampshire. Its first commander was thirty-year-old Major D. W. Jolly, RAVC.

The first fourteen dogs in Germany were demobbed from 21 Army Group on 1 August – to be quarantined at Messrs Spratt's Hackbridge kennels once home. There was worrying news from the Middle East that same day — notification of 'a case of rabies in a war dog'.

No. 1 MQS opened for business a little later than planned, in mid-September 1945, with an exotic collection of adoptees among the early arrivals. A visitor to Chilbolton found the 'first sixty pets' installed, including an Alsatian bitch called 'Zara'. Abandoned by the Germans in Normandy, she had been taken to Brussels by an RASC unit. Miss M. Heighway of Prestbury, Cheshire, an ATS driver, had adopted her, arranged to bring her to England, and dutifully presented Zara for quarantine.

That was quite a rescue dog!

'Lager' was a Dachshund snatched from the ruins of a German town by Brigadier John Vickary, of Seaford, Sussex, a 'keen breeder' who was 'anxious to inject some continental stock into the inbred English variety'. And there was 'Arras', an Alsatian, the adopted pet of a demobbed British soldier, who had found him starving in a Westphalian village and somehow got him home. 'Barty' was an Alsatian 'found in a village in Yugoslavia terrified and hungry by Major H DuPont and came to England in March 1946.' He was enrolled in the Mascot Club. As was 'Blackie', who was 'found at San Severo, Italy in 1943 by an RAF officer, shot through the shoulder but recovered and came to England with her master...'

Among the first demobbed actual war dogs to arrive at Chilbolton was 'Ace', lent to the Army when his owner, Miss Joan Evans of Ely, Cambs, went into the Land Army in 1943. Her one-time pet had 'come back from the continent with the reputation of having seen off enemy saboteurs from a petrol dump.' Ace was 'nervous of strangers', but certainly not in the 'savage' category. His fate looked bright. And there was

War-Dog 'Judy', a 'beautiful Alsatian' owned by an RAF officer, 'who was sensitive and reserved on her arrival, but was now on the best of terms with her kennelmen'. Major Jolly, meanwhile, was supplanted by Major M. Bridgeman, RAVC (the Army Vet who had been keen to save Harry Hollmer, the German bitch captured on D-Day) as Commandant No. 1.

But the real test would come when the war dogs left quarantine and went back to their families. 'Brutus', a demobilised Alsatian from Syston, Leicestershire, met his master at the railway station after three years of war service, but 'failed to recognise him,' according to *The Dogs Bulletin*. But when he reached home, Brutus 'recognised the voice of his mistress at once and was in transports of joy. With the two children, aged five and two, he at once became a firm friend and playmate.'

'Dodo', an Alsatian, had ended up at the GDTS with Major Baldwin after his owner, Mr Gooding from Poole in Dorset, had heard 'a radio appeal'. For three years Dodo had dutifully guarded airfields and factories with his handler, Leading Aircraftsman R. Broad, until after VE Day, when he had been sent to Germany to guard a PoW cage.

Mr Gooding had been warned that Dodo was 'very fierce and could only be managed by his handler,' it was recorded. He was clearly a 'Category B' dog. But Mr Gooding would not be put off and insisted that Dodo be returned when released from quarantine. Dorothea St Hill Bourne recorded the first encounter in December 1945, when a 'worried' Mr Gooding went to meet the London train on which Dodo was travelling. 'Dodo had not forgotten, at the first sight of his old master he went wild with joy. Back at his old home he settled down as if the past three years had never been.'

Michael, the Burnell family's Golden Retriever, had been out of their lives for three years as a mine dog. Other than his handler, anyone else had of course been under strict orders not to make him a pet. A letter arrived from the War Office at their north London home, asking if they would like him back. Of course they would! One day he appeared at their front door with his handler.

As Elizabeth Burnell told the story: 'Michael, on hearing my mother's voice, broke free from his lead, shot through the gate and flew into the house and up the stairs to where my mother was standing. He jumped up, put his paws on her shoulders and licked her face as she started to cry with joy. He then came and sniffed all round us.'

And Airedale cross 'Jim' could at last be reunited with his now demobbed master, Pte Barringer.

On his eventual homecoming in spring 1946 – 'Jim went crazy and knocked me flying. Snarled at me at first and then – boy – what a reception he gave me,' so he recalled. Pte Barringer was delighted when a package arrived in late May from Droitwich Spa containing a 'Commemorative Dog Collar' (see p. 274), marking the completion of Jim's military service, along with a short lexicon of standard Northaw commands, 'Heel', 'Sit', 'Come', etc. – to which Jim turned out to be 'still quite obedient'. Inspired by receipt of the collar, an attempt to enrol Jim in the Camberwell branch of the Royal British Legion was unsuccessful on the grounds that he was a dog.

Ricky, the hero dog of No. 3 Mine Platoon, had 'settled in so well it is difficult to think he was ever away from us. He is still the lovable, silly old dog he ever was,' wrote his owner, Mrs M. V. Litchfield of Bromley, after his triumphant homecoming in August 1946, also wearing his AV&RS-issue commemorative collar.

And the Reynolds family of North Ormesby was reunited with 'Rog', who had been guarding a US airbase in Berkshire (he did not need quarantine). 'When he got off the train, he appeared not to recognise us,' according to Mrs Veronica Hey, who was aged twelve at the time, 'but I could do a yodel in those days and he recognised that straight away.'

And there was 'Wolf', an Alsatian belonging to Mr and Mrs J. Newlove of Willerby, near Hull, who came home with his discharge papers in January 1946, 'after three and a half years' honourable service with H M Forces,' as it was reported. 'He arrived by train, wearing his official dog collar, bearing his name and number.'

Would Wolf have forgotten those he had left behind? Indeed he had not. 'His meeting with his old master and mistress was a rapturous one and then followed a tour of inspection of the old home. There was the drinking bowl, still in the same place. There, too, were the old sleeping quarters just as he had left them. Wolf may not have won any medals, but his name will go down in the illustrious roll of those who have served their King and Country in times of mortal peril.'

War Dog Aces

It was indeed a time for remembrance and recognition of pets who had served their country. The Allied Forces Mascot Club had already led the way with the Dickin Medal award to 'Bob', the 6 QRWK patrol dog whose award had been despatched to Italy in March 1944. Indeed he was the first non-pigeon winner. On 12 January 1945, MAP rescue dogs 'Jet' and 'Irma' were awarded the Dickin Medal by a famous admiral in a ceremony in a chilly north London park. Then it was back to war duties. Brave dogs! Their place in the public's heart was assured — and there would be many more accolades yet.

Not to be outdone, the much statelier RSPCA decided, as the original go-between of the whole loan dog scheme, it too really should start giving awards to animals, whatever some council members' doubts.

In April 1945 the charity asked Brigadier George Kelly, the Army's Chief Vet, to supply details of the war careers of pets loaned by the public for the duration especially deserving of commendation. The Society proposed that qualifying dog heroes should be returned to their owners with 'a collar and medallion' emblazoned 'For Valour', bearing the royal coat of arms befitting the charity's charter.

The Brigadier's deputy, Lt-Col J. C. Bennison, replied enthusiastically – although no 'recommendations had been received in this office to date' (presumably thus far, The Mascot Club had been proceeding on outside commendations for its canine awards to Army dogs). What should the criteria be, the Colonel asked: gallantry in action, hazardous duties, efficiency on guard duty? Was the proposed award for Army dogs only – or did it include dogs 'trained for the RAF or dogs trained by MAP for the RAF and for the US Army [Air Force]'?

'We will commence a list of dogs that have died or been killed on active service,' he said, while he could inform the Society that the directorate itself was considering the issue of 'a certificate or medallion to owners of dogs that passed their course of training,' should there be financial approval.

Thus it was in summer 1945, 'all units holding war dogs ' were circularised and information sought, even though many of those personnel with direct experience had already been demobbed or were about to be. In his signal (sent out globally, including to India, South East Asia, the Middle East and 21st Army Group) Colonel Bennison informed veterinary sub-commands that 'this Society now desires to award a special collar medallion to any War Dogs (provided by loan or *otherwise*) cited for special acts of bravery or devotion to duty in hazardous circumstances.'

All those strays and state-owned dogs might get a gong.

The information was required by 1 August. The AV&RS Directorate would, a little later, decide to itself award a commemorative collar in red, white and blue, along with a certificate of service for all *privately* owned veteran war dog returnees — to which the Society could attach its medallion for especially brave dogs.[48]

And so the commendations began to come in. 'Ricky', the Collie-sheepdog cross from Bromley, who had been wounded in the head while mine hunting in Holland was commended by his former platoon commander, and 'Scamp', a Dalmatian of Rock Ferry, Cheshire, who found twenty-five Schu-mines in the same operation. 'Raf', a mine-hunting Alsatian owned by Mrs A. L. Minchin of Erdington, Birmingham, had been 'blown up during the Ardennes push'. Though physically uninjured, he had 'suffered severe shock and was hypersensitive to sound'. He was now recovered and working with a Corps of Military Police (CMP) Company. And there was 'Paddy', the Glaswegian dog who had made the triumphant demonstration tour of America with Captain Garle.

Lots more commendations were on their way.

'Rob', the Collie who had gone to Algeria with 1st Army, had already received a glowing report. It had come, however, via a different route to Brigadier Kelly's Army-wide appeal for information about especially brave dogs. After a gap of over sixty years, it would turn into a gigantic shaggy dog puzzle. Was Rob the War Dog Who Never Was? Or was he indeed, that lowly thing, a *mascot*?

The story of Rob, the Shropshire farm dog who was loaned to the Army and returned from the war three years later with the combat record of a superhero, was to be told many

---

[48] The US Quartermaster Corps would issue a similar discharge certificate for US war dogs, but after the 'Chips' fiasco, no standard medals would ever be placed on a canine again.

times over, both in the years before his death in 1952 and thereafter.

In his day he was hailed as the 'Ace of War Dogs', proud bearer of both the RSPCA For Valour medallion and the Dickin Medal. He would be the star of personal appearances and numerous press profiles, his reputation proudly embellished by his owner, Mrs Edna Bayne, and later, by her daughter, Heather.

When he had departed the Bayne family home, at Tetchill, Ellesmere, Shropshire, heading for Potters Bar station in summer 1942, he was a lovable pet, his greatest achievement to date helping baby Basil Bayne to walk. His sister, Heather, was not yet born. As she would one day recount, Bob had been bought on the eve of war as a puppy for five shillings to be raised as a farm dog. Two years later, his owners responded to the radio appeal and offered their dog to the Army 'through the ready help of the Ellesmere police'. He passed muster at Northaw, then he had gone to war. From the 78 Division Quartermaster's audit, Rob was posted to an infantry battalion, which had sailed for North Africa in November as reinforcements for Operation Torch. He survived the general catastrophe in Tunisia, which claimed the lives of so many of Northaw's Class of '42.

A Collie, 'Robb' (War-Dog 471/322), is listed in the documentation as being handed over, along with Alsatian 'Rex' (War-Dog 408/503) to No. 3 Veterinary Corps Evacuation Centre, Souk-el-Khemis, by 1 Royal Irish Fusiliers 'early in August', some months after the Axis surrender. The general recall order for tactical war dogs would very soon follow.

He was already a hero just to have survived thus far but neither the war nor canine myth-making was done with Robb. The oft-repeated story was that he was one of two dogs plucked from a holding centre at 'Constantine in Algeria' (the other dog was rejected 'because of a skin disease') to guard from the universal pilfering 'natives' the base camp at Philippeville of 2 SAS. The jeep-borne and parachute-dropped raiding force had been raised in North Africa in spring 1943 by Lt-Colonel William Stirling after his brother, David, the original founder of the SAS, had been captured. The Battalion Quartermaster was veteran soldier Captain Tom Burt, who transferred from the Royal East Kents.

Rob's Northaw tactical training was clear in his silence and discretion. Would he be useful on patrol? In the accepted story, he was somehow set to 'parachute training' in Algeria, using an 'American supplied harness', by Captain Roy Farran, the dashing second in command of 'D' Squadron, who was himself undergoing airborne training in the desert (his 1948 autobiography describes the episode but makes no mention of a dog). Rob's first drop from 800 feet was 'perfect' and 'made without panic', it would be reported. In the developing legend of War-Dog 'Rob', he now went to Italy with 2 SAS, accompanying them into action in an astonishing series of daring, behind-enemy-lines missions.

Which the piratical unit certainly made – the question that would one day be asked is, was Rob there as well? 2 SAS were withdrawn from the Mediterranean in March 1944 for refit and training. Some went to Prestwick in Scotland, the HQ ended up at Wivenhoe Park, a country house near Colchester. Rob, as has been recorded in various accounts, travelled homewards separately by merchant ship to be put into six months' quarantine in Edinburgh. After D-Day, 2 SAS went into action again in France and northern Italy; Rob was not with them.

In early 1945 Rob had showed up in London 'on special leave from his unit' at an exhibition for the 'Returned British Prisoners of War Fund' held at (appropriately enough) the Rover motor car showroom, 78 Piccadilly, flanked by a dramatic 'escort of paratroopers'. One of them was Corporal Victor ('Sam') Redhead of 2 SAS, who, it was said in accompanying reports, had given Rob his 'special airborne training'.

The Allied Forces Mascot Club was there to present him with a Dickin Medal, awarded on 3 February 1945 at the hands of a gallant Victoria Cross bearer, Capt Philip Sidney VC, Conservative MP for Chelsea. What extraordinary wartime adventure had led the farm dog from Shropshire here? Who had alerted the Club to his astonishing bravery?

There was a big fuss in the newspapers as Rob's story came tumbling out ('the soldiers did well, being plied with pints of beer,' it would be written later of the big day). It was truly astonishing. 'At the word of command he would jump from the aircraft without hesitation,' so *PDSA News* reported the words of Corporal Redhead at the ceremony: 'When he reaches earth, he crouches down and keeps still until his parachute is removed and he receives further orders.'

It really was remarkable.

Plucky Rob, 'considered War Dog No. 1 by the War Office,' as he was described, was said to 'have dropped with a patrol of paratroopers behind enemy lines, where they remained for many months.' He had faced 'incredible dangers and through them all Rob never failed to keep guard and play his part manfully.' The amazing Rob had even 'landed from a battleship in the Adriatic Sea.' On one highly dangerous mission, his party was missing for six weeks, all hope of their return given up — 'When they reappeared, their allotted task safely completed, Rob was given the entire credit for their safe return.' The very existence of the SAS had not been admitted to until August 1944, triggering a flood of excitable Sunday newspaper stories. Now they featured a dog.

Rob was trained 'never to bark', it would be breathlessly reported. 'The men could sleep secure in the knowledge that Rob would keep ceaseless vigil, silently pacing around the men. If he saw, heard or scented the enemy, he would move silently back to wake them by licking their cheeks at the sign of any danger' – as the enduring and much-repeated legend would have it. His wondrous Herbert Lloyd training had equally equipped him as a liaison dog (as seen in his June 1943 screen debut in Algeria):

> [Rob] would work between two handlers, often a mile or more apart, carrying messages of such importance that the lives of the men rested on his ability to travel at speed, resist distractions, accept food only from his handlers, and allow no-one but his handlers to remove messages from the special message-bearing case.

Where had this glowing and miraculously detailed record come from? A letter from Droitwich Spa dated 24 January from the AV&RS Deputy Director, Lt-Col J. C. Bennison, informed Mr Edward Bayne (his daughter, Heather, keeps it with pride) of the proposed award of a 'Dickin Medal for Gallantry' – with no explanation of what that was – to War Dog No. 471/322 'Rob', 'which you were good enough to loan for War Service on 19 May 1942'.

Rob 'has given invaluable service [and shown] conspicuous devotion to duty', wrote the Colonel. Should Mr Bayne be agreeable, would he kindly say so, indeed, 'a pre-paid envelope is attached for your convenience'.

A delighted Mr Bayne duly replied, and naturally asked just what the family pet had done to earn such an honour. A terse reply marked 'Secret' came three days later, signed by the AV&RS Deputy Assistant Director, Major H. A. Clay. It said:

> War Dog' Rob' No. 471/322 is attached to the Special Air Service.
>
> He has made over 20 parachute drops including three operational during the past 18 months.

His Mascot Club citation took it a lot further:

> Served with 2nd SAS regt.
>
> Took part in landings in the North Africa Campaign with an Infantry Unit.
>
> From September 1943 he served with a Special Air Unit [sic] in Italy. Most of these operations were of an unpleasant nature.
>
> He was used as patrol and guard on small parties who were lying up in enemy territory. There is no doubt that his presence with these parties saved many of them from being discovered and thereby captured or killed. Rob has made over twenty parachute descents.

Nine months later, in Brigadier Murray's late-summer trawl for dog heroes on behalf of the RSPCA, Rob had been added at the very end — how could he not be? Already he was a medal winner and canine celebrity, after all — even if some of the operations of his 'special air unit' were still girded in secrecy. Indeed he had gone back into their mysterious clutches after his appointment with fame in Mayfair. The press had loved him from the start; his amazing adventures had gained enormous coverage and inspired a hunger for more hero-dog stories.

In response, meanwhile, to Colonel Kelly's original appeal, Eastern Command could report that although its own and London District's return of canine heroes was 'nil', 'War-Dog 471/322 (Bayne)' was 'already in possession of the Dickens Medal [sic]'. 'This dog is at present attached to No.2 SAS Regt, Wivenhoe Park, Colchester,' said the signal of 2 July.

On 2 October, the RSPCA would be sent near-identical wording of Rob's DM citation by the War Office for their proposed For Valour award. The award was duly approved and the medallion sent in November to the Dog Holding Section, Northaw, where plucky Rob was awaiting final release to his family.

Fifty years later, a somewhat different story emerged. It went like this. Being informed in autumn 1944 that Rob was in quarantine, his owners, Edward and Edna Bayne of Tetchill, Ellesmere, Salop, told the War Office that on completion, they wanted him back home. The news duly reached 2 SAS, who were refitting at Wivenhoe Park, Colchester, Essex. Their training officer was James Quentin 'Jimmy' Hughes, who had won the Military Cross and Bar for a daring sabotage raid on Sant'Egidio aerodrome, Italy, in which he had been severely injured and captured by the Germans — and his subsequent daring escape with other Allied PoWs, after which he returned to his unit.

Major Hughes revealed his version of Rob's career in his 1998 autobiographical account, somewhat self-deprecatingly titled by such a brave man, *Who Cares Who Wins?* Rob had certainly been 'somehow' picked up in Tunisia, and perhaps even made the crossing to southern Italy, but far from doing twenty parachute drops, so Hughes stated in his engaging memoir, he had been a barrack-room companion for Capt Tom Burt, the 'burly, rotund' 2 SAS HQ Squadron Quartermaster (always a good berth for a dog).[49]

Instead of saving countless troopers by alerting them to danger on patrols in the Italian mountains, Rob had done little more than wag his tail and cheer up the ground staff at Kairouan Airfield in northern Tunisia, from where some of the missions were mounted (the base later moved to Gioia del Colle, near Taranto).

His amazing war record had been concocted as a result of his Shropshire owners writing to AV&RS at Droitwich Spa in late 1944, asking when he might be coming home out of quarantine. (In fact, the evidence shows it was the AV&RS who first wrote to the astonished Baynes.) Quartermaster Burt was so upset at the prospect of losing Rob that he and Hughes (later a distinguished professor of architectural history) contrived to keep the agreeable Collie by letting the family think he was indispensable to the war effort.

Hughes and Burt further contrived to send him on a parachute jump (in fact, to be his first). 'We had a suitable parachute harness and I phoned through to the RAF and made arrangements for Rob

---

[49] Captain Tom Burt was a career soldier, who had joined the Royal East Kents (the 'Buffs') as a boy bugler in 1914, been wounded at Gallipoli, and twenty-five years later survived the evacuation of the BEF from St Valéry. At the age of almost fifty he had gone to North Africa as 5 Battalion REK CHK Quartermaster (which lost four unnamed dogs in the campaign) — then volunteered for the SAS. Rob was described as the 'battalion mascot' of which 'he was in charge', according to a profile in his local newspaper published on the eve of the medal ceremony for Rob. Capt Burt himself was to be awarded the MBE the same day. 'After D-Day the Captain had been given special training and made many parachute drops,' said the report, while Rob had even visited Captain Burt's Canterbury home when his master had been 'on New Year's leave'.

His MBE citation said: 'Joined SAS March 1943 as Quartermaster when it numbered 100 all ranks, strength now (August, 1944) is 650. It is not too much to say that without this officer's wealth of experience, it is doubtful whether the unit would have survived the many difficulties it has had to face.'

to have a short flight,' so Hughes wrote in his memoirs.
'Unfortunately, quite a strong wind blew up during the flight and
the RAF decided it would be dangerous to drop Rob on that day.'

Thus it was that a letter marked 'Very Secret', wildly extolling
his exploits, reached Ellesmere in January 1945. It was essential,
it said, that the dog be retained 'until the cessation of hostilities'.
On Hughes' account, it was the Bayne family, on receipt of this
letter, who informed the Allied Forces Mascot Club of their
one-time pet's astonishing courage in action.

Dorothea St Hill Bourne in her post-war account of hero
animals (*They Also Serve*), however, was keen to stress, correctly,
that the letter to the Baynes had come direct from the 'War
Office', which, she further stated, had simultaneously
commended Rob's bravery directly to the Mascot Club of
which she was the Secretary, for the award of a Dickin Medal.
He was enrolled as a Club member on 21 January 1945.

Any pending demob of Rob was deferred. Even after his very
public Dickin Medal award in February in London, rather than
be returned to his family, Rob went back to Colchester. He would
be kept there through the summer for 'demonstration purposes'
under the care of Corporal Redhead.

Other than giving quotes to journalists, Corporal Redhead's
role remains obscure (the Mascot Club's records describe him as
Rob's 'Handler'). Mrs Bayne would record in the 1960s that
Sam Redhead was Captain Burt's batman — and that from the
earliest days in Tunisia, he had offered himself 'for special
training as a parachutist and dog handler so that he could
accompany Rob on his drops'.

He was clearly devoted to Rob. His daughter, Mrs Jennifer
Hodges of Lydd in Kent, would one day write that sometime

after the London ceremony, Cpl Redhead himself wrote to the Bayne family, asking if he could keep him, but Mrs Edna Bayne said 'she loved him and wanted him back'.

Her father 'was always receiving letters and phone calls about his time with Rob,' Mrs Hodges told the *Daily Mail*, '[but he] never spoke of his wartime experiences, and kept few photographs. Perhaps they were things he simply did not want to be reminded of.'

That might well be true.

With the war in Europe almost over, the home-based component of 2 SAS meanwhile were enjoying themselves 'in training', conducting mock seaborne raids, playing with novel weapons, making jeep-borne forays to London night-clubs, scoffing champagne and oysters and beating up RAF airfields, stealing cars and hijacking trains on exercises in north Wales, much to the alarm of the local population. Rob apparently spent most of his time snoozing at their Essex HQ, although several accounts have him jumping out of an aircraft operating from RAF Rednal in Shropshire 'over the hills of Llangollen', with Corporal Redhead close besides.[50]

---

[50] An intriguing and highly detailed handwritten account in the Airborne Assault archive made in December 1997 by an ex-2 SAS trooper is of a seven-man team making a mock parachute attack on an RAF airfield in north Wales, in early 1945. A 'highly intelligent German Shepherd' was with them, according to Frank Gleeson, aged twenty at the time. In good Northaw style he would only accept food from his 'dogmaster'. Flying from an airfield near Colchester, 'the dog jumped in the dark with his master over Wrexham,' and, 'after a day or so, including an air supply drop of a bottle of whisky from the QM [presumably Tom Burt], we penetrated the aerodrome defence at night,' so the account continued. The raiders left chalk marks to show their destructive progress. The next day, the mystery dog was further used to act as the roadblock for an ambush in which a column of truck-borne RAF Regiment defenders was shot up and 'all killed'. The station 'CO was furious'.

There was a fascinating doggy diversion for 2 SAS soon after the DM award for Rob. As Jimmy Hughes would recall: 'A few of us were invited in April 1945 to the War-Dog Training School at Potters Bar to see what war dogs could do. We were shown dogs that could sniff out buried mines and would sit down behind them so that sappers could mark their position and destroy them.'

But as well as mine dogs, Herbert Lloyd's team were still experimenting with tracker evasion and patrol dogs. As Hughes wrote:

> We were given ampoules of 'concentrated human sweat' and told to walk across a couple of large fields. Then a dog would be released to follow this scent. What we found was that the dog would not go straight across the middle of the fields, but would follow the hedgerows where the scent, having been blown by the breeze, had landed on the hedges. Finally, we were shown a group of Alsatian dogs that had been trained to move silently across country and, when they heard a strange noise, sit down, thus giving a silent warning that someone was approaching.

Hughes 'took three of these fine dogs to use with our training.' One of them, called (inevitably) 'Rex', turned out to be too 'fierce' but the SAS officer was clearly smitten by a young Alsatian named 'Jan'. 'At the start of any walk she was so full of enthusiasm that she would listen for every sound,' he wrote, 'but she soon tired of the game and would sit down through boredom, so that one never knew whether she had heard something or was merely tired of the whole exercise.'

Any adverse reaction by Rob to the arrival at Wivenhoe of these youthful Northaw graduates is not recorded. Instead Hughes described him as 'lounging around in comfort, living off the fat of the land.' There were diversions, however. In April 1945 Rob was reported to be starring in the SAS Concert Party — 'Cavaliers of Variety', which was raising money for charity at Essex venues in a show telling the story of the regiment's wartime exploits, just as they faced the threat of disbandment by a hostile War Office. Rob's public legend was part of the fight for survival.

In September he was the star of a PDSA fundraising show at the Royal Hospital Chelsea, with an escort of grinning SAS troopers. 'Only quarantine cheated Rob of participating in the D-Day operations,' it was said. 'Undoubtedly Rob saved many British lives,' Major Burt told reporters.

The good times were coming to an end, however, as the unit prepared for disbandment. There was a valedictory service of thanksgiving on 4 October at St Peter's, Colchester and soon thereafter Rob would seem to have been at the Northaw Dog Holding Section in the care of a Lt Biddis, RAVC. Mrs Bayne received an official letter on 9 November, saying, 'with deep regret I have to tell you that Rob's handler was killed on active service.' In a baroque twist she assumed, as she told a local newspaper, that it 'was his keeper and friend Corporal Sam Redhead who died after Rob received his VC'. And she said in a letter to Monty Hunt, almost fifty years later: 'It is so sad because, if Rob was still with him, he might not have been killed.'

Corporal Redhead was very much alive.

At last, on 27 November, Rob was returned by train 'under military escort' from Northaw to Shropshire, proudly wearing his newly awarded RSPCA For Valour collar medallion — this had already been sent c/o Northaw — to be met at Ellesmere railway station by his adoring family. But the 'Dickin Medal awarded ten months earlier to the para-dog, hero of many campaigns,' as Rob was described, had been stolen somewhere en route.

'Rob took up his old life exactly as if he had been away three hours rather than three years,' so Dorothea St Hill Bourne wrote about him not long afterwards. 'He remembered how to deal with the hens and the cattle, and at once renewed his old habits and customs.'

No wonder. War-Dog 'Rob', it seems, was somebody's pet all along. But let Rob have his glory, the Hughes' account simply does not work and, after all, the AV&RS Directorate endorsed his combat record citation *twice*.

By late summer 1945 the Army Veterinary Directorate's hero-dog roster was nearing completion. 'Brian' from Loughborough and 'Bing' from Rochester, the two Alsatians that had parachuted into Ranville on D-Day, were both commended in a list of nine dogs sent on 25 August to Droitwich Spa by Lt-Col R. W. Stalker, Chief Vet (Assistant Director AV&RS) of the British Army of the Rhine. How he had canvassed for citations and who gave them is not recorded.

Both parachute dogs were cited identically but separately as having 'landed in Normandy with the 13 Bn., Airborne Div., and is a fully qualified paratroop in that he has done the requisite number of jumps.'

Also on the list were mine dogs: 'Texas', belonging to Mrs K. Bates of 'Hobbs', Beckley, near Rye, Sussex; 'Rover', belonging to Mrs Bungay of Worksop and 'Bruce', belonging to Mr T.

Oliver of Blackridge, Scotland, all of No. 4 Mine Dog Platoon, still on duty in Germany, were given glowing citations for their fortitude and efficiency in the Reichswald Forest and at the Rhine Crossing. And there was Black Labrador 'Rex', who had worked with 'complete disregard for very heavy enemy shelling. He helped clear a pathway through a thickly sown anti-personnel minefield so saving casualties that would most certainly have occurred but for his devotion to duty.'

No. 4 Platoon Commander Lt Peter Norbury seemed especially keen to honour his dogs. On 26 June 1945 he had sent a signal through 21 Army Group to Droitwich headed 'Canine Awards for Gallantry', inquiring 'just what awards there were, official or semi-official,' for war dogs. 'I wish if it is possible to gain some of the decorations for dogs in my unit,' he said. Could they be awarded 'posthumously'? he asked.

There were guard dogs to consider, all of them at the time inconveniently still in the Mediterranean. Major J. W. Scott, commanding the Middle East CMP dog training school, sent in the commendations. 'Blackie', for example, an Alsatian belonging to Mrs Ligertwood of Maryhill, Glasgow, who had in July 1944 beaten off eight thieves attempting to burgle a clothing store. He had rendered invaluable assistance to his handler in pinioning the chief malefactor and 'taking random bites at the other Italian civilians'.

'Piggy', a Boxer employed by the military police in Cairo, had attacked four 'native thieves' and lost an eye in the fray but had carried on devotedly. She had now recovered and returned to duty. 'Snook', a Doberman Pinscher, had been blown up by a landmine in the Egyptian desert in pursuit of malefactors but was now 'back on duty'. 'Jerry', 'Prince', 'Sheila', 'Ran' and

'Lilith' had all been very brave dogs in the face of seemingly ubiquitous native thieves. 'Simmi', a Boxer, had been tremendously courageous in pinioning a pesky 'native' thief attempting to escape on a train. He had sadly died meanwhile but not before siring a litter of puppies. It was suggested that 'a posthumous award be made to the son'.

A number of unnamed dogs commended for awards by Southern Command were now 'on charge at the Chemical Defence Experimental Station at Porton Down,' it emerged. No further mention would be made of them.

On 2 October a list of eleven dogs was sent by Lt-Col J. C. Bennison, the Deputy Director AV&RS, to the RSPCA. Police dog 'Blackie' was added to the original list of nine war dogs and Special Air Service Rob added at the end, with a citation almost identical to that quoted in January by the Mascot Club. It was now for the Society to inform the Directorate 'to which dogs the award is approved'.

The answer came back by letter on the 9th — 'all of those dogs whose particulars you submitted.' A special mention was made of 'Bing', to whom the charity wished to send the award direct (the typewritten letter is struck through — 'should be "Rob" (Bayne)'). It was duly done. The medallion was sent to Northaw, where Rob was in charge of the Dog Holding Section. The Society next inquired of the War Office the whereabouts of the other nominees, including those 'still with the forces'. Should they be sent their medallion direct or through the auspices of the DAV&RS? Where, in fact, were they? Answering all that was going to prove rather difficult.

The Society was now minded to hold a public presentation sometime when the appropriate dogs might be available 'in

England'. It is evident from the documentation that some owners of brave dogs cited were contacted by the War Office with details of what was intended, including Betty Fetch, triggering her indignation at their near-simultaneous clumsy offer to buy Brian.

Meanwhile Rob's triumphal return from Northaw to the Baynes in Shropshire on 27 November, wearing his shiny new RSPCA For Valour medal, showed just what a publicity bonus could be reaped all round. The charity now proposed a grand ceremony at their London headquarters sometime the following year to coincide with an exhibition of their wartime work.

Telling the press was irresistible. Under the heading 'War Dogs are Coming to Town', the *News Chronicle* ran a story on 4 January 1946 that dogs from all over Britain, recommended for an honour by the War Office, were coming to the capital to receive a handsome collar from the Society engraved with the words 'For Valour'. The recipients were named as 'special air service regiment Rob', guard dog 'Blackie' and mine dogs 'Rover' and 'Raf'. And there was 'Texas', a 'Golden Labrador belonging to Mrs Bates of Beckley, who worked to detect mines under continuous gunfire at the Rhine crossing.'

No other dogs were mentioned.

The newspaper story ran a few days *before* the War Office was informed of the Society's intentions by letter — which further contained a request that they 'be informed of the whereabouts of the other ten animals'. (They knew where 'Rob' was — safely home in Shropshire.)

It all looked terrific for war dogs. Tails, generally, were wagging.

Don't Let the Dogs Out

There was, however, a problem: as at 22 January 1946 the dogs (excluding Rob and the police animals in the Mediterranean), were still on duty in Germany. But more than that, of the roster of Brigadier Kelly's heroes, only Ricky and Brian's owners seemed to want them back. The rest were now listed as 'War Department property'. These exemplary animals, naturally enough, were just what Zellick wanted to keep on charge. The £25 offer to buy them (rejected by Miss Betty Fetch and Mrs Lichfield) was clearly irresistible to everyone else. Eight of them now knew no owner but the state — including Bing, who, spurned by his erstwhile owner in Rochester,[51] was still in Germany.

From being full of enthusiasm in the autumn, the War Office line on canine awards became distinctly prickly. AV&RS Deputy Assistant Director, Major H. A. Clay, informed Mr Arthur Moss, the Society's Assistant Secretary, soon after the publication of

---

[51] Bing's owner, Temporary Lieutenant Cyril William John Cory (aged thirty-seven) of Jackson Road, Rochester, is listed in the Navy List as a Royal Marine Engineer, amphibious construction specialists, which were heading that spring of 1945 to the Far East for the expected climactic battle with Japan.

the list of heroes supposedly on their way to London: 'You may wish to reconsider your original intention to award medals, since the award could only be of interest to a private owner. In any case it is considered inadvisable to communicate with their late owners on the subject.' There might be 'two or three war dogs' out of quarantine in time for the proposed exhibition, Arthur Moss was told, but they would not necessarily be among those cited for awards.

The Porton dog(s) were never to be mentioned. And after the extraordinary claims made for 'Rob' had raised eyebrows, and those pestering letters about 'Brian' and 'Ricky', it seemed that nobody wanted correspondence about hero animals coming through anywhere but official channels.

As winter took hold at the end of 1945, the 'despatch of pet dogs to the UK' from Germany by truck and cross-channel landing was hit by bad weather. For three months the flow of demob dogs stopped. The British Army of the Rhine's Chief Vet admitted meanwhile it was struggling to keep up with demand for dogs as prison guards. The German population were hiding their surviving pets lest they be requisitioned. In Hamburg, it was reported, dogs were being sold as meat. Compelling a town mayor to muster civilian dogs for the WDTS to requisition had been tried but only 'worthless dogs were produced'. A scheme to breed puppies would be started with 'five bitches to be shipped out from the UK'. But how long would that take to produce results?

It was time to be a little less sentimental about war dogs. A startlingly frank article appeared in the Brussels-printed *Soldier* magazine of 2 March 1946, explaining why only forty out of four hundred dogs at the 'War Dogs Training School near Paderborn' had been given their discharge — and why 'de-training to turn them from ferocious beasts into house pets' was taking so long. The 'psychological treatment' was being given by specialist NCOs, it was reported. Northaw veteran Cpl David Cooke, RAVC, explained: 'I do it by taking dogs to a quiet spot and talking to them. Alsatians in particular are very intelligent, far more than human beings.' Meanwhile a number of dogs, including French and German animals 'picked up during the advance into Germany', were being actively trained as guard dogs for PoW camps.

The article's author, Capt E. K. Grove, could further report for the War Office-sponsored news-magazine:

> Some of the more ferocious dogs will never become civilians again, their aggressive training is impossible to eradicate. They will spend the rest of their lives in the army as regular war dogs. Others that will not be demobilised are the expert patrol dogs and the best mine dogs. They will be the nucleus of the Dogs Post War Army.

Among the dogs encountered by Capt Grove were patrol dog 'Bing', a three-year-old Alsatian who had 'parachuted into France on D-Day minus 1 with 6th Airborne Div, who, because he is such an expert,' had been 'bought from his owner by the Government and is now on the permanent staff of the War Dog School.' And there was 'Ricky' from No. 3 Mine Detection Platoon, 'Lassie', a 'French bitch who responded to commands in French and English,' Labrador crosses 'Flash', 'Dan' and 'Blitz', along with 'Revo' and 'Texas' (clearly an Alsatian), who unlike not-to-be-demobbed Bing were 'looking forward to that armchair and cushion on Civvy Street'.

Not long after Bing's photo-call in Paderborn, Betty Fetch wrote another grumpy letter to the War Office regarding 'Brian'. She was told in return that War-Dog 2720/6871 had arrived at Chilbolton Down, near Stockbridge, Hants, on 10 April and the Commandant would be writing to her shortly. The letter from Major Bridgeman duly came on 29 May to say that Brian, in quarantine at No. 1 MQS, 'has settled down well' and would be released to her when appropriate. The local newspaper picked up news of the 'Paradog to Return to Loughborough' ('paradogs' were already part of journalistic shorthand), where 'a hero's welcome was awaiting Brian on his return in a few months time.'

Hero Brian furthermore was 'a fully qualified paratroop having made the requisite number of jumps.' That was a quote from his British Army of the Rhine citation. There was more to come. Brian was on his way to London for a special investiture of 'canine war heroes' to be held shortly by the RSPCA, it would be reported in the *Nottingham Guardian*, a little later in the summer, 'where many dogs from the Midlands would receive medals'. *The Tail-Wagger Magazine* also excitedly reprinted the medal-winning war dogs on the march to the capital yarn.

That was not at all what the War Office had in mind. Who was deciding policy, the RSPCA? The newspapers? Pushy owners? Meanwhile Colonel Bennison's original typewritten list of hero dogs bloomed with pencil annotations – 'cancelled', 'in quarantine', 'WD purchase'. Golden Labrador 'Texas' of Sussex, hero of the Rhine crossing, it turned out, had also been bought outright by the War Department from his owner. In spite of a glowing citation by his platoon commander, Lt Peter Norbury, there would be no medal for him.

Brave Black Lab 'Rex', War-Dog 3564/S.12, mine-hunting hero of the Reichswald Forest, who had also been recommended directly by Lt Norbury, meanwhile turned out to have been 'a stray'. He did not even have an ex-owner and was struck off the list altogether.

Alsatian-cross 'Rover', from Worksop, for all his 'keenness and reliability under the most hazardous conditions' had been purchased by the WD while awaiting repatriation. There could be no medal for him. Nor for 'Bruce', another Reichswald hero not wanted on demob by his erstwhile owner, Mr T. Oliver of Blackridge, West Lothian.

Government-owned Raf, unusually, did get a medal, handed to his ex-owner, Mrs Minchin (now living in Lowestoft), in December by an RSPCA local inspector as a 'memento'. But when she asked for a photograph to be taken of somewhere-in-Germany Raf to be 'treasured' alongside it, the AV&RS directorate replied that this would be 'impossible due to the large number of such requests for photographs of War Dogs sold by their owners'. Police dog Blackie from Glasgow, meanwhile, died before demob.

The only medal-cited heroes actually going *home* were Ricky and Brian. Ricky's handler, Pte Maurice Yelding, had meanwhile written directly to his owners with handwritten details of their pet's July 1945 citation for bravery – plus further intimate details of his fortitude. Now the Litchfields were badgering the AV&RS directorate by letter for news of 'an award'. The RSPCA was urged to communicate directly with them to avoid further embarrassment.

For months the RSPCA Council clearly agonised over what to do with its roster of heroes. Formally it was for them to decide, not the War Office, just as it would be for the Allied Force Mascot

Club to enrol members and make further Dickin Medal awards, should they choose to do so. As the Commandant of the Chilbolton quarantine camp was told by Lt-Col Bennison in April 1946, 'these are recommendations only and may not result in an award being granted by the organisation[s] concerned.' The Mascot Club was mentioned in the signal as an interested party.

And it had been the RSPCA, apparently, that had stressed in the original trawl for information in July the year before that brave dogs were eligible for medals whether 'on loan or not'. That is how the commendations had come in – as collated by the Chief Vet of the British Army of the Rhine. It was about the dogs, not their social status. Who cared who 'owned' them? Now it was the deciding matter.

It would seem that by spring 1946, while claiming it was for the charities to decide, the Directorate of the AV&RS wanted to escape the canine minefield they had so carelessly laid on their own doorstep. The return of publicly loaned dogs to their original owners was difficult enough to deal with, let alone with medals attached.[52] Dogs were still in huge demand in the British Army of the Rhine for guarding millions of prisoners of war. Four hundred thousand more were held at hundreds of locations in Britain, Canada and elsewhere. (Their detention would go on for three more years – the last Afrika Korps PoWs, remarkably, would not return from Egypt to Germany until December 1948.) Corporal David Cooke would tell his local newspaper in summer 1946 that,

---

[52] Almost twenty years later the British Army 'Training of War Dogs' manual would comment on the 'Procurement of Dogs' and how wartime arrangements were flawed: 'Hundreds of dogs were loaned by civilians for the duration. This entailed endless correspondence as owners desired to be regularly informed of their pet's welfare. Again with the coming of peace these dogs had to be returned to their owners and their services lost to the army.'

as well as repatriating British war dogs, the Sennelager School was 'taking *in* and training more than seventy dogs a month,' most of them destined to patrol PoW cages.

Still referred to as 'VP dogs', they were now trained to 'attack and hold on command [by] means of a course in baiting' (men dressed as 'Germans' in padded clothing, teasing the dog), which 'brings out their aggressive nature', as the new school headmaster, Major G. D. Young, RAVC, would explain. That took at least a month, and longer for a dog that could attack 'loose' and bring down an escapee 'at a distance from its handler'.

Like War-Dog E533 'Afra', for example, who, so his handler L/Cpl Rodway reported in summer 1946, 'made a kill' at PoW Camp 2233, near Munster, when a large number of prisoners broke out through an escape tunnel beyond the perimeter wire, 'like people coming out of a rush-hour train'. After that, he would report: 'An escaping German PoW would not stop running if he saw you were just an armed guard, but as soon as he saw a dog after him he would stand very still.'

Ex-Wehrmacht Rottweilers proved especially effective. Bull Terriers in cold weather, however, refused to leave the comforts of the guard room apparently. But snoozing or snarling, these were the 'Class A' dogs the Treasury Solicitor had been consulted on, the ones 'too ferocious [ever to] become civilians again'.

Destined to return home or not, the service dogs in Germany were having it tough. Most of the puppies in the experimental breeding programme died in two outbreaks of distemper and hard pad disease. The breeding bitches sent from England were destroyed as being 'too nervous in temperament for retraining as guard dogs,' according to the War Diary. The destruction rate of Class A animals was about twenty-five dogs a month. The

procurement of dogs locally was by now proving impossible —
and the veteran wartime trainers had been released, while 'new
arrivals at the school are mainly very young men with very little
time to serve.'

The line to the charities was clear — although all sides could
agree the proposed award was for the *dog* and not its owner, it was
policy not to facilitate the giving of medals to animals on War
Department charge. Why draw attention to the doomed-to-be-
destroyed animals by awarding medals, even to those with
distinguished wartime records, to dogs who, for whatever reason,
happened to still be in the service of the state.

It was just as the Quartermaster General had warned at the start
of it all, four years earlier. War dogs were equipment, after all.

The RSPCA was not going to fight. But writing their history
of the charity at war, *Animals Were There* (published in March
1947), authors Arthur Moss and Elizabeth Kirby went out of
their way to include medal-less Bing's story at length, including
his Rhine-crossing role. The book also reverentially reproduced
the 'citations' as received from Colonel Bennison the October
before, for all the brave dogs, including those for police guard
dog 'Blackie', the transatlantic demonstration dog 'Paddy',
mine dogs 'Ricky', 'Scamp', 'Bruce' and 'Texas' — who had
'contributed largely to the clearing of the approaches for the
bridging of the Rhine on both banks.'[53]

---

[53] The book also reprised the story of Red Army canines — including one called 'Dootik'
('tailwheel') — a flying mascot who brought aid to the crew of a shot-down Shturmovik.
'The RSPCA has offered to recognise this exploit and those of other Soviet war dogs
by presenting medallion inscribed collars, similar to those being given to British Army
dog heroes,' wrote Mr Moss. The proposal seems not to have survived the end of the
Anglo-Russian love affair post-war. Very mysteriously, the book also referenced
another airborne 'Bing', who had somehow operated behind enemy lines in Yugoslavia,
presumably with the Special Operations Executive.

Would they get medals?

Some would. 'So meritorious was the work of these dogs that the Council of the RSPCA decided to award special collars with a medallion "for valour" to the *most distinguished* of them,' the authors said very disingenuously.

That meant just three.

There would be no grand ceremony in London, whatever the papers might have promised. In the end the Society decided to ignore the dogs without owners. 'So useful have these dogs become they will either be demobilised among the last of the war veterans or retained for peacetime purposes,' wrote Mr Moss in his published wartime tribute without further explanation.

For Brian and Ricky, lucky dogs, however, it was a different matter. 'Brian' was returned from quarantine to his owner, Miss Betty Fetch, on 10 October 1946 and after his press build-up through the spring was already a local celebrity. But he would not be coming to London. Not yet. He was awarded the 'For Valour' medallion by Mr Arthur Tinley, Branch President, at the Loughborough and North Leicester RSPCA meeting in December and 'barked his thanks' at a splendid municipal ceremony.

And the 'For Valour' award for plucky Ricky, the famous 'Bromley War Dog', was on the front page of the London *Evening News* in January 1947 when he came out of quarantine and was presented with his RSPCA gong by the Mayor of Bromley. The feted 'Rob' of Ellesmere already had his collar medallion.

The PDSA, which had already led the way with its Dickin Medal awards for Royal West Kent War-Dog 'Bob' of Tunisia fame and several London rescue dogs, was much more populist than the stuffy RSPCA and had a genius for attracting national publicity. Its Mascot Club had been a masterstroke from the start. The charity was naturally keen not to be upstaged by its statelier rival. Might not the People's Dispensary for Sick Animals of the Poor, with its concern for the underdog, embrace this canine *salon des refusés*?

The amazing adventures of 'special air unit Rob' had been a sensation when revealed in February 1945 at his Dickin Medal award. And so it had continued — the Cameronian patrol dog, Rifleman Khan, hero of the Walcheren Causeway, was smartly enrolled in the AFMC on 25 February and presented with his Dickin Medal a month later, at a full battalion parade before being returned to the Railton family in Tolworth, Surrey (then later adopted by his handler, L/Cpl Jimmy Muldoon, after a tempestuous tug-of-canine-love episode).

Since VE Day, Dickin Medals had been awarded to the unofficial ARP rescue dogs, 'Beauty' and 'Rip' of 1940–41 Blitz vintage, plus London rescue dogs 'Peter', 'Thorn' and 'Rex' (on the direct recommendation of Sir Edward Warner, the London Senior Regional Civil Defence Officer), all with identifiable 'civilian' owners. The PDSA did not need ponderous Whitehall ministerial citations, rather (as seemed to be the case with Rob), the written testimony from 'some official quarter', preferably close to the potential recipient.

Reports from the front line on MAP rescue dog 'Rex', for example, on his six-month life-saving campaign in the capital were exemplary. And he had an owner, Mr Sydney Ramshaw of 2 Lily Avenue, Jesmond, Newcastle, who was more than happy to have him returned. Born at Catterick Camp in March 1943, Rex had been 'loaned to the RAF when a few months old' and 'during his career, been gassed, bombed, buried alive, his paws burned and his head injured.' He was presented with his Dickin Medal in April 1945 at the 'Wembley World War Dogs Heroes Parade' and Mr Ramshaw would continue to be a proud exponent of Rex's bravery at many fundraising events thereafter. In 1948, Rex sent Mrs Dickin, on holiday in Saltdean, Brighton, a congratulatory telegram on her eightieth birthday. Rex told her just how valued was her work for animals. 'I fear the work is just beginning,' she replied.

All the MAP rescue dogs made numerous and hugely popular public appearances with their Mrs Dickin-awarded honours. Jet, billed as 'The Dog with the Magic Nose, hero of the Blitz, burglars' enemy and children's friend', made guest appearances with her Liverpudlian owner and breeder, Mrs Hilda Babcock-Cleaver, and entertained Londoners at West End stores and fashionable restaurants in the company of young film actresses. And on 10 June 1945, Rescue Dog 'Peter' was chosen to lead the Civil Defence stand-down parade in Hyde Park, during which he was presented to the King and Queen (taking an interest in Her Majesty's fur stole), and Princess Elizabeth. Peter would be awarded the DM in November, with his owner beaming proudly.

Then there was 'Judy', a pedigree Pointer, 'a liver and white bitch born in the Shanghai dog kennels in 1937,' as *The Tail-Wagger Magazine* would report, who had briefly been a Royal Navy warship mascot, before being caught in the Japanese tide of conquest on the island of Sumatra in March 1942. She had survived, miraculously, over three years of captivity, produced a litter of puppies and narrowly avoided being herself eaten.

Judy was now the property of her fellow prisoner of war, Leading Aircraftsman Frank Williams, who had protected her through all kinds of dire perils and got her back to England from Singapore very unofficially on a troopship in late 1945. Soon after her arrival,

The Tail-Wagger published the full story and invited subscriptions from club members to pay for six months of quarantine at the commercial Messrs Spratt's Hackbridge kennels, announcing the award of its own *Tail-Wagger* 'For Valour' medal, 'regarded by many as the Dogs' VC,' as it pronounced. Not to be outdone by such a claim, the Mascot Club swooped.

As release from quarantine neared, news of a pending Dickin citation covered Judy in 'a blaze of glory', wrote Dorothea St Hill Bourne, and, after being 'interviewed and photographed dozens of times', her bravery was formalised in the Allied Forces Mascot Club medal citation as being: 'For magnificent courage and endurance in Japanese prison camps, which helped to maintain morale among her fellow prisoners and also for saving many lives through her intelligence and watchfulness'. 'If the old bitch can hang on for release, we can make it too,' said fellow prisoners, according to an unusually worded press release sent by Miss St Hill Bourne to news editors.

The medal would be duly fastened to her collar on 2 May 1946 by Major Viscount Tarbat MC, chairman of the Returned British POW Association at its No. 57 Cadogan Square HQ, and Judy was enrolled as 'the association's only dog member', so wrote Miss St Hill Bourne. (War-Dog 'Mac', captured by the Germans with his master, Major J. F. H. Hudson MC, on the mist-shrouded Dejebel Tanngoucha Mountain evidently did not come home.)

Then there were 'Punch' and 'Judy', Boxer dog and bitch CMP guard dogs, given awards in November 1946. They had saved the lives of two British officers in Palestine the previous August — 'by attacking an armed terrorist who was stealing upon them unawares and thus warning them of the danger. Punch sustained 4 bullet wounds and Judy a long graze down her back.'

The actual awards were made at the Royal Tournament in London, on 14 June the following year, before a huge crowd. Judy's owner was named as Lieutenant-Colonel Hugh G. G. Niven, Adjutant General in Palestine, one of the apparent assassination targets.

All had been heroes, all had beaming owners, happy children or adopters-in-uniform to whom they had been safely returned after their years of service. It made wonderful publicity all round. And there were more dogs out there like them. Except that in certain cases the rival RSPCA had got there first.

When Dorothea St Hill Bourne, Secretary of the Allied Forces Mascot Club, contacted the War Office at the end of January 1947 about the possibility of an award for the already medal-bearing 'Ricky', she was informed that the RSPCA had been sent a citation. 'Should you desire to award the Dickin Medal [to Ricky] there is no objection in this department,' she was informed. And there was War-Dog 'Brian', 'who may be of interest', who had been returned to his owner, Betty Fetch. A copy of Brian's citation for bravery in Normandy was enclosed.

But of the others, the ownerless animals, Major P. W. Dean, the embattled officer now in charge of what he called 'canine awards' at Droitwich Spa, told Miss St Hill Bourne in the same letter on behalf of his director that, 'since all other citations received refer to dogs which the owners have sold to this department, [no] useful purpose would be served by granting them a medal. In any case they could not be present at any ceremony.'

It was just as the RSPCA had been advised: no owner, no medal. The Mascot Club, although still actively recruiting members, was not minded to push the matter further.

But the dogs with photogenic families were ready for their close-up. Ricky had been swiftly enrolled in the PDSA's Mascot Club on 8 January 1947, on the eve of his 'For Valour' presentation, and became additionally Ricky, DM, at a ceremony on 26 March at PDSA House, Cork Street, Mayfair, London. And 'Brian' had come from Loughborough with his young owner to receive his DM from Air Chief Marshal Sir Frederick Bowhill at the same splendid Mayfair function, celebrating the opening of the 'animal war hero portraits exhibition' by veteran animal painter, Mrs Georgina Shaw-Baker.

It was reported: 'Sir Frederick, after attaching the medals to the dogs' collars, stood to attention and saluted each animal in turn.' Fritz, the 'ex-Nazi dog' captured just after D-Day, was in the audience and doubtless barked approvingly. Betty Fetch beamed.

All this was fundraising publicity gold for the veterinary charity — and why not? It would go on and on, a glint of canine cheer amid post-war austerity. Nor was it too late to join the Mascot Club. 'Do you have an unsung war hero?' so the Club advertised in the press in July 1947, asking for details of services rendered during the war by dogs. 'If there is evidence from some official quarter as well, your dog might win a medal.' Mine dogs 'Guinevere', a Springer Spaniel owned by Maj G. Wilson, RA and 'Niggar', a Retriever owned by Mr J. Black, both were thus enrolled that summer.

Rob was back on parade at *The Star* newspaper's Dog Tournament at Wembley Stadium in July 1947, described by BBC sports commentator Raymond Glendenning, as 'Britain's first parachute dog, the ace of war-dogs and the king-pin of the show.' Rex, the rescue dog from Jesmond, was among the other canine celebrities under the spotlights. After a further flurry of pigeons, the last wartime DM was awarded in July 1949 to 'Tich', an adoptee mongrel mascot, before another huge Star Dog Tournament crowd at Wembley Stadium with his desert army master, Mr J. Walker of Newcastle.

Rescue dog 'Jet' would also get an RSPCA For Valour collar medallion presented by the Lord Mayor of Liverpool on 20 April 1948, both for his war work, and for his role in the rescue of trapped miners at Whitehaven, Cumbria, the same year.[54] But when the Home Office that year looked at enlisting its own rescue dogs for such emergencies, and it was suggested that Mrs Margaret Griffin might be consulted, an official noted: 'There is nothing to say that Mrs Griffin ever came into the picture, although she might have provided some of the animals,' that were used in the London rescues. She was tracked down to an 'Easter fete', where she was giving 'demonstrations with some of her dogs of the detection of mines and one thing and the other'. She was 'extremely interested and very keen to help us if we should want her help in the future.'

Margaret Griffin was awarded the British Empire Medal and Herbert Summers Lloyd the OBE in the 1946 New Year Honours.

Not only brave dogs got gongs.

Of the other heroes, 1st Army/2 SAS veteran, Rob, DM, FV, moved with the Bayne family to a new house, 'Springfields', at Kenwick Park, Ellesmere, where he 'lived out his days until old age and infirmity overtook him and he was put painlessly to sleep in 1952'. It was further recorded:

---

[54] In March 1971 the comedian Ken Dodd unveiled a 'luxurious memorial kennel' to Jet at the RSPCA Animal Home, Edge Lane, Liverpool.

He was buried at Springfields and a marble stone, the gift of sculptor F A Cox, engraved with Rob's head and behind the planes and parachutes, stands in the garden — a tribute to a loyal and gallant dog.

On their deaths both Brian and Ricky would go to the canine Valhalla, the PDSA pet cemetery in Ilford, to be buried alongside more obscurely named wartime pets such as 'Hitler' ('In Memory of a Good and Faithful Pal', the tombstone was inscribed), 'Timoshenko', 'Joffre', 'Dinky', 'Dusty', 'Ginger' and 'Peter', the Home Office cat. Other wartime heroes would follow.

The fate of Bob DM, the hero of Green Hill, Tunisia, and CQMS Cleggett's best pal through the Italian campaign, was sadder still. Bob Cleggett was especially concerned that he should bring the Collie back to England himself lest someone who 'did not know his ways' should lose him. But it was not to be. Cleggett was demobbed in Austria soon after VE Day. Bob would follow when it was possible to get an animal home under the Special Services Scheme. Disaster struck. On his way (in the care of another member of the regiment) in February 1946 to the RAVC Dog Holding Unit at Milan railway station, 'Bob broke his collar and disappeared into the blue.' His 'description was circularised and broadcast throughout Italy,' but, like Mine-Dog 'Judy' who disappeared one day in Brussels, Bob had vanished from the face of the earth.

'No trace has ever been discovered but his medal was presented to his owner in 1947,' wrote Dorothea St Hill Bourne (she meant Bob Cleggett, listed both as 'owner and handler' by the Mascot Club). It was heartbreaking. Bob was the most loyal of dogs and his wartime adoptive master the most caring.[55] But their relationship had turned into something very much not what had been intended when the young Collie Labrador-cross with the white patches had been despatched from Northaw to join 1st Army on his great African adventure.

It was sad but inevitable perhaps. It suited both the publicity-conscious charities and the War Office that there should be a happy-seeming end to the war-dog story — which required a loving family or a former handler to come home to. Nobody ever mentioned the 'Class A dogs' that were too savage ever to return — or those whose families, for whatever reason, were unwilling or unable to take them back. And not just the savage dogs. It had all been decided. There was no consultation. At the end of 1945 the Veterinary Directorate had signalled the British Army of the Rhine: 'War dogs that have been purchased from their owners are now War Department property. Accordingly when they become surplus to military requirements they are either to be sold to Allied governments, if required, or humanely destroyed.' No wonder there had been a change of mind.

All would have medals, and even more medals, except those who came from the Dogs' Home, Battersea, or those who knew no owner but the state. Parachuting Bing, veteran of Normandy and the Rhine crossing, blown-up Raf and Mine-Dog Rex, the

---

[55] 'Bob' was a tug-of-love War-Dog. Monty Hunt would record the anguish of L/Cpl Plumridge, Bob's handler in Tunisia, at the claims made by CQMS Cleggett that he was Bob's true master, and that Cleggett, now a postman in Kent, was placing press adverts for the missing dog and telling newspaper reporters that 'he still hoped to see Bob again'. Cleggett, it was said, merely had 'his photograph taken with Bob' before his return. L/Cpl Plumridge meanwhile was now at the WDTS Zellick, wearing German uniform and padding as a 'baitman' for guard dog training, told *Soldier* magazine in June 1945 how proud he was to have been Bob's handler for twelve months with the 1st Army in Africa.

'stray', were ignored, along with the other ownerless heroes for whom Brigadier Kelly's army-wide trawl for especially brave dogs had drawn forth citations. The amazing story of Rhine-storming 'Texas', for example, from Beckley, Sussex, and his rooting out of the Bouncing Betties on the hot side of the river under mortar fire was not to be told.

As one by one they departed, they were buried un-mourned, save by a few ATS-girls, in a corner of the Sennelager military range. They will be remembered.

'Brian' and 'Bing':
A Special Note

Accounts of 'hero' animals published since the mid-1990s and repeated many times online have conjoined 'Brian' (War-Dog 2720/6871) and 'Bing' (War-Dog 2738/6218), both of 13 (Lancashire) Battalion, Parachute Regiment, into one and the same animal. The courageous dog, it seems, won two medals for the same act of gallantry at the outset of a wartime career that would take him from Normandy to the Baltic – before returning home to a hero's welcome and a loving owner.

Because medal-winning dogs tend to be the only ones to have had their stories told, the Bing–Brian conundrum has made telling the wider war-dog story problematic. There is an alternative solution – there were two dogs but one of them did not come home.

In the one-dog version, the dog who jumped into action in June 1944 was known as 'Brian' at home and 'Bing' in Army service. Explanations offered include that 'Bing' was the name used by the men of 13 Bn as being more 'warlike', or that it had 'a sharper sound to it when being given commands by his handler'. It has also been claimed that Bing is buried at the PDSA Pet Cemetery, Ilford, in a grave marked 'Brian'.

The resting place for companion animals in northeast London is distinguished by the graves of winners of the 'Dickin Medal'. It was revived with a posthumous award in 2001 and awards have continued thereafter — for dogs in Operation Telic (Afghanistan) and 'honorary' DMs to animals for bravery before the medal's actual instigation in 1943 — for example, in the First World War. The charity does not permit access by outside researchers to its archives.

War Office records, however, show that 'Brian', loaned to the War Office between 1943 and 1946 by Miss Betty Fetch of Glyndyr, 6 Edelin Road, Loughborough, and 'Bing', on loan (until he was purchased by the War Department in 1945) from (Temporary) Lieutenant Cyril William John Cory of the Royal Marine Engineers and his wife, Marjorie, of 56 Jackson Avenue, Rochester, Kent, to be different animals.

The documentation for the auction in September 2006 of the Dickin Medal awarded to Brian, offered for sale by a Canadian medal collector (it realised £13,000), directly reinforced the proposition that there was one dog, not two. This was endorsed in public statements by the PDSA at the time of the sale and repeated ever since. That Brian was somehow Bing had been given the stamp of authority.

It was not always so. The one-time family pet from Loughborough who won two medals (the first of which was the RSPCA's For Valour) was famous in his day — with never a hint in contemporary reports, in the RSPCA's published post-war history, or for fifty years thereafter that the 'paratroop dog' was anyone other than 'Brian'. Then it changed.

In mid-1996, Steven Blackbourn, the newly appointed curator of the Airborne Forces Museum, Browning Barracks, Aldershot, proposed an exhibition about 'para-dogs'. That November, it was mounted in the Medal Room and centred on a display featuring Brian's Dickin Medal, bought at auction six months before by a collector, Ronald Penhall. Alongside were Brian's Mascot Club DM certificate 'for service with the 13th Battalion in Normandy, in June 1944', plus an oil painting of Brian, commissioned by Mr Penhall.

The show was very 'popular with veterans and children', so it was recorded at the time. But there was another dog in the airborne canine story, an Alsatian called 'Bing', whose wartime record, among other dogs of the battalion, was being researched in parallel by Major Ellis 'Dixie' Dean, D-Day veteran and 13 Bn archivist. He had reminded veterans, a decade earlier, of the existence of 'Bing' in a letter to *Pegasus* magazine, referring to him as the one dog of *three* who had dropped into Normandy on the night of 5/6 June 1944, who 'could cope with the incessant mortaring and shelling'. Bing had been returned to quarantine in the UK in September and had then gone into action again at the Rhine crossing, said the letter. A picture showed the dog, described as being 'Bing', on a Baltic beach near Wismar, in May 1945, with members of the Scout Platoon.

Maj Dean had been posting requests in the association newsletter for more information on the 13 Bn dogs. One account that emerged was by former Pte David Robinson of the A/T Platoon, HQ Company, published in August 1996 in his local Leicester paper. Referring to 'Brian' throughout, he told the reporter, 'we would keep an eye on the dog as he was the first to hear enemy shells and mortars being fired. Brian would dive into the nearest slit trench and we'd be close behind.' After Normandy, Brian 'went on to the big push through to Germany,' he added.

Mr Blackbourn, the museum director, quoted Mr Robinson's words directly in his narrative written to accompany the Aldershot exhibition. But, for whatever reason, the dogs' names were switched: '*Bing* would dive into the nearest slit trench and we'd be close behind', he wrote. 'At other times he found his way working through enemy lines working as a sniffer dog.' The display was mounted meanwhile that autumn with a straightforward telling of the 'Brian' story, his bravery in Normandy and return to Loughborough, where he would 'growl at anyone in uniform' — including bus conductors. There was a short line in the accompanying press coverage that 'when he won his wings, he was known as Bing'.

To build on the exhibit's success, Lt-Gen Sir Peter Downward, 13 Bn Scout Platoon Commander in spring 1945 (who had never encountered 'Brian'), proposed the creation of a life-size resin canine mannequin of an Alsatian para-dog. Clad in faux-fur, it was commissioned from a specialist west London company, along with a replica pack and harness from the Irvin Parachute Company of South Wales. Having handed over a 'generous cheque', Sir Peter was naturally keen, as he said by letter, that the resulting tableau based on original photographs he had supplied should portray the dog who had accompanied him from the Rhine to the Baltic — 'Bing'.

But as 'Project Bing', as it was referred to, moved forward, Sir Peter grew baffled. 'There is a little confusion over some of the dogs' names,' he wrote in July 1997 to Ken Bailey (Brian's wartime handler — who by now had been traced with some difficulty to his home at Sale, Cheshire), 'as the name "Brian" appears in some accounts. Is he in fact Bing under another name?'

It would seem to have been easier all round to say that he was.

War Office files in the National Archives, however, pointed to the two-dog resolution of the conundrum. As did contemporary press reports. When Brian, the 'Alsatian-Collie cross born in early 1942', was returned from quarantine in Chilbolton to Loughborough in October 1946, it was well publicised — as was the award of his RSPCA For Valour medallion, a month later.

More pointedly, Bing had been pictured in *Soldier* magazine, in a feature from the BAOR headquarters at Paderborn-Sennelager in March the same year, described as a 'three-year-old Alsatian', who had 'parachuted into France on D-Day minus 1 with 6th Airborne Div [who] has been bought from his owner by the Government and is now on the permanent staff of the War Dog School' (which had relocated to Germany in November 1945).

War Office files meanwhile showed that in 1945 two dogs, 'Bing' and 'Brian', with quite distinct owners and WDTS kennel numbers had been given separate 'For Valour' citations for service with 13 Parachute Battalion by the Chief Vet of the British Army of the Rhine. They further showed in a list of dogs on charge with the BAOR as at January 1946, where Brian was due for return to Miss Fetch post-quarantine, and Bing had been bought outright by the War Department for continuing service, a circumstance that disbarred him from receiving a civilian-originated medal.

When Mr Monty Hunt, the WDTS veteran, pointed out by letter that to his knowledge there were two dogs, the Airborne Forces Museum curator replied in July 1997:

> Brian was a male Alsatian known as 'Bing' during periods of active service, to prevent him being confused with soldiers in the battalion who had the same name (there were several!). Handled by Ken Bailey, he first parachuted operationally on D-Day, landed in a tree. He served in Normandy until September 1944 when he returned to Britain and was quarantined before being released early in the New Year. He parachuted into action again during the Rhine crossing in April 1945. This information is from members of his handling platoon, the PDSA and the owner of his VC [sic].

Bing was in business. The completed museum-display mannequin was taken in triumph to the 54th anniversary reunion of the 13 Bn, held in October 1997 at the Novotel, Coventry, also attended by Betty Fetch and medal collector Ron Penhall of Vancouver. The model, described as being of 'Bing', proved the 'highlight of the weekend', according to *Pegasus* magazine. Miss Fetch, who had acquired Brian as an eighteenth birthday present to herself, seems not to have objected to her wartime pet's revised identity.

When the mannequin of Bing was installed at the museum soon afterwards, a replica of Brian's DM was included in the re-launched display, along with a Normandy to the Baltic war record and heart-warming details of the war dog's return to Miss Fetch.

Unlike the dogs without owners denied medals fifty years earlier (of which Bing was one), it was more family-friendly perhaps that a reunion with a young woman at war's end, plus two gallantry awards should make for a suitably happy ending. So Brian had to become Bing — on active service, at least.

The real Bing, meanwhile, never won a medal and did not come home. His likely resting place is the small war-dog cemetery at Sennelager. That was not to be mentioned. Based on information doubtless perceived as accurate at the time, a charity-fundraising children's book about medal-winning 'Bing' from Loughborough's amazing true story was published in 2010, attracting considerable press attention.

Ken Bailey died in 1999 and on 6 June that year, 'his ashes were scattered on the spot in Normandy where he and the dog Brian landed on D-Day'. Betty Fetch died in October 2010, and Pte David Robinson in 2012. His ashes were scattered at Putot-en-Auge War Cemetery among parachute regiment war graves. Ron Penhall died in 2013. Airborne Forces Museum curator Steven Blackbourn died tragically young, aged thirty-seven, in March 2009.

The mannequin labelled 'Bing', featuring Brian's Dickin Medal, his WDTS number and Bing's service record, was reinstalled at the Airborne Assault Museum, IWM Duxford, in 2008, where it remains very popular with children and veterans — and indeed, everyone else.

Postscript

How did the mine-hunting dogs do it? The puzzle had never been solved. Other than being guards, war dogs had been briefly in but mostly out of favour through the travails of war — and had only just about come right in the mine-infested polders of Holland and the rubble of V2-blasted London. It was all in the nose. But how did it really work? Seventy years later, the question was still being asked and in military terms was more urgent than ever.

The first training document drafted for the post-war British Army War Dog School at Sennelager admitted that 'the nature of the faculty by which dogs can find mines cannot be stated — it is highly probable it is aided by some *mysterious sixth sense*.' In the new world of atom bombs[56] and rockets, that would not do. Secret research began. Because it drew on wartime experience

[56] Like the rest of the Army, the RAVC had to adjust to the prospect of atomic weapons on the battlefield. An early analysis concluded, 'There will be an enormous animal casualty list after an atomic explosion, the line between surviving and dying is so very narrow that training should aim to make actions instinctive.' Underground stables and kennels might be required. Meanwhile, planning for conventional war must continue. A bizarre General Staff plan in 1951 to introduce 'Dog Companies' into infantry regiments mustering 6,000 canines with a range of fighting skills, including infantry patrol and 'combat', came to nothing.

(and used veteran war dogs), it is both part of this story – and the link to the twenty-first-century comeback of the British war dog, hunting for 'Improvised Explosive Devices' in the heat and dust of Afghanistan.

Just as in the US, wartime contracts had been given to British electronics companies to find an answer to non-metallic mines. None had been successful – mine dogs had just about worked, and they might be useful again. But the one-man, one-dog rule was impractical and all that wartime recruiting of 'dog-lovers' to be handlers and embarrassing public appeals for family pets had sentimentalised the whole business. The Ministry of Supply concluded, 'dogs are temperamental and unreliable and cannot be used over battlefields strewn with distracting litter.' Indeed the results were little better than those of mystic human diviners who had 'helped find large unexploded bombs'. When Northaw-trained 'Peggy', veteran of No. 1 Platoon RE, died in January 1950, the *RAVC Journal* gave a fulsome tribute to the 'distinguished War Dog' who had spent the years since VE Day as a mine-dog demonstrator showing off her 'amazing technique' to astonished audiences and latterly her skill in finding deeply buried unexploded bombs – 'She was admired by all.'

But Peggy was exceptionally gifted. What was wanted was a mine dog that would function like a standardised piece of equipment. Better still would be a mechanical device – a 'dog-homologue working on physico-chemical principles', as it was described, which would be the subject of a doomed, decade-long British research effort.

To begin with, a certain Major R. Cawthorne (who had fielded Lt Davison's mine-dog reports from northwest Europe at the War Office as Scientific Adviser to the Army Council) was given the job of collating recent experience and establishing a technocratic way forward. He started in 1947 by testing the presumption that dogs *probably* detected landmines by smelling the explosive. Six trained mine dogs were chosen for an experiment; four had their olfactory nerves surgically cut. Five 'reject' VP guard dogs acted as controls, three subjected to surgery without having their nerves cut. According to the War Office records, two of them died during the procedure. If the smell hypothesis proved correct, the dogs surgically deprived of their senses would be unable to detect landmines. But under tests in Germany, in mocked-up minefields, they showed only a marginal decline in performance. Had the surgical procedure failed? This possibility was tested by exposing the animals to a substance (a compound in solution of aniseed, gresol, phenol and ammonia) known to cause an acute reaction.

Their non-reaction seemed to confirm they could not smell. That, and the fact they would not eat until food was actually put in their mouths. To make certain, Cawthorne introduced the same dogs to a bitch in season, only to find that mine dogs 'Tang', 'Jasper', 'Billy', 'Tech', 'Kein' and 'Bruce' (of ownership unknown — but presumably dogs' home strays), all of whom had been subjects of a trans-frontal brain operation, reacted normally.

It was still all a giant puzzle. The 1943 US work on buried object detection by radioactivity, seismic vibrations, ultra-high frequency waves, etc. was re-examined to see if it offered any clues. On the advice of the physiologist and Nobel-laureate, Professor E. D. Adrian, an 'electroencephalograph' was brought into the experiment. Even this clever device, for recording changes in the electrical activity of the brain, failed to determine that smell was the primary way that trained dogs could find mines. Nothing was proved. It could be that the mine sensing was by a different group from olfactory, or 'a complex group of senses', concluded Major Cawthorne. It was even suggested dogs somehow sensed mines through their paws.

In 1947 Cawthorne gave up, insisting the work required a 'physiological and psychiatric approach', something beyond his competence. A second opinion would be sought. It would come, on Prof Adrian's recommendation, from Prof Solly Zuckerman, animal behavioural expert, anatomist and government scientific adviser. During the war he had both studied the effects of landmine blast and been an architect of 'operational research' that sought to apply scientific method to military undertakings, most famously the area bombing of German cities (it was ineffective, he concluded). His very involvement showed how seriously Whitehall took the issue of mine dogs. It would take almost a decade to reach a conclusion.

Work began in 1949, funded by the Ministry of Supply, with the insistence by Zuckerman that the War Office abandon its 'tale' that 'dogs can be trained to detect mines'. There was much chuckling among those involved, who assumed the programme had its 'Secret' classification to avoid 'alarm and despondency at Cruft's'. They were happy, meanwhile, to take the ministry's 'bow-wow' money.

What was new was the insistence that human—dog empathy be entirely removed from the process. The dog must work consistently and predictably, and do so for anyone.

First, there was a re-run of the Aldershot field demonstrations of May 1944 with Battersea dogs 'Ron' and 'Nigger', trained on the meat reward principle. They were set to look for mines buried in the ground — explosive-filled, entirely empty, made of metal, plastic, wood, and glass (in fact, they were Pyrex 'casserole covers') working on a range constructed at the Army Veterinary and Remount Centre at Melton Mowbray (to where the WDTS relocated from Germany in 1948). All of the objects were detected equally readily but the success rate fell off sharply as the 'age of the minefield increased', so Zuckerman would write. 'Detection was definitely related to the extent of discernible disturbance of the ground, and we had to conclude [at this stage] that the mine itself did not contribute much to the ability of the dog to point correctly.'

Next, an obstacle course was devised with a run of four breeze-block wells closed on top by metal grids covered with hessian. Placing objects in the wells (there was no 'disturbed' soil), and letting the dogs snuffle round them should reveal whether or not dogs could respond to unseen stimuli alone.

And they did. The test dogs 'demonstrated a remarkable capacity to detect a variety of concealed objects, wooden and metal cubes, glass dishes and landmines.' Even a breeze block in a breeze-block well brought a response. Success rates diminished in proportion to the dwindling size of the hidden object. Zuckerman inferred it was smell, most likely a chemical detected by the dogs' olfactory senses.

The tests went on with all sorts of variables introduced — sound, fans to move the air, humidity, temperature, blindfolded dogs, even blindfolded handlers. A further series of experiments were designed to explore the smell hypothesis by assuming the deeper a mine was buried, the harder it would be to detect.

'The broad conclusion we drew from the results of these experiments was that up to a point dogs can detect chemical substances that are diffused in molecular state from any hidden object,' Zuckerman would write.

There was no sixth sense.

Many years later, when dogs were proposed as mine clearers after the 1982 Falklands War, Lord Zuckerman outlined in *The Times* the story of the wartime mine dogs and described the clinical postscript to his own team's field trials. 'We then moved on to an extensive series of laboratory experiments,' he wrote, (using animals from Battersea and Porton[57]), which 'showed that while all dogs are blessed with a large number of smell cells in their nose and have a sense of smell vastly superior to man's, they differ greatly in their individual smelling ability'.

'The general conclusion of all our work was that though trained dogs can locate mines in open grassland for a short period after planting, their performance rapidly deteriorates to a level which is of no operational value as the ground over the buried mine settles.'

Mine-hunting dogs were next to useless, he concluded. Their wartime 'success' had been an illusion. Proper statistical analysis had been rudimentary, Zuckerman suggested. Had false points been accounted for, the dogs' detection rate would have been 'little more than that expected from chance'.

As for the dogs, they of course would not perform as machines, 'indeed they proved consistently inconsistent, working successfully in one instance and not at all at another.' All that wartime anguish about suitable breeds, mongrel versus pedigree,

---

[57] Section 3(5) of the Dogs Act (1906) forbade the release of stray dogs for the 'purpose of vivisection'. The Cruelty to Animals Act (1876) forbade painful experiments on animals without licence. Zuckerman wrote to the Home Office Inspector in 1954 to alert him to 'secret work on mine dogs' that 'does not concern experiments under the [1876] Act because it is not calculated to cause pain'.

etc. was explained away by 'temperament'. It was further observed:

> Differences in ability seem to be correlated with differences in temperament. A placid dog is easier to train and handle and is more reliable. For this reason Labradors and their crosses are preferred, the cross-bred proving more amenable than the pedigree. 'Temperamental' dogs like Alsatians, terriers and spaniels are distractible and difficult to train.

Lord Zuckerman also revealed that as part of the government-sponsored work three decades before he had visited Dr Joseph B. Rhine's faculty of parapsychology at Duke University in North Carolina, the 'leading American authority on, and believer in extra-sensory perception (ESP)'. The Pentagon had contracted Dr Rhine to investigate ESP in homing pigeons, he recalled in his newspaper article. What he did not say was that his own British government-funded visit was part of the continuing UK mine-dog programme.[58]

Indeed Dr Rhine, already famous for his work on 'trailing' animals, pets that mysteriously turned up in remote locations,

---

[58] The US air attaché at the London Embassy asked for special security clearance. Prof Zuckerman at the time was under observation because of his apparent 'communist sympathising' scientist friends. MI5 had first taken interest in his acquisition of monkeys from the London Zoo for some mysterious purpose in 1940.

having somehow followed their families over hundreds of miles,[59] was working on a contract from the US Army Engineer Research and Development Laboratories at Fort Belvoir, instigators of the wartime M-Dog program, to explore whether dogs could find mines using extra-sensory perception. Some perfectly sensible people called it a dog's 'sixth sense'.

Dr Rhine designed his 1952 experiments around model 'environments', constructed on a Californian beach, north of San Francisco, with replica wooden Schu-mines covered at various times with sand and seawater. At first the subjects, German Shepherds 'Binnie' and 'Tessie', showed a high level of ability to detect mines. Rhine was convinced they were employing ESP. Then, for reasons unexplained, success rates fell off to a point below that expected by chance. The Army contract was terminated. The dogs had been trained, as he noted, writing seventeen years later when the experiments were declassified, by the 'older method of punishment with a steel trap, a method which happily has been abandoned'.

Professor Rhine's experiments had, however, admitted a degree of empathy between handler and animal, while the

59 Wartime American newspapers delighted in tales of soldiers overseas being trailed by their loyal dog. In 1944, a 'little black Cocker spaniel' named 'Joker' came to national fame, having travelled 6,000 miles from his Pittsburg, CA, home via Oakland docks to a South Pacific Island, where he successfully located his 'master', Captain Stanley C. Raye.

Dr Rhine was also in contact after the war with Dorothea St Hill Bourne, Secretary of the Mascot Club and PDSA publicist — who also acted as his researcher on British wartime psychic pets, especially those evacuated cats and dogs who had seemingly made incredible journeys homeward. Doing ESP work for Dr J. B. Rhine, she investigated a story that had appeared in US newspapers about a British naval officer who had been torpedoed, spent five days adrift in an open boat and was then picked up by a US Navy destroyer in the Atlantic. At home in London, his dog 'Jeepers Creepers' had stopped eating when his master was first endangered and started eating again the moment he was rescued.

new-wave British research sought to eliminate just that — along with the human—canine training that created a mine-dog 'team'. It was a moral concept. How could 'confidence' or 'trust' be quantifiable in scientific terms? One could not ask a man to wager his life against a Schu-mine on the 'love' of a dog.

But that is what had happened time and again in Holland and on the German frontier in 1944–5. On canal banks, on smashed-up railway lines, by demolished bridges, in the Reichswald Forest, mine dog, dog handler and Royal Engineer mine-lifters cleared a vast expanse of frozen, mine-infected landscape.

Lieutenant-Colonel Peter Norbury RE, who almost forty years earlier had been the youthful CO of No. 4 Platoon and had led them into action across the Rhine, would write in response to Lord Zuckerman's *Times* outburst: 'I worked with ten dogs which consistently found mines in varied terrain,' he said, 'and under all sorts of conditions. They did not miss mines either and I have two feet to prove it.'

He was convinced that 'although a sense of smell played a part, so too did other senses. And in particular, the animal's very highly developed *sixth sense*.'

A few British mine dogs were used in the Korean War on rear area minefields, and 'patrol' dogs were used in the British Army's wars of colonial disengagement in Malaya, Kenya and Cyprus. 'Sniffer' dogs were employed in Northern Ireland to find roadside culvert bombs and arms caches, and as prison guards.

In Vietnam the US Army used dogs to detect 'explosive artefacts and trip wires', and 'tunnel dogs trained to detect open and camouflaged holes and trip wires'. According to a USAF history: 'The need for tracker dogs to assist US combat units in maintaining contact with the Vietcong in jungle areas was recognized early in the war. We turned to the British for assistance in developing this tracker dog capability and received their support in training some 14 Army tracker dog teams in Malaysia, beginning in October 1966.' War dogs had been used in the often clandestine jungle warfare operations by British forces in the so-called 'Confrontation' with communist Indonesia. More than four thousand dogs were recruited for service through public donation in the Vietnam War, at the end of which, scandalously and tragically, they were designated as 'surplus military equipment', and only a few hundred made it home.

Explosive-detecting dogs meanwhile were becoming intellectually respectable again. Talk of 'ESP' had gone quiet. A report called 'Mine-Detecting Canines', published in 1977 by the US Army Mobility Equipment Research and Development Command, Fort Belvoir, concluded that, 'dogs are the most effective and versatile mine/booby-trap/explosives detection systems available for immediate use in either military or civilian applications.' This was an acknowledgement of the gigantic task now looming in those post-colonial, proxy battlefields in Africa and Asia, like Cambodia and Angola (and later, post-Cold War, in the Middle East and the Balkans), which would require decades of 'humanitarian demining' – as opposed to 'mine clearance' as part of combat operations at which the wartime US M-Dogs had so spectacularly failed.

The first attempts at using dogs had brought 'very mixed results'. 'Some organisations swore by them; others swore at them,' according to an authoritative report. It continued: 'There were claims of excellent performance, whereas with others, even in the same theatre of operations, dogs were deemed a failure. While there was good knowledge of how to breed and give basic training to dogs for explosive detection, there was less knowledge of how to achieve the right interaction between handlers and dog.'

A system called REST ('Remote Explosive Scent Tracing') had been developed meanwhile in South Africa, in which air and dust samples were hoovered up from suspected mine-infected areas and taken back to a central station for 'sniffing' by trained explosive-detecting dogs. It was used by the humanitarian Norwegian People's Aid organisation for demining in Angola and the Balkans before finding a more lucrative commercial home in airline security.

All this came at a time when the 'civilian' world of dog training was going through its own cultural revolution. Books like Karen Pryor's *Don't Shoot the Dog* (1985), in which 'positive reinforcement' was emphasised, became bestsellers — and new techniques, such as 'clicker' training, in which a sound acts as a reward for desired behaviours became highly popular, along with concepts such as 'operant conditioning', 'shaping' and 'relationship based training'. Most novel of all was 'dog-led training', in which the dog offers a desired behaviour before being rewarded. The new wave was based on animal behavioural science as much as timeworn experience. All this was mainly about 'pets' — could it apply to mine-detecting dogs too?

In 1999 the first global 'mine dog' conference was held with UN backing in Slovenia. It reportedly began in an 'initial atmosphere of suspicion and mistrust', as new-wave clickers and shapers came up against the old guard war-dog trainers.

Most of the early MDD programmes had been established by ex-military or police dog trainers, who had little understanding of landmines and none at all of how vapour sensing for explosives might actually work. Dogs missed mines with no clear explanation. Post-war Bosnia-Herzegovina especially had become a 'Klondike', as it was described, for commercial demining. It was a shambles. Strict efficiency tests were introduced. 'Demining organisations outshone each other in making excuses for the appalling results,' so it was reported, 'yet some managed to pass the test with most of their dogs. Nevertheless, the overall credibility of MDDs had been significantly affected.'

International standards for using canines in humanitarian demining were needed urgently. As they emerged then and ever since, the guidelines have strong echoes of those that came back from the polders of Holland in 1944–5 as 'Rover', 'Ricky' and co. sniffed their way through the Schu-mines. It was agreed:

> The fundamental task of the detector dog trainer is to teach the animal two lessons: First, the animal must learn an association between a target odour and some highly rewarding stimulus, and second, it must learn to give a specific response in order to gain access to that reward.

It was all good Herbert Lloyd stuff.[60]

[60] A major US commercial mine-dog training company outlined its basic technique: 'The normal incentives are "kongs" (a rubber ball on a short throwing rope), balls and rag-balls, used from the onset of search-response training. Small boxes with trigger mechanisms that contain odours of explosives are used to develop the link between the reward (toys) and the stimulus (odours). The dog searches among several small boxes on the ground, which contain different odours and various playthings (kong, ball, etc). When the correct box is identified by the dog, a ball, rag-ball or other plaything is ejected. The dog is released and goes after the plaything. Sometimes the plaything is given directly to the dog by the trainer. The trainer then starts to play fetching with the dog at a high intensity for a short period. On command or prompt the dog is taught to drop or sit-drop.'

It had been very similar at Northaw.

Dogs were at their best when 'delineating minefield boundaries, clearing roads and railways', according to the report of the United Nations Mine Action Service, and in 'the rapid sampling of cleared areas which can be done behind both manual and mechanical demining'. But it also noted:

> Mine dog detection has proved efficient and cost effective [however] the increased use of dogs has created new challenges since there are many contradictory views about mine dog detection capabilities.

It was that old problem. Could a mine dog really be trusted? Was it even a 'technology' at all? The search for a dog 'homologue', an artificial nose, abandoned by Britain four decades before, had been revived meanwhile in the US as a military priority. In 1998 the Pentagon's Defense Advanced Research Projects Agency's $25 million 'Dog's Nose Program' showed its first result, an MIT-developed electronic vapour sensor that could respond to tiny traces of airborne explosive molecules close to the ground. It was called 'Fido'.

'Fido doesn't have the computational power or the agility of a dog, but it has a similar sensitivity for certain things,' so its developer, Timothy Swager, said a few years after it was first revealed to the world (it works on a limited range of explosives), but the company that makes the hand-held device continues to promise 'canine-comparable performance with lower cost and higher reliability'.

Fido was an early stab at what would become a huge research effort. The question remained: could a dog's nose ever be truly replicated or bettered, both in humanitarian demining and in high-intensity warfare? The day of the mine dog appeared to be ending.

But it was not. What happened in the new wars of the twenty-first century was the resurrection of the 'Military Working Dog'. The 'Protection' dog was still useful, guarding bases and supplies, which required old-fashioned wariness of strangers and aggression. But it was the 'Specialist' dog that was really new, exquisitely optimised for a particular role with a level of training that would have made Herbert Lloyd gasp (although his methods were still at its heart). A US military working dog cost an estimated $80,000 to train and care for, it was stated in 2013. In 1939, Mr Lloyd was offering trained guard dogs to the War Office for '£12–15'.

The intervention in Afghanistan necessitated these new-wave war dogs, especially the use by the Taliban enemy of 'Improvised Explosive Devices', which, to begin with, made overland patrols from fortified encampments so hazardous. They would eventually claim the lives of over 220 British soldiers.

In response, the Pentagon pursued the $19 billion 'Joint Improvised Explosive Device Defeat Organization'. Its director would later admit that dogs were the best bomb detectors and Congress insisted on boosting the canine research budget. There was no ESP this time. After much controversy, the British Army also set up a task force to study the IED threat and develop new tactics and equipment, much of it secret. What was not secret was the continuing use of dogs – in several rôles – as 'Arms and Explosive Search' (AES) animals used to sweep for bomb factories and precursor chemicals, as 'Vehicle Search' dogs (a separate skill-set), and as dedicated mine and

IED hunters along contested routes and patrol areas[61]. It was all still about that astonishing nose.

In March 2010 the 1st Military Working Dog Regiment RAVC headquartered at Sennelager, Germany (site of the post-war WDTS), assumed command of five independent MWD squadrons to continue support for the Afghan operation with 284 soldiers and officers and 200 dogs. The training process for an Arms and Explosives Search dog was described:

Training dogs ('scent imprinting') is achieved through rewards. The scent for which a dog is being conditioned to search – an explosive such as TNT or PE4 – is placed in a cage with the dog's toy on top. The dog will run to the cage, and then be 'rewarded' by having a ball thrown. Soon the animal associates the smell from the cage with the reward. The 'game' is then made more complicated, with the cage placed in different places.

A dog indicates a 'find' by sitting. Further scents are easily introduced. The dog must also be prepared for the strangeness of Afghanistan and the noise and confusion of war. Rattles are used, along with recordings of loud bangs, noises made by other animals such as chickens and of children.

If a dog fails to measure up as 'gun steady', it is re-homed. The final proving stages are full-scale exercises with helicopters, aerial drones, mortar fire and explosions.

[61] As well as AES dogs, the British Army's Counter-IED Task Force in Afghanistan included Royal Engineers Search Teams (REST) and Royal Logistics Corps Ammunition Technical Officers (ATO). An RLC ATO has been described as the 'expert's expert', relying on 'hand detection with a mine probe, a two-inch paint brush, and a hand-held Vallon Minehound dual sensor detector, which combines a Ground Penetrating Radar and Metal Detector'.

A report from the ground by an RAVC dog handler was more revealing. 'If you're going to put a dog on a helicopter, he will need his hearing protected, so you need Mutt Muffs,' Cpl Richard Marshall told a military journal. 'There are Doggles for his eyes and boots in case you're walking over glass or anything like that. We have cooling jackets as well, if they get too hot, though we find they acclimatize as easily as we do.'

The mine dogs of 1944–5 had no such comforts but their handlers treated them with equal concern and respect. And instead of toys as rewards in training they got chunks of meat. There were more echoes of the wartime past, especially how the presence of dogs can generally lift morale among troops, if unofficially. A US Army veteran posed an online account of his time as an infantry platoon leader in East Zhari:

> We had dogs accompany us on many patrols. There was not a single incident where a dog found an IED. They were often too tired/over-heated by the time we walked a quarter mile to be of any use. The most effective way to find IEDs is just by being vigilant and knowing what to look for. That being said, I loved having the dog on patrol just because he boosted morale. He and his handler usually stuck by my side [and] rarely led the way.

But the casualty rate among MWDs shows they were much more than just passengers in the wars of the new century. They were as vulnerable as the dogs of 1st Army had been in the mountains of Tunisia. Before the final British Army pullout from Iraq, after eight years of conflict, 'Hero', a German Shepherd protection dog, was killed on patrol in August 2007. Labrador 'Max' was killed searching for weapons in Basra in February 2010. AES dog 'Benji' was killed while supporting a convoy in April 2010.

In Afghanistan, on 24 July 2008, Lance Corporal Ken Rowe RAVC attached to 2 Parachute Regiment and AES dog Golden Labrador 'Sasha', were both killed in a rocket attack while 'searching compounds for enemy weapons in the Sangin area'. Six years later, Sasha would be awarded a posthumous Dickin Medal.

German Shepherd Protection Dog 'Oz' was killed at Musa Qala in September 2008. Malinois 'Ric', so it was reported, 'died as a result of enemy fire' in Helmand in August 2013 on operations involving special forces. In January the same year a Labrador called 'Scout' was killed in an IED explosion. A year earlier, 'Fire' was badly injured by an IED and flown back to Britain for treatment. In July 2012, MWD 'Bull', a Labrador, died of injuries, having jumped into an irrigation ditch in Helmand, where he was hit by a water turbine. Springer Spaniel cross 'Theo' suffered a fatal seizure when his handler, Lance Corporal Liam Tasker, twenty-six, was shot dead in March 2011.

But the battlefield was not the most dangerous place for a war dog: the number being put down rose with the numbers engaged on operations – from 20 in 2002, the first full year of the Afghan conflict, to 125 in 2009. The danger intensified when it was getting near time for a dog to quit the stage after around eight years of service. While a veteran AES dog will 'usually go on to live with its handler's family', as the MoD explained, Protection Dogs, trained to be aggressive, have 'behavioural issues which make them less likely to make good pets'. Although they were given 'training to calm their temperament and find them a new home, [this] did not always work out'.

They were in the same perilous boat as the 'Class A' dogs of 1945.

One Afghan war dog rehomed in spectacular circumstances was an MWD (original name unknown), captured by the Taliban in December 2013 after a British special forces mission went wrong, a Royal Engineer captain was killed in action and some exotic weaponry embarrassingly captured. The dog, now renamed 'DaGarwal', the Pashto for 'Colonel', was shown in a video posted online, showing the nervous-looking, but keen-to-please Malinois wearing a 'K9 Storm Intruder' combat jacket.[62] A Taliban spokesman soon said that Colonel was being kept 'in a safe place' and 'was in good health — he is not like the local dogs which will eat anything and sleep anywhere'. DaGarwal was living on 'chicken and beef kebabs', his captors claimed. He was the first British war dog captured in battle since 'Mac' and Major J. F. H. Hudson disappeared on Djebel Tanngoucha in Tunisia, in April 1943.

The incident led to calls for both a full-scale rescue mission and for the award of a Dickin Medal, a move described as 'worthy of consideration' by the PDSA. But to receive a medal, 'Colonel' would have to be nominated formally by his regiment or the Royal Army Veterinary Corps, it was pointed out. The Ministry of Defence refused to comment — because the PoW dog incident involved special forces. Meanwhile the shadow of SAS hero 'Rob', of Italian mountain patrol fame, hovered over the affair.

---

[62] A Canadian-developed device fitted with a GPS tracker, a torch and infrared camera and transmitter to beam back digital images as the dog searches a building. US Navy SEAL super-dog, Belgian Malinois 'Cairo', wore one in the raid on the Abbottabad, Pakistan, compound of founder and head of the Islamist militant group al-Qaeda Osama bin Laden in May 2011.

But there would be a whole clutch of medals for 'hero' dogs, which tapped a deep well of public sentiment — at a time when the Afghanistan mission overall was becoming a matter of increasing public indifference, if not hostility. In 2007, 'Sadie', a nine-year-old black Labrador, a veteran of Bosnia and Iraq, discovered a secondary explosive device amid the bloody wreckage of a suicide blast outside the UN headquarters in Kabul. Sadie received the DM at a ceremony at the Imperial War Museum in London and she retired thereafter to live with her handler, L/Cpl Karen Yardley, RAVC.

In 2010 'Treo', another eight-year-old Labrador, a veteran of Northern Ireland and VIP security (bomb-sniffer-in-chief to former British Prime Minister Tony Blair), received the award from Princess Alexandra. He had turned up two 'daisy chain' bombs, multiple explosives wired together, in Sangin Province, Afghanistan. His handler, Sgt Dave Heyhoe, RAVC, left the Army at the same time as Treo was retired and the father of three was able to take on his wartime comrade as a family pet. It was happy timing and a deservedly bestselling book resulted.

But detraining an AES dog could not put back the inner puppy entirely. It was reported: 'Each morning, Treo searches every room in the house for non-existent explosives and it's the same if he is ever visiting another property.' Some war dog returnees of 1945–6 had been observed to crouch down low every time a diesel engine rumbled close by.

Not to be outdone by its charity rival, in 2013 the RSPCA announced its 'Animal Hero' awards, with a public service category open to military animals, in effect a revival of its For Valour medallion of 1945. A year later, the obligatory hero dog who had 'saved countless lives' was 'Hertz', a German Short-haired Pointer, a former narcotics-sniffer, who with his RAF handler had detected multiple banned mobile phones and MP3 players secreted in the clothing of Afghan civilian workers at the Camp Bastion base.

The twenty-first-century medal-winning dogs were military animals, on the 'ration strength', as the old definition had it. That was why they were eligible for awards. They were not adopted strays, mascots or civil demining dogs but sophisticated, war-fighting assets. But it was the relationship with their handlers, and not their military role, that fitted the many populist narratives that appeared at the time – of animals being 'faithful unto death' and 'heart-warming stories of canine devotion'. In fact, in direct contrast, commercial companies supplying the US Army with Contract Working Dogs (CWDs) for use in war zones were using new-wave training techniques such as 'shaping' that sought to overturn the one-man, one-dog tradition that had so informed the British wartime experience.

It was an uphill struggle. The language being used around war dogs in their new incarnation tipped over the edge. The famous anonymous epigraph: 'He is your friend, your partner, your defender, your dog. You are his life, his love, his leader. He will be yours, faithful and true, to the last beat of his heart', began to be widely quoted in the context of military canines. Variations were inscribed on the many lovingly wrought memorials that bloomed across America to military and police K9s in the years after 9/11.

And in his splendid account of 'Treo', Sergeant Heyhoe vows at the outset of their deployment to Afghanistan (man and dog already know each other – they had worked together before in Ulster) – to protect 'my best buddy, my dog, with my very life if I have to'. But he does confess in his moving account that 'with some K9 teams the love between handler and hound becomes so strong the dog actually stops working properly'.

That was the dilemma that the RE Dog Platoons had recognised seven decades earlier. Could you really trust a dog against a Schu-mine? And if you loved the animal too much, would not the dog just 'pretend' to work to please you (or get that meat reward)? The professionals tried as they might to take 'love' out of it — and were trying still.

In 2004, the American Kennel Club presented its first 'Heroic Military Working Dog Award' to 'Frenke', a German Shepherd veteran of Afghanistan and Iraq. In 2011, the American Humane Association inaugurated its first annual American Hero Dog Awards, for civil and military canines who had shown 'unconditional love, devotion and intuition'. Explosive detection dogs 'Gabe' and 'Carlos' were winners, along with the US Army Military Police narcotics search dog 'Bino'.

It turned political. After much impassioned lobbying, in January 2013 President Obama signed into law legislation which made provisions for transporting retired veteran war dogs back to adoptive homes in America and for ongoing veterinary care — but did not meet the full ambitions of the Congressional sponsors of the 'Canine Members of the Armed Forces Act', that military working dogs should be reclassified as 'members of the armed forces' rather than being considered 'equipment'. It did, however, 'direct the Defense Secretary to create a decoration or other appropriate recognition to recognize such dogs that are killed in action or perform an exceptionally meritorious or courageous act during their service.'

Non-military dogs do not get medals. 'Major', for example, a black Labrador demining dog who began life as a family pet in

Wigan and was taken on by a commercial working-dog training company, the long-established 'Karenswood Dog Academy' of Birmingham. Described as 'a friendly, well-bred dog with a tremendous sense of fun', Major (full name 'Major Kipper-Ridge') held the record for the number of mines detected in Somalia — he was responsible for detecting sixty-seven Pakistani-made[63] P4 plastic A/P mines, notoriously difficult to make safe. He also located more than one hundred items of unexploded ordnance, and seventeen anti-tank mines. In 2006, clever Major detected fifty-three cluster bombs during an emergency tour in Lebanon.

He was adopted by a UN deminer, Mr John Dingley, who took him now in retirement, as a companion animal to his next assignment in Laos, where Major fathered five sons and six daughters in a mid-life encounter with a much younger Southeast Asian bride. Eventually, his knees and hips weakened (by osteoarthritis, which affects so many war dogs) after years of toil in the minefields of Somalia and Lebanon, and Major was humanely put down in 2012, aged fourteen.

I suspect Lieutenants Davison, Norbury and Pritchard would have found room for Major in their platoon. Texas and Rover would have surely made him welcome. Someone might even have recommended him for a medal.

---

[63] Pakistan, along with the United States, Russia, China, Myanmar, North Korea, United Arab Emirates, Cuba, Egypt, India, Israel and Iran, among others, is a non-signatory of the 1997 Ottawa A/P Mine Ban Treaty banning production, development, stockpiling and transfer. Britain was one of the first signatories and before her death, Diana, Princess of Wales, its most famous champion.

Acknowledgements

The authors are indebted to the archivists, librarians and concerned individuals who kindly helped us to discover so much hidden information on wartime dogs and the War-Dog Training School in particular. Thank you especially to Veronica Morrison of the Royal Society for the Prevention of Cruelty to Animals, Clare Boulton, librarian of the RCVS, Jean Rosen of the IWM Department of Documents, Simon Manton-Milne, IWM Department of Film, Jon Baker of the Airborne Assault Museum, Duxford, Ciara Farrell, librarian of the Kennel Club, Becks Skinner of the Army Medical Services Museum, Keogh Barracks, Aldershot, and Ada van Hoof of the Dijk-En Oorlogs-museum, Polderhuis, Westkapelle, Walcheren, Holland.

We are additionally grateful to Mrs Joyce Lloyd Carey for sharing childhood memories of her father Herbert Summers Lloyd, Maj-Gen Sir Peter Downward for giving us his personal insight into the dogs of 13th Parachute Battalion in 1944–5 and to Heather Bayne, for sharing original War Office correspondence about War Dog Rob which disproved revisionist versions of events.

We are grateful to the publishers of *The Dog World* and *Our Dogs* for permission to quote from wartime issues of their fine publications. The *Manchester Guardian* newspaper is quoted by permission of the Guardian Media Group, the extracts from the published works of Lionel Montague and Arthur W. Moss appear by permission of the Random House Group. Extracts from Crown Copyright documents in the National Archives at Kew and Army Medical Services Museum Veterinary Archive appear by permission of the Controller of HM Stationery Office. We are grateful to the Trustees of the Imperial War Museum and the individual copyright holders for granting access to the collections of private papers held by the IWM — especially Mr Timothy Hunt. Copyright in the extracts from the WW2 People's War online archive of wartime memories contributed by members of the public belongs to the contributors as credited, licensed to the BBC. The archive can be found at www.bbc.co.uk/ ww2peopleswar.

Every effort has been made to trace the copyright holders of further unpublished documents and published works in print or electronic form from which quotations have been made.

We would also like to thank our publisher, James Gurbutt, and agent Felicity Blunt for getting behind this book so enthusiastically from the start, Emma Herdman at Curtis Brown for her continual support, as well as editors Jane Donovan and Clive Hebard for their intelligent and insightful comments.

Finally, we would like to thank our daughters, Maria and Katy, and son Joseph, for their patience with our canine obsession, but who meanwhile seem to have inherited their parents' passion for pets.

Bibliography

Bourne, Dorothea Saint Hill, *They Also Serve (On Animal Mascots in the Allied Forces)* (Winchester Publications, London, 1947).

Clabby, J., *The History of the Royal Army Veterinary Corps, 1919– 1961* (Allen, 1964).

Cooper, Jilly, *Animals in War* (Corgi, London, 1984).

Cummins, Bryan D., *Colonel Richardson's Airedales: The Making of the British War Dog School, 1900– 1918* (Detselig Enterprises, Calgary, 2003).

Dickin, Maria Elisabeth, *The Cry of the Animal* (PDSA, London, 1950).

Douglas, Nina Mary Benita, Duchess of Hamilton and Brandon, *The Chronicles of Ferne* (The Animal Defence Society, London, 1951).

Downey, Fairfax, *Dogs for Defense: American Dogs in the Second World War 1941– 1945* (Trustees of Dogs for Defense Inc., New York, 1955) http://tera-3.ul.cs.cmu.edu/NASD

Downward, Peter, *Old Yourself, One Day: Personal Memoirs* (privately published, 2008).

Edwards, Thomas, *Regimental Mascots and Pets* (Hutchinson, London, 1940).

Home Office (ARP Dept.), *Air Raid Precautions Handbook No. 12* 'Air Raid Precautions for Animals' (HMSO, London, 1939).

Hughes, Jimmy Quentin MC, *Who Cares Who Wins* (Charico Press, Liverpool, 1998).

Le Chêne, Evelyn, *Silent Heroes: The Bravery and Devotion of Animals in War* (Souvenir Press, London, 1995).

Lemish, Michael G., *War Dogs: Canines in Combat* (Brassey's Washington, London, 1996).

Lind-af-Hageby, Louise, *Bombed Animals-Rescued Animals-Animals Saved From Destruction* (Animal Defence & Anti-Vivisection Society, London, 1941).

Lloyd, Herbert Summers, *The Dog in War* in *The Book of the Dog* ed. B. Vesey-Fitzgerald (Nicholson & Watson, London, 1948).

——, *The Popular Cocker Spaniel* (4th edn.) (Popular Dogs Publishing Co., London, 1939).

Montague, Frederick, *Let the Good Work Go On (On the Work of the People's Dispensary for Sick Animals of the Poor)* (Hutchinson, London, 1947).

Moss, Arthur W., *Animals Were There: A Record of the Work of the RSPCA* (Hutchinson, London, 1947).

Richardson, Edwin H., *British War Dogs, Their Training and Psychology* (Skeffington, London, 1920).

——, *Fifty Years with Dogs* (Hutchinson, London, 1950).

US Army Medical Department Office of Medical History, Chapter XVII *Army Dogs* http://history.amedd.army.mil/booksdocs/wwii/vetservicewwii/chapter17.htm

US War Department, *War dogs—Technical manual TM 10-396* (Washington, 1943) http://www.easypetmd.com/tm-10-396

Waller, Anna M., *Dogs and National Defense* (Department of the Army, Washington DC, 1955) http://www.qmmuseum.lee.army.mil/dogs_and_national_defense.htm

Journals: *After the Battle*, *The Animals Defender*, *Animal World*, *Der Hund*, *Die Hundewelt*, *The Dogs Bulletin*, *The Dog World*, *The Field*, *Horse &* *Hound*, *The Journal of the Parachute Regiment*, *The Journal of the RAVC*, *The Journal of Veterinary History*, *Our Dogs*, *Pegasus*, *PDSA News*, *The Tatler*, *The Tail-Wagger Magazine*, *The Veterinary Journal*.

War Diaries of battalions, regiments, brigades, divisions, etc. are in the National Archives. The War Diary of the Directorate Army Veterinary & Remount Services (a vital source) is in Box 14, Veterinary Archives, the Army Medical Services Museum, Keogh Barracks, Aldershot, as are The Captain James Rankin Davison papers, including reports of No. 2 Dog Platoon sent to Northaw, the reports from Washington DC of US M-Dog experiments, and secret correspondence regarding the acquisition of mine dogs. Mr H. M. 'Monty' Hunt's four-volume scrapbook, 'The War Dog Training School', is in the Imperial War Museum (henceforth IWM Hunt WDTS), with further unbound material in the Army Medical Services Museum Veterinary Archives (AMSMVA).

Source Notes

p. xxi 'DOG TO JOIN SERVICES ...' *Ruislip Advertiser and Gazette*, 12 May 1944, cutting in AMSMVA.

p. xxi 'SNIFFER DOGS LEAD ...' *Daily Telegraph*, 20 January 2011.

p. xxi 'BRAVE ARMY DOG ...' BBC News, 30 April 2014.

PART ONE: 'SIT!'

p. 1 'In their great struggle ...' H. S. Lloyd, *The Book of the Dog*, p. 190.

Chapter 1: Dogs in the Service of the State

pp. 3–11 The story of police dogs 'Smut' and 'Nigger', plus Herbert Lloyd's correspondence with the Home Office and Metropolitan Police on the eve of war are in TNA MEPO 2/6208.

pp. 6–8 Press reports from Washwater are from *The Times*, 15 January and 20 May 1938.

p. 11 Home Office advice to pet owners in the event of war is in TNA HO 186/1418 and TNA MEPO 2/6478.

Chapter 2: A Splendid Collection of Dogs

pp. 15—19 Quotes from Col Richardson are from *British War Dogs* (1920) and latterly from *My Fifty Years with Dogs* (1950). The Colonel's 1939—40 correspondence with the War Office is in TNA WO 199/416.

Chapter 3: The 101 Alsatians

pp. 21—8 Early wartime experiments with dogs for the Army are in TNA WO 199/416 'Employment of Dogs with Guards at Vulnerable Points' and TNA WO 199/2061 'War Dog Section, formation in Southern Command'.

p. 21 'told to enlist as Police ...' *The Dog World*, 3 May 1940, p. 414.

p. 22 'It is a peculiarity ...' *Gloucestershire Echo*, 12 January 1944, p. 5.

p. 23 'snuffling sound ...' *Dundee Courier*, 6 February 1940, p. 5.

pp. 23—4 'Dogs — usually Alsatians ...' *Aberdeen Journal*, 18 December 1939.

p. 24 'Their method was ...' Lloyd, op. cit., p. 186.

pp. 24—5 'The officers of this regiment ...' *Horse & Hound*, 1 December 1939.

p. 25 'foxhounds for British officers ...' ibid., 12 January 1940.

p. 25 'Secretary of State for War ...' Hansard, 9 October 1939.

p. 26 'Dogs' homes could provide ...' TNA WO 199/416.

pp. 26—7 'saboteur tendency ...' 'Vulnerable Points' retrospective summary referring to 1939 in TNA CAB 112/26.

p. 27 'I believe you will find ...' Lloyd to Cox, 27 October 1939, TNA WO 199/416.

p. 28 'The dog supplied ...' ibid.

Chapter 4: 'Army Dog No. 1'

pp. 32–7 The formation of the first War Dog section is in TNA WO 199/2061. Vulnerable Points and the suitability of dogs as guards is in TNA WO 199/416.

p. 34 'Army Dog No. 1 ...' Letter to Mr W. Adams (ex WDTS) from Lt-Col John Clifford CO No. 1 ADTU RAVC Sennelager, 5 July 1982 in AMSMVA.

Chapter 5: The Dismal Jimmies

pp. 39–44 The story of the fledgling War Dog Section continues in WO 199/2061. High-level political concern over Vulnerable Points is in TNA CAB 112/1 and CAB 112/26. Suitability of dogs as VP guards is in TNA WO 199/416.

PART TWO: 'SEEK!'

p. 45 'Nothing will teach ...' TNA WO 163/183.

Chapter 6: 'The War Office invites dog owners ...'

pp. 47–9 The adventures of freelance war dogs in the Western Desert are movingly recorded in Montague, *Let the Good Work Go On*, pp. 77–81 and St Hill Bourne, *They Also Serve*, pp. 58–72.

pp. 50–4 Herbert Lloyd's account of the War Dog public appeal is in *The Book of the Dog*, p. 183. His recruiting trip to Leeds is recorded in *The Yorkshire Post*, 30 April 1941 and *PDSA News*, August 1941, p. 5 and also in a letter to *The Tail-Wagger*, May 1941, p. 99.

pp. 54–60 The 1941 battle between War Office doubters and dog advocates is recorded in TNA WO 199/2061. Lt-Col J. Y. Baldwin's early efforts to establish a Guard Dog Training School are recorded in TNA AVIA 9/15 and TNA WO 199/2061.

p. 58 'Canine Warriors ...' http://www.britishpathe.com/video/canine-warriors

p. 58 'Pets Train for War ...' *Illustrated*, 22 November 1941.

p. 58 ' "doggy" people ...' *The Times*, 6 November 1941.

Chapter 7: '... To lend your dog to the Army'

p. 63 'In May 1942 ...' DAV&RS War Diary, AMSMVA Box 14.

p. 63 Huskies for winter warfare is in DAV&RS War Diary, 23 April; 4, 13 July 1942.

p. 64 'present Training School ...' DAV&RS WD, 19 January 1942.

p. 64 'gone off the rails. ...' DAV&RS WD, 30 January 1942.

p. 65 'l was much exercised ...' Brigadier C. A. Murray, *Animal World*, August 1944, p. 60.

p. 66 'condemned meat roll ...' DAV& RS WD, 1 April 1942.

p. 66 'ensure a regular ...' DAV&RS WD, 9 February 1942.

pp. 67–8 'tattooing the ear flap ...' 5 March 1942, TNA WO 199/416.

p. 68 'The owner is also ...' *Animal World*, August 1944, p. 60.

p. 68 'If [civilian-loaned dogs] ...' 16 March 1942, TNA WO 32/10800.

p. 69 'they were the property ...' DAV&RS WD, 3 July 1942.

p. 69 'gradual infiltration ...' DAV&RS WD, 29 April 1942.

p. 69 'Government Appeal ...' See, for example, *Western Daily Press*, 5 May 1942, p. 5.

p. 70 'Well, pals ...' 'The War and Us Dogs by Rex', *The Tail-Wagger Magazine*, September 1944, p. 175.

p. 70 'I do not have much time ...' 19 June 1945, TNA WO 32/10800.

p. 71 'she could not wait ...' TNA WO 32/10800.

p. 71 'chasing cats ...' *Bath Chronicle*, 2 October 1943, p. 5.

p. 72 'A Bull terrier was ...' *Evening Telegraph*, 15 May 1942, p. 4.

p. 73 'I had been a kennel man ...' Pte David Cooke, IWM Hunt WDTS, vol. 3, p. 139.

Chapter 8: Disciplined Pets

p. 75 'The team of eight dogs ...' 16 April 1942, TNA AVIA 9/15.

p. 75 'The dogs of Britain ...!' *The Dog World*, 22 May 1942, p. 313.

p. 76 'armed and fully ...' From Dir of Military Training, 29 June 1942, TNA WO 199/416.

p. 76 'with message and patrol ...' Monty Hunt 'My Memories of the War Dogs Training School', AMSMVA Box 14.

p. 77 'placed in kennels ...' Sgt Dennis Hipgrave, RAVC in Hunt pps. AMSMVA Box 14.

p. 77 'Rex' ... 'Adolfs' ...' AFMC Records, IWM.

pp. 77–8 'Each dog was given ...' IWM Hunt WDTS, vol. 1, p. 44.

p. 78 'Entrants are then ...' 'A War Dogs' Training School' by Capt D. C. E. Danby, RAVC, *RAVC Journal*, vol. 15, pp. 42–4.

p. 79 'I moved into camp ...' Private D. M. Pilkington, IWM WDTS, vol. 2, p. 132.

p. 79 'My first location ...' Gay Agocs, IWM WDTS, vol. 3, p. 194.

p. 80 'Every building had ...' Kay Manning, IWM WDTS, vol. 3, p. 179.

p. 81 'Some dogs were ...' Pilkington, IWM Hunt WDTS, vol. 2, p. 132.

p. 82 'It may be reckoned ...' Brig-Gen Murray, 'War Dogs', *The Animal World*, September 1944, p. 67.

p. 82 'house dogs rather ...' ibid., p. 69.

p. 84 'It must be understood ...' Lloyd, *The Popular Cocker Spaniel* (4th edn.), p. 54.

p. 84 'L/Cpl Plumridge had to learn ...' IWM Hunt WDTS, vol. 4, p. 217.

p. 85 'the dog immediately ...' Lloyd, op. cit., p. 187.

pp. 85–6 '"Reveille" is either ...' Danby, op. cit.

p. 86 'entirely by kindness ...' Murray, *The Animal World*, September 1944, p. 68.

p. 87 'Any dog debarred ...' 9 July 1942, TNA WO 199/416.

p. 87 'Green vegetables will be ...' 18 July 1942, TNA WO 199/2537.

p. 87 'subsist on the cookhouse …' 18 July 1942, TNA WO 199/2537.

p. 89 'It was like raising a regiment' … *The Animal World*, December 1942, p. 91.

p. 89 'A patrol dog [will be] …' *Morpeth Herald*, 31 July 1942, p. 4.

pp. 89–90 'All men on the short VP …' TNA AIR 2/8734.

Chapter 9: Don't Make Friends with these Dogs

p. 91 'The Tactical Employment of War Dogs …' TNA WO 199/416.

pp. 93–4 The story of the Falkland beagles is in TNA WO 176/60 'Falkland Islands: Headquarters Force 122 May–Dec 1942' and in DAV&RS WD entries for the period.

p. 94 'We can no longer …' TNA MAF 84/57, 2 December 1942.

p. 94 'rationed foodstuffs …' DAV&RS WD, 24 August 1942.

p. 95 'any pure-bred dog of either sex …' Downey, *Dogs for Defense*, p. 25.

p. 96 '*War Dogs*' https://archive.org/details/war_dogs

p. 96 'roving patrol and messenger …' Waller, *Dogs and National Defense*, p. 6.

p. 96 'Throughout the learning …' https://archive.org/stream/1943-01IntelligenceBulletinVol01No05#page/n73/mode/2up/search/dogs

p. 97 'The few animals that were …' Waller, op. cit., p. 24.

Chapter 10: Dogs of the Desert

pp. 99–100 'Frightened by the noise …' *Derby Daily Telegraph*, 30 November 1942, p. 4.

p. 100 'horrified to see …' *Evening Telegraph*, 4 September 1945, p. 2.

p. 100 ' "Benghazi", "Boozer" …' AFMC records, IWM.

p. 101 'attractive Dachshund …' St Hill Bourne, op. cit., p. 72.

p. 101 'Shoofty …' *The Tail-Wagger Magazine*, December 1945, p. 204.

p. 102 'a tiny terrier …' *The Tail-Wagger Magazine*, April 1944, p. 73.

p. 102 'One soldier who …' Montague, op. cit., p. 81.

p. 102 'No mascots are so popular ...' *The Tail-Wagger Magazine*, July 1945, p. 129.

p. 103 'the duty of all war dogs ...' Hunt, pps. AMSMVA Box 14.

p. 103 'Large dogs should be fed ...' Hunt, pps. AMSMVA Box 14.

pp. 103–4 'HEEL Dog to walk ...' Hunt, pps. AMSMVA Box 14.

p. 104 'Brushes, Dandy, small ...' WO Memorandum for Home Commands, Canadian Command and 1st Army HQ, 13 November 1942, TNA WO 199/2537.

Chapter 11: Tiger Country

pp. 106–117 The fates of the 78 Division animals, 'Gyp', 'Bob', 'Mac', etc., are listed in 'Summary of War Dogs supplied to the Division, HQ Allied Armies Italy – Q2 Branch – Military Police Dog Units Organisation', 31 January 1944, TNA WO 204/7732.

p. 112 'War dogs attached to ...' 'War Dogs on Patrol with 6th West Kents; War Dogs In Action', IWM film archive 'dope sheet' AYY 290/1.

p. 116 'A Vickers machine gun ...' 'The Battle of the Oued Zarga-Medjez El Bab Road'. IWM film archive 'dope sheet' AYY 390/4/2. See also 2 Lancashire Fusiliers War Diary, 16 April 1943, TNA WO 175/512.

p. 117 'although the Germans ...' Clabby, *The History of the Royal Army Veterinary Corps, 1919–1961*, p. 68.

Chapter 12: What about 'Scruff'?

pp. 121–2 'E Company, 4 Battalion ...' Clabby, op. cit., p. 97.

pp. 122–3 'Brigadier waiting ...' *Daily Telegraph*, 26 April 1943, p. 5.

p. 123 'Preliminary reports ...' Waller, op. cit., p. 24.

pp. 123–4 'Patrol dogs were used ...' Lloyd, op. cit., p. 185.

p. 124 'We were sent a message dog ...' Miskin, Arthur Henry, IWM sound archive 29484, reel 7.

p. 124 'Thinking it was just another ...' Moss, *Animals Were There*, p. 124.

Chapter 13: 'Cowardly, Noisy and Useless'

p. 125 'with Infantry battalions ...' Capt Ashley Bramall for GS, 11 February 1943, TNA WO 199/416.

p. 125 'army dog training centre ...' *The Tatler*, 7 April 1943, p. 14.

p. 126 'Dogs are not satisfactory ...' 18 March 1943, C-in-C Home Forces to Under Secretary of State War Office, TNA WO 199/416.

pp. 126—7 'photographs from Tunisia ...' *Manchester Guardian*, 3 June 1943, p. 3.

p. 127 'an army message dog in action ...' IWM film archive, A471.

p. 128 'in respect of future ...' DAV&RS War Diary, 3 June 1943.

p. 129 'cowardly, noisy and useless ...' ibid.

p. 130 'attacked an enemy machine gun ...' Waller, op. cit., p. 40 and Lemish, *War Dogs: Canines in Combat*, p. 75.

p. 131 'The British press ...' See, for example, *Derby Daily Telegraph*, 15 January 1944, p. 5.

p. 131 'Order of the Golden Kite ...' TNA WO 208/1337.

p. 132 'pilfering proclivities ...' Clabby, op. cit., p. 54.

p. 132 For RAF police dogs in Middle East, see TNA AIR 63/6002.

p. 133 '1lb meat and 2lb cornmeal ...' DAV&RS WD, 5 January 1943.

p. 133 'loan dog escaped ...' DAV&RS WD, 5 May 1943.

p. 134 'Captain Garle arrived ...' DAV&RS WD, 6 January 1943 and Waller, op. cit., p. 24.

p. 134 'Success in field trials ...' US Army TM 10-396 *War Dogs Technical Manual*, Section II para 10 (d) http://www.easypetmd.com/tm-10-396-chapter-1-section-ii-history-military-use-dog

p. 135 'North Africa reports ... ' Paper BZ GS policy Committee on Weapons and Equipment: Employment and Training of Dogs for War Purposes WO 163/183; see also TNA WO 32/10504.

pp. 136—7 'Khaki Mongrels ...' *The Tail-Wagger Magazine*, May 1941, p. 100.

p. 138 '10,000 killer dogs ...' *Daily Sketch*, 24 April 1943 (cutting in TNA MAF 35/495).

p. 139 'not having ...' T. J. Edwards, *Mascots and Pets of the Services* (2nd edn.), p. xvi.

p. 140 'bronzed and tired-looking soldiers ...' St Hill Bourne, op. cit., pp. 75–6.

p. 140 ' "Abdul" and "Steve" ...' St Hill Bourne, op. cit., p. 66.

p. 141 'There is no doubt ...' TNA MAF 84/61.

PART THREE: 'FIND!'

Chapter 14: Beyond a Dog's Instinct

p. 143 'Patience and ...' Lt J. R. Davison, *History of No. 2 Dog Platoon*, RSPCA Archives.

p. 145 'used to belong to ...' *The Times*, 6 November 1941.

p. 145 'BBC receiving station ...' Lloyd, op. cit., p. 188.

p. 146 'became uninhabitable with the smell ....' http://services.english-heritage.org.uk/ResearchReportsPdfs/110_2010

pp. 148–9 'The first task is to find ...' quoted in *The Milwaukee Journal*, 27 March 1943, http://news.google.com/newspapers?nid=1499&dat=19430327

p. 150 'The accepted manner ...' 'Brian', 29 June 2003, BBC WW2 People's War, http://www.bbc.co.uk/history/ww2peopleswar/stories/27/a1092827.shtml

p. 152 'fed in his kennel ...' 'Mine Detection Dogs' anon. (probably Lloyd), 11 August 1944, TNA AVIA 22/871. See also Robert G. W. Kirk *'In Dogs We Trust, Intersubjectivity, Response-Able Relations, and the Making of Mine Detector Dogs' Journal of the History of the Behavioural Sciences*, January 2014. http://www.ncbi.nlm.nih.gov/pmc/articles/PMC3908362/#fn11

p. 154 'intelligent appreciation ...' Davison, op. cit., p. 4.

p. 154 'noises off – such as Bren guns ...' Lloyd, op. cit., p. 188.

p. 154 'Several solutions ...' ibid.

Chapter 15: No Owner But the State

p. 157 Anglo-US communications on mine dogs are in 'Reports and Correspondence between UK and USA on Training and Trials of Use of Dogs as Mine Detectors 1943–44', AMSMVA, Box 14.

p. 157 US non-metallic mine detection research is outlined in US Army Corps of Engineers Report obtained by the Ministry of Supply in 1946, enclosure in TNA AVIA 22/3312.

p. 158 'bites of venomous snakes ...' US Army Medical Department Office of Medical History, Chapter XVII Army Dogs, p. 627 http://history.amedd.army.mil/booksdocs/wwii/vetservicewwii/chapter17.htm

p. 159 'The dog's world differs ...' US War Department: War dogs—Technical Manual TM 10-396, Washington, 1943.

p. 159 'trapping in reverse ...' 'Report on M-Dogs, California', 12 June 1944, AMSMVA Box 14.

p. 161 'detect and dig out ...' TNA WO 208/1337.

p. 161 'whilst most people ...' Kelly to King, 14 June 1943, AMSMVA Box 14.

p. 161 'If it becomes known ...' ibid.

p. 162 'dangerous dog ...' *Nottingham Evening Post*, 22 September 1943.

p. 163 'ferocious ...' *Ruislip Advertiser and Gazette*, 12 May 1944.

p. 163 'Juno ...' Letter from Clifford to Adams, 5 July 1982, AMSMVA.

pp. 164–5 '9 patrol dogs ...' Lloyd to Commandant WDTS, 18 August 1944, AMSMVA Box 24, chemical weapons.

p. 165 'little encouragement ...' BAS Washington to WO London, 15 September 1943, AMSMVA Box 14.

p. 167 'The dogs are also ...' Col. C. Browning, BAS, from Fort Belvoir VA to Chief Engineer BAS Washington, 24 September 1943, AMSMVA Box 14.

p. 168 'may be used freely ...' TNA AIR 2/8734.

p. 169 'dogs to guard secret installations ...' *Evening Standard*, 8 October 1943, p. 5.

p. 169 'light kit only in case ...' TNA AIR 2/8734.

p. 169 'thirty war dogs embarked UK ...' AV&RS WD, 9 March 1944.

p. 170 'Diet is liberal ...' *The Dog World*, 17 December 1943, p. 1223.

p. 171 'We had a lovely Golden ...' Elizabeth A. Burnell, *Animals In War – a treasured memory from a rather older 'young girl'* http://www.animalaid.org.uk/images/pdf/michael.pdf

p. 172 '"Larry", "Vic" and "Charlie" ...' Records of the PDSA Allied Forces Mascot Club, IWM 25460.

p. 172 'a battalion of parachutists ...' TNA CAB 112/26.

p. 173 'Experimental training ...' 'Notes of a Meeting Held at the WDTS, 23 January 1944', AMSMVA Box 14.

p. 175 'There is a requirement for ...' 15 February 1944, TNA WO 163/194.

p. 175 'girls wearing the Leningrad ...' *Daily Telegraph*, 12 February 1944.

p. 176 'secret purchase ...' Director of Staff Duties to DAV&RS, 31 January 1944, AMSMVA Box 14.

p. 176 'Cocker, Springer ...' DAV&RS WD, 18 March 1944.

p. 177 'care should be taken ...' 'Mine Detection Dogs', 9 August 1944, TNA AVIA 22/871.

p. 177 'Dogs with black eyes ...' 'Mine Detection Dogs' anon. (probably Lloyd), 11 August 1944, TNA AVIA 22/871.

pp. 178–9 'The American hospital ...' loose leaf in WDTS Memories and Description IWM [o] k. 94/56a.

p. 179 'mine hunting dogs had discovered ...' *The Animal World*, August 1945, p. 61.

p. 180 'Nazi killer dogs ...' *Daily Mail*, 16 February 1944.

p. 180 'that thousands of [British] dogs ...' *The Dog World*, 5 May 1944, p. 282.

p. 180 'to enrol *all* animals and birds ...' St Hill Bourne, 1 November 1943, TNA AIR/5306.

p. 182 'the sentiment of a wagging tail ...' 21 November 1943, TNA AIR/5306.

pp. 182–3 '39 Huskies and 8 puppies ...' DAV&RS WD, 22 April 1944.

Chapter 16: Airborne Dogs

p. 185 'the only dog in the British ...' *The Dog World*, 17 December 1943, p. 282.

p. 186 'In January 1944 ...' 'Parachuting the War Dog' by 'Pegasus', *The Journal of the RAVC* vol. XXI, No. 1, March 1950, pp. 6–11.

pp. 187–8 'From January 1943 ...' http://www.pegasusarchive.org/normandy/james_hill.htm

Chapter 17: 'Not to be Returned'

pp. 191–3 Full reports on the Claycart Bottom trials on 24 March 1944 and Lt Davison's handwritten inventory of war dogs ('Smiler' etc.) employed as mine detectors in No. 2 Platoon are in AMSMVA Box 14.

p. 191 'come from owners ...' '"M" Dogs' undated, AMSMVA Box 14.

p. 194 'a patrol out into enemy lines ...' St Hill Bourne, op. cit., p. 13.

p. 194 'Bob, our Company dog ...' ibid.

p. 195 'special menu ...' ibid., p. 12.

p. 195 'Neither skill nor ...' Treasury to WO, 15 June 1944, TNA 32/11100.

p. 196 'I was actually in the Highland ...' Chris Tarrant, *Dad's War*, 2014, p. 107.

p. 196 'There have been dogs in the Army ...' 11 May 1944, TNA WO 32/11100.

p. 196 'the platoon is a mine detection ...' 13 May 1944, TNA WO 32/11100.

p. 196 'Schu-mines' TNA AVIA 22/871.

p. 196 'holding rejects ...' DAV&RS WD, 24 April 1944.

p. 197 'Home Service ...' DAV&RS WD, 8 May 1944.

p. 197 'stray dogs' DAV&RS WD, 9 June 1944.

Chapter 18: The D-Day Dogs

p. 200 'Considerable light flak ...' No. 296 Sq. Operations Record Books, TNA AIR 27/1645.

p. 201 'he was caught in a tree ...' Moss, op. cit., p. 127.

p. 201 'endured heavy mortar' http://www.dnw.co.uk/auction-archive/ catalogue-archive/lot.php?auction_id=94&lot_id=54027 (22 September 2006, conflates Brian with Bing).

p. 201 'Private Lloyd Neale ...' '13th Battalion the Parachute Regiment: Luard's Own by Major Ellis "Dixie" Dean MBE, MC' http://www. pegasusarchive.org/varsity/repLuardsOwn.htm

p. 202 'From that day ...' James Baty, IWM sound archive 21192, Reel 3.

p. 203 'for the first time ...' Laurie Goldstraw, 'The Paratrooper and His Dog', *After The Battle*, Issue 74, p. 30.

p. 203 'I had with me ...' http://www.pegasusarchive.org/normandy/ james_hill.htm

p. 204 'Somehow or other ...' St Hill Bourne, op. cit., p. 77.

p. 204 'Sailor ...' *The Tail-Wagger Magazine*, August 1944, p. 146.

p. 205 'a Major from a parachute ...' *Daily Mail*, 2 August 1944.

pp. 205–6 Documents on 'GPW Harry Hollmer' and her pups are in TNA MAF 35/918.

p. 206 'for the quarantine ...' DAV&RS WD, 30 July 1944.

Chapter 19: 'Too kind and trusting'

pp. 208–9 Sapper Les Coates's memoir of No. 1 Platoon is in IWM WDTS vol. 2, pp. 86–89.

p. 209 'Thirty French mongrels ...' *Aberdeen Journal*, 4 July 1944.

p. 209 'pets at British homes ...' *Sunday Despatch*, 9 July 1944.

p. 210 'A secret panel ...' *Daily Express*, 29 October 1944.

p. 210 'Heinz Hounds ...' *The Times*, 9 August 1944.

p. 210 'It is with deep regret ...' *PDSA News*, 10 October 1944, CHK p. 10.

p. 211 'I was waiting my turn ...' Les Coates, IWM WDTS vol. 2, p. 88.

p. 211 'A lane 30 yards wide ...' Report on Accident to OIC Dog Platoon, 12 July 1944, TNA WO 205/1173.

p. 212 'There was much gunfire ...' Report on Employment of No. 1 Dog Platoon, 15 July–11 August, TNA AVIA 22/871 and TNA WO 205/1173.

p. 213 'After Normandy our luck ...' Coates, IWM WDTS vol. 2, p. 89.

p. 214 'particularly observant officer ...' Lloyd, op. cit., p. 190.

p. 214 'Mobilisation completed ...' No. 2 Platoon War Diary, 24 August 1944, TNA WO 171/1824.

p. 214 'at hearing barking ...' Tarrant, op. cit., p. 106.

p. 215 'The dogs look forward ...' Davison, op. cit., p. 6.

p. 215 'I had sausages for breakfast ...' Don May, IWM WDTS, vol. 2, p. 162.

p. 215 'too much sweet grass ...' 2 Platoon WD, 7 September 1944, TNA WO 171/1824.

p. 215 '1 tin of Spam and 1 Jerry helmet ...' Davison, op. cit., p. 7.

p. 216 'several dogs off ...' TNA WO 171/1824.

p. 216 'Make sure no mines ...' Technical Report to Commandant WDTS, 7 October 1944, Davison, pps. AMSMVA Box 14.

p. 217 '"Mick" ... "Judy" ...' TNA WO 171/1824.

p. 217 'a few apparently in good ...' Technical Report, 7 October 1944, Davison, pps. AMSMVA Box 14.

p. 217 'A well-disciplined soldier ...' ibid.

p. 218 'regarded sarcasm ...' ibid.

p. 219 'gun-shy and very nervous ...' War Diary AV&RS HQ 21 Army Group TNA WO 171/191B.

Chapter 20: Good Dogs

p. 221 'their staff difficulties ...' 7 July 1944, TNA MEPO 2/6589.

p. 222 'Black out was the rule ...' Kay Manning, IWM WDTS, vol. 3, p. 178.

p. 222 'the many times the sirens ...' Gay Agocs, IWM WDTS, vol. 3, p. 194.

p. 223 '"Lady Paula", "Boy" and "Thorn" ...' *Gloucestershire Echo*, 1 March 1944.

p. 226 'quartz in pebbles ...' TNA WO 171/1825.

p. 226 'We found nine Tellermines ...' TNA WO 171/1825.

p. 226 'Quite by chance ...' Burnell, op. cit.

p. 226 'like the Rock of Gibraltar ...' St Hill Bourne, op. cit., p. 185.

p. 227 'the dog pulled hard ...' 17 January 1945, TNA WO 205/1173.

p. 228 'A patrol dog ...' 'The Possibility of Combining in One Dog the Duties of a Patrol Dog and a Mine Dog', 15 January 1945, Davison, pps. AMSMVA Box 14.

p. 229 'Every day, men were coming ...' 'Brian', 29 June 2003, BBC WW2 People's War, http://www.bbc.co.uk/history/ww2peoples war/stories/27/a1092827.shtml

p. 229 'those that were used ...' 'Note on Visit to British War Dog Training Centre 13 March 1945', Chief Engineer BAS Washington TNA WO 205/1173.

p. 229 'Dogs do not like ...' 7 March 1945, Davison pps. AMSMVA Box 14.

p. 230 'dirty area, mines ...' No. 1 Platoon War Diary, 19 February 1945, TNA WO 171/5376.

p. 231 'The only activity ...' TNA 32/10800.

p. 231 '[u]nder fire are absolutely worthless ...' Lemish, op. cit., p. 265; see also http://doglawreporter.blogspot.co.uk/2011/06/why-did-mine-dogs-work-for-brits-but.html

p. 231 'The mine-dogs went ...' Don May, IWM Hunt WDTS, vol. 3, p. 182.

p. 232 'shock at finding ...' Davison, op. cit., p. 14.

p. 232 'There have been no casualties ...' Davison, pps. AMSMVA Box 14.

p. 233 'Dog killed "Gerry" ...' No. 2 Platoon War Diary, 30 March 1945, TNA WO 171/5377.

p. 233 'I blush, but every year ...' Davison to Pitkin, IWM Hunt WDTS, vol. 1, p. 62 and obit. *BMJ* vol. 314, p. 757.

p. 233 'which was under water ...' Don May, IWM Hunt WDTS, vol. 3, p. 186.

p. 234 'What I have heard ...' Davison pps. AMSMVA Box 14.

p. 235 'HQ V & R who ...' Davison pps.

p. 235 'simplex ...' Davison pps.

p. 235 'in a storm boat' No. 4 Platoon War Diary, 24 March 1945, TNA WO 171/5378.

pp. 235–6 'worked under continuous ...' ibid.

Chapter 21: The Dog with the Magic Nose

Extensive documentation on the London rescue dogs is in TNA HO 186/2671 and HO 186/2572. There are secondary accounts in St Hill Bourne, op. cit., pp. 156–175 and extracts from Mrs Griffin's diaries are reproduced in Le Chêne, *Silent Heroes*. The Imperial War Museum archives have the record sheet of Rescue Dog 'Peter' and post-war correspondence concerning 'Rex'.

Chapter 22: 'Jump!'

pp. 244–6 Sir Peter Downward's primary account of the 13th Parachute Battalion in northwest Europe is in his *Old Yourself, One Day, Personal Memoirs*, pp. 179–211.

p. 246 'Only once do I remember ...' Letter in Airborne Assault archive, Box 'Dogs', 2 February 2001.

p. 246 'I tried not to ...' Interview with Gen. Peter Downward, Windsor, July 2014.

pp. 247–8 'I remember leaving ...' Vera Cooke, IWM WDTS, vol. 3, p. 136.

p. 248 'day when we were due ...' Kay Manning, IWM WDTS, vol. 3, p. 179.

p. 249 'I was always out long ...' Gill Eager, IWM WDTS, vol. 3, p. 197.

PART FOUR: COMING HOME

Chapter 23: 'On VE Day we all went mad ...'

p. 253 '[your dog] will continue ...' Moss to Maj Clay, 1 October 1945, TNA 32/10800.

p. 254 'He had come through ...' *The Tail-Wagger Magazine*, October 1946, p. 6.

p. 255 'On VE Day we all went mad ...' Gill Eager, IWM WDTS, vol. 3, p. 198.

p. 256 'the ballast caused ...' Davison, op. cit., p. 13.

p. 257 'Seven weeks after loss ...' No. 2 Platoon War Diary, 1st September 1945, TNA WO 171/5377.

p. 257 'a sweet little beast' Davison, pps. AMSMVA.

p. 257 'Following VE Day ...' Irene Cornish, IWM WDTS, vol. 3, p. 140.

p. 259 'On our arrival ...' Irene Cornish, IWM WDTS, vol. 3, p. 140.

p. 259 'transferring to Sennelager ...' Kay Manning, IWM WDTS, vol. 3, p. 181.

p. 260 'on each occasion ...' *RAVC Journal*, November 1946, p. 21.

Chapter 24: Demob Dogs

p. 261 'Special Services Scheme ...' TNA ADM 1/20854.

p. 262 'Commanding officers ...' ibid.

p. 262 'Accomplished with very few ...' Anon., 30 November 1945, TNA WO 170/7404.

p. 263 'The service departments ...' *The Dogs Bulletin*, spring 1946, p. 10.

p. 263 'I myself have brought ...' ibid.

p. 263 'Nothing gave more trouble ...' Clabby, op. cit., p. 164.

pp. 263–4 'About 200 have been ...' *Dundee Evening Telegraph*, 4 September 1945, p. 2.

p. 264 'Now that hostilities ...' *RAVC Journal*, November 1946, pp. 20–1.

p. 264 'two officers and seventy other ranks ...' Geoffrey Williamson, 'Service Pets in Quarantine', *Illustrated*, 12 January 1946, p. 18.

p. 265 '(A)Those too savage ...' DAV&RS WD, 20 July 1945.

p. 266 'Cockabendie ...' TNA WO 32/10800.

p. 267 'I am now demobbed ...' St Hill Bourne, op. cit., p. 182.

p. 268 'found in a village in Yugoslavia' AFMC records IWM.

p. 268 'first sixty pets ...' *Illustrated*, 12 January 1946, pp. 18–19.

p.269 'Brutus ...' *The Dogs Bulletin*, spring 1946, p. 11.

p. 269 'a radio appeal ...' St Hill Bourne, op. cit., p. 179.

p. 270 'Michael, on hearing ...' Burnell, op. cit., p. 359.

p. 270 'Jim went crazy ...' Barringer pps. Airborne Assault archive, Box 'Dogs'.

p. 270 'settled in so well ...' TNA WO 32/14999.

p. 271 'When he got off the train ...' http://www.thefreelibrary.com/Roger+the+dog+of+war+guarded+his+tales+well.-a0365954388

p. 271 'after three and a half years ...' *Hull Daily Mail*, 18 January 1946.

Chapter 25: War Dog Aces

pp. 273–5 Correspondence between DAV&RS, the RPSCA and Allied Forces Mascot Club (PDSA), 1945–49 about canine awards, proposed recipients plus citations is in TNA WO 32/14999.

p. 277 'on special leave ...' *PDSA News*, March 1945, p. 12.

p. 278 'special airborne training ...' ibid.

p. 278 'the soldiers did well ...' Hughes, *Who Cares Who Wins*, p. 236.

p. 278 'landed from a battleship ...' Article by Edna Bayne, April 1985, cutting in Airborne Assault archive, Box 'Dogs'.

p. 279 '[Rob] would work ...' ibid.

p. 279 'Served with 2nd ...' St Hill Bourne, op. cit., p. 17.

p. 282 'burly, rotund ...' Hughes, op. cit., p. 235.

p. 282 'We had a suitable ...' ibid.

p. 283 'War Office ...' St Hill Bourne, op. cit., pp. 16—17.

p. 284 'he was always ...' *Daily Mail*, 12 September 2000.

p. 284 'highly intelligent German Shepherd ...' Letter from Sgt Frank Gleeson, 25 September 1997, in Airborne Assault archive, Box 'Dogs'.

p. 285 'A few of us ...' Hughes, op. cit., p. 234.

p. 286 'under military escort ...' St Hill Bourne, op. cit., p. 17.

p. 287 'Rob took up ...' ibid., p. 18.

p. 287 'landed in Normandy ...' TNA WO 32/14999.

p. 290 'War Dogs are Coming ...' *News Chronicle*, 4 January 1946, p. 3.

Chapter 26: Don't Let the Dogs Out

p. 292 'you may wish to reconsider ...' 22 January 1946, TNA WO 32/14999.

p. 292 'despatch of pet dogs ...' TNA WO 267/588.

p. 292 'de-training to turn ...' 'Taking the Bite Out', *Soldier*, 2 March 1946, p. 7.

p. 293 'Some of the more ...' ibid.

p. 294 'has settled down well ...' Airborne Assault archive, Box 'Dogs'.

p. 294 '"cancelled", "in quarantine" ...' TNA WO 32/14999.

p. 296 'Hundreds of dogs' TNA WO 279/338 p. 34.

p. 297 'taking *in* and training ...' *Gloucester Echo*, 11 August 1946, p. 3.

p. 297 'attack and hold on command ...' *RAVC Journal*, November 1946, pp. 18—19.

p. 297 'made a kill ...' TNA WO 267/589.

p. 299 'So meritorious was ...' Moss, op. cit., p. 125.

p. 300 'barked his thanks ...' *The Animal World*, January 1947, pp. 8–9.

p. 300 'loaned to the RAF ...' 'Rex' papers IWM.

p. 301 'The Dog with the Magic Nose ...' Bill Cleaver and Ron Brown, *Jet of Iada DM MFV* 2006, http://jetofiada.tripod.com/Story.htm

p. 302 'a liver and white ....' *The Tail-Wagger Magazine*, December 1945, p. 229.

p. 302 'a blaze of glory ...' St Hill Bourne, op. cit., p. 12.

p. 302 'If the old bitch...' PDSA press release, 30 April 1946, TNA AIR 2/5036.

p. 303 'Should you desire ...' Maj P. W. Dean to Secretary, AFMC, 7 February 1947, TNA WO 32/14999.

p. 304 'Do you have ...?' IWM EN2/1/ANI/001.

p. 305 'There is nothing to say ...' 8 April 1948, TNA HO 186/2671.

p. 306 'Hitler ...' *The Times*, 9 May 1955, p. 12.

p. 307 'War dogs that ...' DAV&RS WD, 12 November 1945.

Chapter 27: 'Brian' and 'Bing': A Special Note

p. 309 'Brian ...' (War Dog 2720/6871) War Dogs: Awards of Royal Society for the Prevention of Cruelty to Animals, TNA WO 32/14999.

p. 309 'Bing ...' (War Dog 2738/6218), TNA WO 32/14999.

p. 309 'warlike ...' Text for display of 'Brian' by Lawrence Goldstraw, 29 September 1999, Airborne Assault archive, Box 'Dogs'.

p. 310 'Lieutenant Cyril William John Cory ...' TNA WO/14999 (see also ADM 159/115/681for service record).

p. 310 'repeated ever since ...' Statement from PDSA to author via e-mail, 26 September 2014.

p. 311 'for service with the 13th Battalion ...' DM citation, 26 April 1947 (copy), Airborne Assault archive, Box 'Dogs'.

p. 311 'could cope with the incessant ...' Letter from E. (Dixie) Dean, 6 September 1985, *Pegasus*, December 1985, p. 121.

p. 312 'we would keep an eye on the dog ...' 'Remarkable Story of Wartime Canine Courage', *Leicester Mercury*, 3 August 1996, p. 10.

p. 312 '*Bing* would dive into the nearest ...' 'History of Paradogs' exhibition notes, circa. November 1996, Airborne Assault archive, Box 'Dogs'.

p. 312 'when he won his wings ...' 'The Dog Who Won the VC', *Camberley News*, 16 November 1996.

p. 312 'generous cheque ...' Peter Downward to Ken Bailey (copy), 21 July 1997, Airborne Assault archive, Box 'Dogs'.

pp. 312–13 'There is a little confusion ...' ibid.

p. 313 'three-year-old Alsatian ...' *Soldier*, 2 March 1946, p. 7.

p. 314 'Brian was a male Alsatian ...' Blackbourn to Hunt, 7 July 1997, letter in War-Dog Training School scrapbook, vol. 4, p. 258, IWM, Lambeth.

p. 314 'highlight of the weekend ...' *Pegasus*, December 1997, p. 102.

Postscript

p. 317 'the nature of the faculty ...' 'Outlines of training of various types of war dogs at War Dogs Training School, British Army of the Rhine (BAOR) Training Centre', TNA WO 291/2673.

pp. 318–20 Major Cawthorne's mine-dog experiments are documented in TNA WO 291/1048. US experiments on detection by technical means are in TNA AVIA 22/3312 and TNA WO 195/9544-9545 'Physics of Armaments Committee: non-metallic mine detection'. See also Kirk, op. cit., for Zuckerman pps.

p. 320 'alarm and despondency at Cruft's ...' 'Ministry of Supply, financing of research into detection by dogs of land mines, traps and trip wires, 1949–1956' TNA T 225/477.

p. 320 '"Ron" and "Nigger" ...' *Manchester Guardian*, 31 May 1950, p. 2.

p. 321 'demonstrated ...' Kirk, op. cit., http://www.ncbi.nlm.nih.gov/pmc/articles/PMC3908362/#fn11

p. 322 'We then moved on to ...' *The Times*, 3 September 1982, p. 10.

p. 324 ' "Binnie" and "Tessie" ...' J. B. Rhine, 'Location of hidden objects by a man-dog team', *Journal of Parapsychology*, 1971, 35: pp. 18–33.

p. 324 'Jeepers Creepers', Dorothea St Hill Bourne to L. B. Bradley, 21 August 1955, correspondence file IWM.

p. 325 'I worked with ten dogs ...' 'Using dogs as mine detectors', *The Times*, 13 September 1982, p. 9.

pp. 325–6 'The need for tracker ...' William H. Thornton, *The Role of Military Working Dogs in Low Intensity Conflict*, February 1990, USA, p. 6, http://www.dtic.mil/dtic/tr/fulltext/u2/a224049.pdf

p. 326 'dogs are the most ...' Nolan and Gravitte, *Mine-Detecting Canines*, 1977, US Army Mobility Equipment Research and Development Command, Fort Belvoir VA.

p. 329 'the rapid sampling ...' http://www.scribd.com/doc/20332866/A-Guide-to-Mine-Action Geneva International Centre for Humanitarian Demining, 1998.

p. 329 'Fido doesn't have ...' 2 April 2007, http://www.businesswire.com/news/home/20070402005357/en/Chemist-Inventor-Sniffs-Prestigious-500000-Lemelson-MIT-Prize#

p. 331 'Training dogs ...' Robert Chessyre, 'Dogs of War', 20 January 2011, http://www.telegraph.co.uk/news/worldnews/asia/afghanistan/8269095/Dogs-of-war-sniffer-dogs-lead-the-way-in-Afghanistan.html

p. 332 'If you're going to ...' November 2011, http://aviationweek.com/awin/ruff-

p. 333 'usually go on to live with ...' 6 April 2012, www.dailymail.co.uk/news/article-2125974/Hundreds-army-dogs-thought-fierce-pets-serving-time.html

p. 334 'K9 Storm Intruder ...' http://www.k9storm.com/cataloguenew12.html

p. 335 'Each morning, Treo ...' 'The Doomed Dogs of War', 21 September 2013, http://www.express.co.uk/news/uk/431049/The-doomed-dogs-of-war-What-happens-to-military-dogs-when-they-are-no-longer-needed

p. 336 'He is your friend ...' http://www.cpwda.com/k9_monuments.htm

p. 337 'with some K9 teams ...' Dave Heyhoe, *It's All About Treo*, Quercus, 2012, p. 9.

p. 338 'a friendly, well-bred dog ...' 10 January 2012, http://www.telegraph.co.uk/news/uknews/defence/9003186/Major-the-demining-dog-dies-after-saving-more-than-200-lives.htm